Mercury Cyclone GT.
Fast-backed. 4-stacked. Radial-tracked.

The golden girl in our picture ordered her Cyclone GT with a 4-stack Marauder 390 GT V-8. And with optional wide-tread whitewall radials.

Which is a pretty neat way to get around the wild West. Or South. Or East.

You may like something tamer in engines. A 390 2-barrel V-8. Or our basic 302. But in any case you'll still get our special GT performance package. Extra-stiff springs, fore and aft. Heavy-duty shocks. A big D sway bar. And wide wheel rims for the wide oval tires.

Our GT double side striping is unique. So are the turbine-type wheel covers. And the racer-oriented black-out job in the grille area.

Inside, the Fine Car Touch of our Lincoln Continental designers has worked tailored wonders.

In the clean, elegant, functional lines of the dash. In bucket seat richness, without a bit of fussiness.

Give yourself a whirl in a Mercury Cyclone GT.

The Fine Car Touch inspired by the Continental.

LINCOLN-MERCURY DIVISION Ford

(Courtesy Ford Motor Co)

Some other great books from Veloce:

Bahamas Speed Weeks, The (O'Neil)
British at Indianapolis, The (Wagstaff)
British Cars, The Complete Catalogue of, 1895-1975 (Culshaw & Horrobin)
Camaro 1967-81, Cranswick on (Cranswick)
Chevrolet Corvette (Starkey)
Chrysler 300 – America's Most Powerful Car 2nd Edition (Ackerson)
Chrysler PT Cruiser (Ackerson)
Cobra – The Real Thing! (Legate)
Cobra, The last Shelby – My times with Carroll Shelby (Theodore)
Dodge Challenger & Plymouth Barracuda (Grist)
Dodge Charger – Enduring Thunder (Ackerson)
Dodge Dynamite! (Grist)
Dodge Viper (Zatz)
Ford Cleveland 335-Series V8 engine 1970 to 1982 – The Essential Source Book (Hammill)
Ford F100/F150 Pick-up 1948-1996 (Ackerson)
Ford F150 Pick-up 1997-2005 (Ackerson)
Ford Focus WRC (Robson)
Ford GT – Then, and Now (Streather)
Ford GT40 (Legate)
Ford GT40 Anthology – A unique compilation of stories about these most iconic cars (Allen & Endeacott)
Ford Maverick and Mercury Comet 1970-77, Cranswick on (Cranswick)
Ford Midsize Muscle – Fairlane, Torino & Ranchero (Cranswick)
Ford Model Y (Roberts)
Ford Mustang II & Pinto 1970 to 80 (Cranswick)
Ford Small Block V8 Racing Engines 1962-1970 – The Essential Source Book (Hammill)
Ford Thunderbird From 1954, The Book of the (Long)
Ford versus Ferrari – The battle for supremacy at Le Mans 1966 (Starkey)
Inside the machine – An engineer's tale of the modern automotive industry (Twohig)
Legend of American Motors, The (Cranswick)
MOPAR Muscle – Barracuda, Dart & Valiant 1960-1980 (Cranswick)
Northeast American Sports Car Races 1950-1959 (O'Neil)
Nothing Runs – Misadventures in the Classic, Collectable & Exotic Car Biz (Slutsky)
Patina Volkswagen, How to Build a (Walker)
Patina Volkswagens (Walker)
Pontiac Firebird – New 3rd Edition (Cranswick)
Porsche, Cranswick on (Cranswick)
Racing Camaros (Holmes)
Racing Mustangs – An International Photographic History 1964-1986 (Holmes)
Runways & Racers (O'Neil)
Sleeping Beauties USA – abandoned classic cars & trucks (Marek)

www.velocebooks.com

First published in May 2016, this paperback edition published February 2023 by Veloce Publishing Limited, Veloce House, Parkway Farm Business Park, Middle Farm Way, Poundbury, Dorchester DT1 3AR, England. Fax 01305 268864 / e-mail info@veloce.co.uk / web www.veloce.co.uk or www.velocebooks.com.
ISBN: 978-1-787119-28-4; UPC 6-36847-01928-0.
© Marc Cranswick and Veloce Publishing 2016 & 2023. All rights reserved. With the exception of quoting brief passages for the purpose of review, no part of this publication may be recorded, reproduced or transmitted by any means, including photocopying, without the written permission of Veloce Publishing Ltd. Throughout this book logos, model names and designations, etc, have been used for the purposes of identification, illustration and decoration. Such names are the property of the trademark holder as this is not an official publication. Readers with ideas for automotive books, or books on other transport or related hobby subjects, are invited to write to the editorial director of Veloce Publishing at the above address. British Library Cataloguing in Publication Data – A catalogue record for this book is available from the British Library. Typesetting, design and page make-up all by Veloce Publishing Ltd on Apple Mac.
Printed and bound by CPI Group (UK) Ltd, Croydon, CR0 4YY.

FORD MIDSIZE MUSCLE
FAIRLANE, TORINO & RANCHERO
V8 Dynamite 1955-1979

MARC CRANSWICK

VELOCE PUBLISHING
THE PUBLISHER OF FINE AUTOMOTIVE BOOKS

Contents

Introduction – The Car With No Name 5

Chapter 1: Hooking Up With Fairlane 6

Chapter 2: Ranchero – The Tuxedo-Wearing Pickup! 29

Chapter 3: Midsize Fairlane – The Right-Size Ford! 40

Chapter 4: Ranchero's Compact to Midsize Transition 53

Chapter 5: Fairlane Becomes a Muscle Car 1965-69 63

Chapter 6: Torino the Muscle Car 1970-73 95

Chapter 7: 1968-1979 Ranchero. From Cobra Jet to Disco Delight 139

Chapter 8: Torino Moves from Turin to Lincoln Type Design 1974-1979 152

Appendix 167
    Ford's four on the floor! 167
    Forums and websites 169
    Bibliography 169
    Footnotes 170

Index 175

Introduction – The Car With No Name

Henry Ford and his company have been innovators. Mass production, the V8 for the common man, even the pony car. Henry didn't invent the muscle car, but he did invent the size category that gave rise to the same, the intermediate, compact II or midsize. Even so, the car associated with this class and muscle car genre, has been one of Dearborn's quiet achievers.

What started off as a top trim level became a nameplate, and to some folks a legend. That ride was Fairlane, and as fashion and culture changed, Ford's midsize became Torino and then LTD II. But an intermediate by any other name would still seat six, if one didn't get hung up on that transmission tunnel! History also shows Henry's midsize begat a car-based pickup called Ranchero. Can you say red headed stepchild?!

All these names and models got caught up in the rises and falls of the postwar period. Consistently Ford's better sellers: Henry raced, sold and promoted Fairlane, Torino and Ranchero for 25 years. They were the better ideas Ford put on wheels, and to many the 'Right Size Ford.'

Tailfins were the height of fashion by the late '50s, but the muscle car market was still in its infancy. (Courtesy Larry Stanley Business 500 Auto)

1

Hooking Up With Fairlane

Henry's Fairlane to full-size fun, 1955-61

CAR magazine's Chris Harvey summed up the legend that was the 1964 GTO: "… a new kinda car attracted those young at heart – defined as the 18 to 34 year-olds, or anybody who had never really grown up."[1] Three cheers for John Z DeLorean, Pete Estes and Jim Wangers for elevating the family intermediate above mere transportation. Without them Jan & Dean wouldn't have had anything to sing about. Fortunately, there was indeed a mighty GTO with triple deuce 389, 4 on the floor and insurance premiums to make a grown Allstate man salivate!

The GTO may have set the muscle car pattern, but things were brewing underhood soon after World War II. The 1950s showed that Detroit's engineers were intent on taking the V8 to the moon! Each manufacturer was offering a quicker way for that little old lady from Pasadena to get to church. Leading the way away from asthmatic flatheads, the 160 horse Cadillac 331ci OHV V8 of 1950 brought breeding and breathing! Lincoln matched those horses with its 317ci V8 in 1952. Ford and Mercury said goodbye to the sidevalve with the final 110bhp 1953 Strato-Star.

Chevrolet introduced performance to the masses with its 1955 small block, making it 'The Hot One.' By 1957 the Chevy Fuelie injected 283 V8 was making 283bhp on a 10.5 comp ratio. In 1956 the optional 354 Hemi V8 of the Chrysler 300B made 355 horses. It was the first domestic V8 motor to beat one horse per cube, making Chrysler's Hemi 'Firepower V8' nomenclature very apt. Let's also not forget AMC's 1957 special 288 horse electronic-injected Electrojector 327 V8![2]

There was even some understanding in Detroit about handling. In 1956 the Studebaker Golden Hawk used a 275bhp Packard 352 V8. In 1957 the Golden Hawk flew on Studebaker's supercharged 289 V8. This V8 had the same ponies, but was 100lb lighter in the nose.

For all this, the idea of a performance car in North America was pretty alien, much like an MG import. Even the hallowed Corvette had a shaky Blue Flame start. Cars were sold on features to generate excitement, not speed. Ford's Fairlane was no exception: on the subject of the Crown Victoria Skyliner, an option that started as a fancy tinted transparent plastic roof on the 1954 Crestline Skyliner was followed by 1957's expensive, troublesome, and not very popular, powered retractable metal folding hardtop.

Showroom bait was the name of the game. However, aside from having the V8's torque rating on Edsel rocker covers, it seemed likely that safety and speed didn't sell. But look a little closer, and once the late 50's recession was in the rear view

In 1955 the Fairlane Crown Victoria two-door sedan sported a decorative chromed Landau bar in the B pillar area. This wasn't structural. The optional 272 V8 Power Package made a reported 190 horse. This gave Fairlane CV the dash to match the flash! (Courtesy Dennis Crenshaw)

Looking like it came out of the movie *American Graffiti*, the '57 Fairlane two-door hardtop was born to be a low rider! The optional supercharged 312 V8 tided one over until the '58 MY FE V8's arrival. (Courtesy Dennis Crenshaw)

1: Hooking Up With Fairlane

mirror, there were signs that sporty driving could be a youth market sales booster. It started with the sedately named Fairlane. The model took its name from Henry Ford's Dearborn, Michigan estate of the same name. The Fairlane car replaced the full-size Crestline, and would remain full-size until the departure of 1961 model year.

Ford's slogan of the hour was 'Watch the Fords go by,' and prospects got an eyeful with three new trim lines. They were Mainline, Customline and the upscale Crown Victoria (CV). With Fairlane Crown Victoria, two-tone paint and creased-profile sheetmetal afforded fancy jukebox charm, as Ford's family cars rolled off the line in Claycomo, Missouri. Frenched-look headlights from the custom scene, and plush seating underlined Ford's desire, like other companies, to make its low cost cars appear fancier than a peacock! Fortunately, there was substance underfoot and underhood, to give Joe Q Public genuine butter and egg value.

Both Ford's latest OHV sixes and eights shared a wedge-shaped combustion chamber, plus other design aspects and components, like anti-fouling sparkplugs. At 120bhp, the 223ci I6 was 10 horses stronger than the final Ford Flathead V8! Most eyes were on the Y block V8 displacing 272 cubes. The Y block was a 1954 debutante and made 162 horses in base guise, 182bhp in higher 8.5:1 comp ratio style. Answering calls for even more zotts under the hood was the optional 272 'Power Package.' This late '55 MY inclusion added a hot distributor, 4-barrel carb, special radiator and intake manifold to the duals, that were enjoyed only by Fairlane V8 and Thunderbird in the Ford line.

Figures for the normal optional premium fuel 272 were 182bhp at 4400rpm and 268lb/ft at 2600rpm. In line with the general showroom anti-racing pact between the automakers, Ford didn't disclose the effect of duals or special equipment. However, as *Motor Life*'s December 1954 issue showed, the top

With growing length, width and height dimensions of 208/77/57in, the 118in wheelbase 1957 Fairlane four-door sedan stretched the idea of the traditional good-handling 'Right Size Ford.' (Courtesy Larry Stanley Business 500 Auto)

Ford Midsize Muscle – Fairlane, Torino & Ranchero

Still sporting its original power team, this 1957 Fairlane 500 sedan has a 292 V8/Ford-O-Matic combo. In June 1956 Bill Holland of *Motorsport* magazine said the T-Bird sourced Y-8 292 would jump a Fairlane sedan away from traffic lights fast enough for anyone but a fanatic! (Courtesy Larry Stanley Business 500 Auto)

Fairlane CV had a 'V8' front fender chrome badge, and 0-60mph in 12.6 seconds and 98.7mph top speed credentials. Enough for a modern Bonnie & Clyde or Dillinger! However, don't discount handling. Family Fords were known to be moderately sized, roadable cars, and 1954 had been a big year for Ford suspension.

The 115.5in separate chassis featured revised balljoint/torsional systems with four lubrication points. There had been 16, and altered front end geometry brought reduced brake dive and less roll. At 198in long, 76in wide and 61in tall the 3236lb sedan with 192in² brake lining area was heftier than past Fords, but still controllable. A 3.89 rear ratio was also possible to cut ETs! Working on the new Fairlane, PH Pretz was chief test engineer, and the senior project engineer was Dick Heathfield.

Supremely practical folks could choose a Ranch Wagon, also available with the 272 Power Package and suspected 190 gross ponies. In the era of Lucky Strike being advertised on *The Jack Benny Show*, the only concern was rising smoke from the Fairlane's ashtray tarnishing the dials of the factory-fitted Ford valve radio. For trends, a few were going for the chrome free Mainline, some with the part chrome Customline and many for the full chrome Crown Vic. However, the humble 223 I6/Overdrive manual power team was getting overshadowed by the Fairlane's V8/Ford-O-Matic combo.

It was noted at the time that although the six was a vaunted format for road and racing cars in Europe, the OHV V8 was the rising star Stateside. The straight six with overdrive was once respected by the American family man, looking for no nonsense, low cost operation. However, with postwar affluence, Mobil economy runs were losing out to the traffic light drag race. The six was increasingly left in the corner, as most yearly manufacturer

Bill Boyer and Chuck Mashigan were on the design team for Ford's new-look 1957 family car. It established a style that would feature on Fords until 1964. (Courtesy Larry Stanley Business 500 Auto)

Uncle Tom McCahill tested a '57 Fairlane 500 292 sedan just like this! In *Mechanix Illustrated*, Uncle Tom reckoned Fairlane cornered as flat as a mailman's feet! (Courtesy Larry Stanley Business 500 Auto)

upgrades were showered on the V8. So it was for the 1956 MY, where the six alone had a manual choke, and many favoured the shiftless Ford-O-Matic.

It was also increasingly unnecessary to re-engine one's family car. It had been common practice to buy a new low cost car and replace its motor, using a unit from a high price line. A Caddy OHV V8 into a formerly flathead Ford was a normal occurrence nationwide, with specialist shops doing neat conversions. The low cost line didn't have the fancy trim or high horsepower, large displacement, advanced V8 design motors of expensive automobiles. To get a V8 with the valves upstairs, and size well over 300ci, required an engine swap to turn one's family lead sled into a racer!

With increasingly fancier trim and the latest OHV V8, offered by the Big 4, low-cost line life was getting lively. For '56 MY Ford introduced uprated versions of its Y series V8. Displacement was now 292 cubes: with an 8.4:1 compression ratio, this implied 202bhp at 4600rpm, and 289lb/ft at 2600rpm, using 4bbl carburetion. Ford had dubbed its motor the 'Y8' due to its deep block design. It was a development of the 1955 Mercury luxo car motor. In 1956 the 292 had bigger intake passages and revised intake manifold for improved breathing.

A smaller diameter camshaft of new alloy material had higher lift lobes. There was precision extrusion of better steel alloy exhaust valves. Deeper capped, umbrella-fitting design over the valve stem brought improved valve stem lubrication. An optional premium fuel version of said 292 took compression ratio to nine to one, and power on to 208 horses with torque at 299lb/ft at the same respective rpms as the regular gas 292. If this wasn't enough there was a later '56-released 312 V8, with a rumored 250 horses at announcement time. It was a far cry from the 110bhp of the strongest V8 Ford had in the 1953 model year.

The new normal '56 Fairlane with 202 horse, 8.4 CR 292/Ford-O-Matic weighed

Top: Compared to the circular instruments of '56 MY, '57 Fairlane possessed a fashionable crescent speedo in a redesigned dash. The high mount universal joint interior reversing mirror was ergonomic for all sizes of driver.
(Courtesy Larry Stanley Business 500 Auto)

Bottom: 1957 Fairlane 500 opened the door to late '50s fancy Detroit, with a base sticker of $2300. The 'Thunderbird Special' 245 horse 312 V8 was optional.
(Courtesy Larry Stanley Business 500 Auto)

Ford Midsize Muscle – Fairlane, Torino & Ranchero

Above: Ford made big separate chassis changes to its family car for '57 MY. These included kicking up the frame's side rail to clear a rear axle moved 12in rearwards. This liberated more rear compartment space.
Below: The ubiquitous Continental kit showed the road to Edsel was paved with good options! Boost the price and make a car dealer smile (^o^). (Both pictures courtesy Larry Stanley Business 500 Auto)

3280lb, and could do 0-60mph in 10.4 seconds according to *Motorsport*. *Road Test* said the Fairlane CV of 1955, with base 162bhp 272 V8, and Ford-O-Matic took 14.4 seconds. So things were really moving, and what about that 312 motor? On the subject of glamor the optional 9.0:1 292 carried Thunderbird script on its rocker covers. Yes, there was a time before the Mustang halo effect. In the '50s the Ford sports icon to associate with was that lil' 2 seater T-Bird, and hotter Fairlanes essentially used Thunderbird power teams sans fresh air induction.

Even in the '50s, go faster kids were obsessed with duals. *Motorsport*'s Bill Holland made the observation that set-ups with exhaust outlets tidily exiting the bumpers of T-Birds et al looked neat, but had too many bends for practical throughflow. However, years before Ford's Total Performance mindset, Mr Holland said of the '56 Fairlane, "It is still one of the best handling cars on the market today." The only fly in the ointment was the limited 180.1in^2 brake lining area. However, this was common on all Detroit low cost and upscale offerings.

Building safer Fords

The story wasn't all about speed. Even though Henry said safety doesn't sell, Ford was engaged in a two year safety program involving full scale crash tests at its Dearborn test track. A range of 1956 'Lifeguard Design' standard and optional safety features were available. Apart from optional front seat lapbelts, there were items involving dashboard padding, dished steering wheels, safety door latches and locking seat rack positions on non-powered seats. A booklet was available from Ford dealers, titled *Report to the Public on the National Safety Forum*, informing on the current passive safety situation. This was all before Robert McNamara came to Ford. Chrysler Corp was engaged in a safety R&D program too.

For all the above-mentioned engineering and safety advances, the public generally said meh. It was acknowledged by critics at the time, that the average North American car buyer had little understanding or interest in what went on mechanically under a car's bodywork. Reliable transport from A to B was the order of the day. The youth market hadn't started yet, so spec sheets on hotter Y block V8s were only pored over by minority tinkerers and hot rodders with cigarette packets rolled up in their T shirt shoulders!

The one thing the average buyer did comprehend was flash. Fancy styling, chrome, a deluxe interior and radio, plus a flavor of the month gadget with an imagination-sparking name. After

all, this was a time when TV dinners on compartmented foil trays, and TV remote controls, were first appearing. In this automated paradise, offering the highest standard of living in the world, one would switch channels and come across a car commercial for … The Retractible!

Suddenly, Fairlane's 1956 range of 21 two-tone exterior color combos flew out of mind, the fact Ford hadn't given the Y series hydraulic lifters didn't register: it was 'The Retractible' mon amor! Or at least Ford hoped it would be. This feature and model would lower its steel-paneled top at the push of a button in just 40 seconds, courtesy of 7 electric motors.

All that hardware would concertina into the trunk, clear out of sight. This Skyliner variant was $300 to $400 over the normal Fairlane 500. However, the look of astonishment on neighbor's faces as one lowered the top was priceless!

With Skyliner, one was the new king of suburban one-upmanship. Unfortunately, pride comes before a fall. The concertina top made the trunk unusable when out of sight. The mechanism was also hardly gremlin-free, so most buyers passed this expensive option/variant on the other side of the street. More commonly enjoyed was Fairlane's 8 tube factory valve radio. With this device one could enjoy Jo Stafford, Perry Como, or something more serious. The radio dial was marked for the Conelrad civil defense emergency stations. The Cold War reality was that this was how someone might be informed that a Soviet nuclear attack was under way, and

By 1957, family Fords ran from 116in wheelbase Custom and Custom 300 through to highline 118in wheelbase Fairlane, and displayed Fairlane 500. As ever, a top trim level soon became a formal model nameplate. Stylewise, the roof trim chrome basket handle of '56 Crown Vic had given way to trendy tailfins. Inside, transistors replaced valves on Ford's optional factory radios. (Courtesy Larry Stanley Business 500 Auto)

Ford Midsize Muscle – Fairlane, Torino & Ranchero

Whether it was pioneering auto safety, car-based pickups, or powered metal roofed convertibles, Ford was an innovator. (Courtesy Marc Cranswick)

Below: Bob Lee originally owned a '57 Ford Tudor back in the early '60s, as a teenager. This similar Custom 300 revives the memories, and realizes past dreams, hence the license plate. (Courtesy Bob Lee & Jim Smart)

make their way to the nearest nuclear shelter/bunker post-haste. Ford owners were ready for the Cuban Missile Crisis!

In the '50s many middle class Americans had two cars, two television sets, a refrigerator, and often a shelter for when the balloon went up. The Cold War mood contributed to living in the moment, and perhaps automotive planned obsolescence. With nothing older than last year's ride, all eyes were on the new model year fall releases. Make 'em fast, and get the rides to the dealer for fast sale. Build quality was the price of impatience. Fords assembled in low volume CKD operations, in locales like Mexico and Sweden, have exhibited a much higher-quality feel, honoring the Ford designer's original intentions.[3]

Stateside family Fords, and other low-

1: Hooking Up with Fairlane

Back in 2004, when this custom Ford was being built, Ford crate motors didn't exist. So, you had to create your own! In this case, a special worked 351W, which took inspiration from a similar job in *Hot Rod* Magazine. With Edelbrock RPM heads and Paxton-Novi 1200 blower, figure 500 stallions at the rear wheels! Paxton also made the Ford factory blowers, optional on '57 Y blocks! (Courtesy Bob Lee & Jim Smart)

cost line family vehicles, were known for being rough and ready on assembly quality, but very durable nonetheless. This was a testimony to the ruggedness of Henry's power teams, frames and hardware. Thus, buyers still had a reason to choose high-priced lines, for bank vault quality. However, with Ford's '57 MY revisions, one could at least maintain the pretense of 'hi line.' Ford had eliminated the Mainline, leaving just Custom and Fairlane.

With the Lincoln influence of slim chrome pillar trim for a hardtop look, the Fairlane 500s appeared decidedly natty. Ford had handled the '57 MY release well, getting new ones out early, and stockpiling sufficiently to meet demand. Tick the right option box, and power was aplenty, courtesy of the 9.7:1 comp 245 horse 312 V8 and three-speed Thunderbird power team. *Motor Trend* offered the following on the latest Fords in January 1957, "If you enjoy the act of driving, you'll like a Ford …" If the Skyliner/Retractible '50s gadget business was a dead end, Ford had a new avenue with Customline.

Customline was available in a shorter

wheelbase. Add the T-Bird 312 and one had big power in a smaller ride, 7 years before GTO. Contemporary critic speculation wondered where this might lead. The low-cost family sleds had acceleration and handling to make sportscars redundant. It could only lead to the '60s muscle car, but in the late '50s things weren't so focused. The press

On the outside a Santini paintjob featuring House of Kolor Blue, and Honda Pewter metallic with metal flake fade side trim. Inside, this custom leather interior with luxury not even a '50s Lincoln product planner could have dreamt of! (Courtesy Bob Lee & Jim Smart)

Ford Midsize Muscle – Fairlane, Torino & Ranchero

This show winner, with proud owner, was originally built at Ford's Terminal Island Facility, in Long Beach, California on September 27 1957. Number 247 from the end of the model year. The Custom 300 now resides in Alamitos, CA. (Courtesy Bob Lee & Jim Smart)

You don't want to peer too closely at the gas gauge around town. Even with a manual 5 speed OD TKO 600, 8mpg is the norm! (Courtesy Bob Lee & Jim Smart)

was noticing that the average family car was getting bigger and flashier, but was it getting better? At least Ford had introduced a real automatic!

Shifting gears with Ford-O-Matic

The first commonly used fully automatic unit utilised by Ford automobiles was the Ford-O-Matic of 1951 model year. Ford had been tardy concerning the introduction of a real automatic box. In the late '40s Ford got into discussion and agreement with Borg Warner, concerning what would become the Ford-O-Matic. Smoothing the shift in Ford's transition was new Ford Engineering VP Harold Youngren. Youngren was an ex Borg Warner man, and had been working on the Ford-O-Matic design before moving to Ford.

Ford-O-Matic brought the modern 'PRNDL' shift pattern to Henry's hacienda. It also involved a Ravigneaux three-speed planetary gearset with torque converter. Ford-O-Matic's arrival was timely, because more and more Americans wanted the convenience of a fully automatic gearbox, three-speed 'on the tree' manuals were falling by the popularity wayside. Ford-O-Matic evolved into Cruise-O-Matic, as Ford maintained those annual horsepower increases to keep pace with rivals. In Ford parlance the smaller Cruise-O-Matic was the FX, the larger, heavier-duty unit was the MX.

There was most certainly call for heavier-duty automatics at Ford. The Y series 312 V8 had been racetrack inspired, and Ford had some super heavy hitting options by 1957. Fairlanes and Thunderbirds could have the 312 with two 4-barrel carbs, this E-code motor was rated at 270bhp. Over this was a supercharged F-code 312 boasting 300 galloping horses.

The blower was a McCulloch centrifugal unit courtesy of Paxton. If that still wasn't elegant sufficiency, Ford offered a NASCAR racing kit that took the 312's output to 340

1: Hooking Up with Fairlane

ponies, long before anyone had heard of the Mustang nameplate. Detroit rivals had their V8 catalogue candy at the ready too. It looked like the nation's roads would become awash with copious horsepower and tiresmoke. Short-circuiting this development was the Automobile Manufacturer's Association. This august body said whoa! A pact developed between the automakers whereby actions to push the horsepower sales angle were cooled.

You can't stop the horsepower!

Power to weight ceilings were set, the best motors were reserved for full-size cars only. However, one didn't have to wait for the 1964 GTO for things to improve. Horsepower and engine sizes continued their upward spiral with each new model year release. Companies just got subtle with the introductions. That said, one couldn't miss Ford's new FE big block series release for 1958 model year. Two new V8 sizes to know were 332 and 352 cubic inchers. The police issue oriented 'Interceptor' term started to be publicly spoken, in relation to Ford's showroom fare.

The average American car was growing. Come 1960, with the Falcon compact, Ford would need a range of V8 designs to suit different size classes. To help with this trend, the new FE (Ford-Edsel) V8 family was technically a medium block development of the Y series. Once again a deep V, cast iron head and block with OHV arrangement. The deep skirt FE block, saw the cylinder block extend below the crankshaft centerline by 3.625in. This permitted greater block rigidity and improved crankshaft bearing support, along with displacements from the aforementioned 332, to a very large 428 considering the modest block exterior dimensions.

It may have been cast iron, but Ford engineers used a special, advanced thinwall casting technique. This involved consistent mold pouring sans wasted metal. As a result an FE long motor with aluminum intake manifold and water pump fitted was under 600lb in weight.

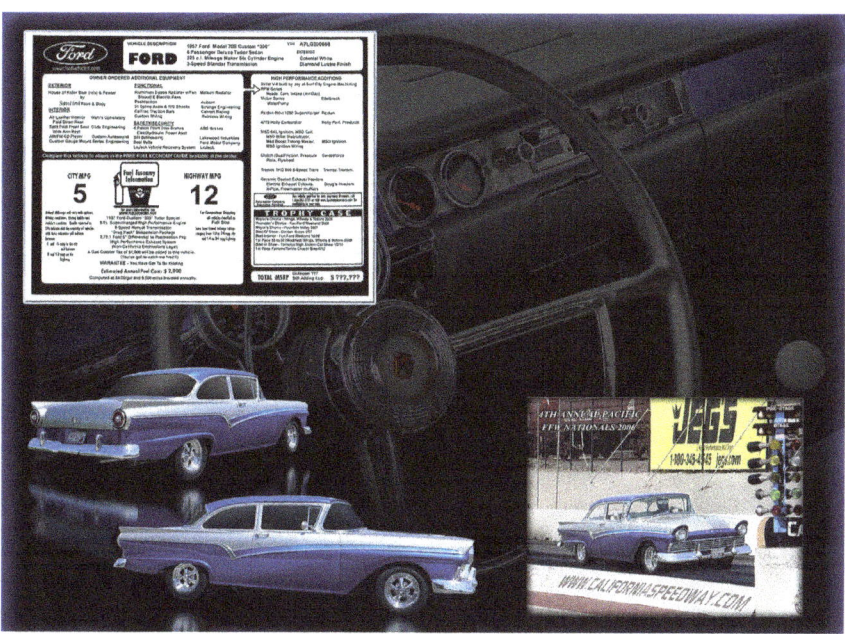

This beauty still struts its stuff in the ¼ mile. 1988 T-Bird sourced rear disks provide whoa! to match the go! (Courtesy Bob Lee & Brian Pancoast)

As a lifelong surfing enthusiast, Californian owner Bob Lee modified the trunk to accept his surfboard. He prefers this location to the usual roof-mounted style. (Courtesy Bob Lee & Jim Smart)

This was less than the 700lb-plus units GM and Chrysler were installing between the shock towers of their family cars. Less weight equaled improved handling and apart from marine applications, the FE

Window stickers didn't exist in the '50s. This custom creation describes all the upgrades bestowed on this very Custom Tudor. The highway figure should be 17mpg, because the TKO 600 five-speed's 0.64 OD now makes it so! (Courtesy Bob Lee & Jim Smart)

Ford

www.fordvehicles.com

VEHICLE DESCRIPTION

FORD

1957 Ford Model 70B Custom "300"
6 Passenger Deluxe Tudor Sedan
223 c.i. Mileage Maker Six Cylinder Engine
3-Speed Standar Transmission

VIN A7LG200668

EXTERIOR
Colonial White
Diamond Lustre Finish

OWNER ORDERED ADDITIONAL EQUIPMENT

EXTERIOR
House of Kolor Blue (mix) & Pewter by Santini Paint & Body

INTERIOR
All Leather Interior Fold Down Rear — Wahl's Upholstery
Split Fold Front Seat With Arm Rest — Glide Engineering
AM/FM CD Player — Custom Autosound
Custom Gauge Mount — Seriec Engineering

FUNCTIONAL
Aluminum 2-pass Radiator w/Fan Shroud & Electric Fans — Matson Radiator
Positraction — Auburn
31 Spline Axels & H/D Shocks — Strange Engineering
CalTrac Traction Bars — Calvert Racing
Custom Wiring — Painless Wiring

SAFETY/SECURITY
4 Piston Front Disc Brakes ElectHydraulic Power Asst — ABS Brakes
SFI Bellhousing — Lakewood Industries
Seat Belts — Ford Motor Company
LoJack Vehicle Recovery System — LoJack

HIGH PERFORMANCE ADDITIONS
351W V-8 built by Jay at Surf City Engine Machining
RPM Series Heads, Cam, Intake (Air-Gap)
Victor Series WaterPump — Edelbrock
Paxton-Novi 1200 Supercharger — Paxton
4779 Holly Carburetor — Holly Perf. Products
MSD 6AL Ignition, MSD Coil, MSD Billet Distriubutor, Msd Boost Timing Master, MSD ignition Wiring — MSD Ignition
Clutch (DualFriction, Pressure Plate, Flywheel) — Centerforce
Tremac TKO 600 5-Speed Trans — Tremec Transm.
Ceramic Coated Exhaust Headers Electric Exhaust Cutouts, X-Pipe, Flowmaster mufflers — Doug's Headers

Ford Motor Company Insurance Services

Compare this vehicle to others in the FREE FUEL ECONOMY GUIDE available at the dealer.

CITY MPG
5

Fuel Economy Information

HIGHWAY MPG
12

For more information see WWW.FUELECONOMY.GOV

1957 Ford Custom "300" Tudor Special
5.8L Supercharged High Performance Engine
5-Speed Manual Transmission
"Drag Pack" Suspension Package
3.70:1 Ford 9" Differential /w Positraction Pkg
High Performance Exhaust System
(Non-California Emmissions Legal)
A Gas Guzzler Tax of $1,000 will be added to this vehicle.
(You've got to catch me first!!)
WARANTEE - You Have Got To Be Kidding
Estimated Annual Fuel Cost: $ 2,000
Computed at $4.00/gal and 5,000 miles traveled annually.

For Comparison Shopping all vehicles classified as Full Size have been issued mileage ratings ranging from 10 to 24 mpg city and 14 to 34 mpg highway.

TROPHY CASE
Mayor's Choice - Wings, Wheels & Rotors 2006
Promoter's Choice - Fun Ford Weekend 2006
Mayor's Choice - Fountain Valley 2007
Best Of Show - Garden Grove 6/07
Best Interior - Fun Ford Weekend 10/08
1st Place 55 to 59 (Modified) Wings, Wheels & Rotors 2008
Best In Show - Torrance High Alumni Car Show 10/11
1st Place Fairlane/Torino Cruisin' Bros 6/12

TOTAL MSRP — Unknown ??? Still Adding it up — $???,???

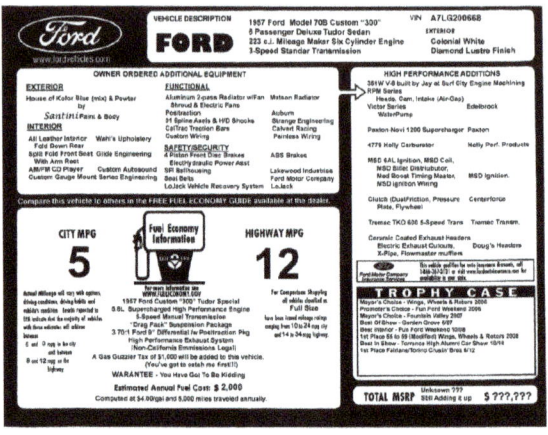

The '57 Custom below was originally an I6 car. It has had one respray of its original Willow Green exterior, and is a two-owner car. It has a fan club! (Courtesy Todd Matthies)

was much used in road coarse racing. The motor found its way under the AC Cobra Mk III's hood. It powered future Mustangs, and, in 427 side oiler form, was the driving force behind Ford's 1-2-3 defeat of Ferrari utilising the GT40 at Le Mans in 1966!

So it was that Ford created a high quality V8 with FE. A tighter tolerance, fewer cores process was used to create molds to cast the FE's thinwall blocks. GM and Chrysler used more material to obscure production flaws when casting their V8 blocks. As a performance legacy Ford took the lessons learned from FE, and applied them to the later 4.6-5.4 liter modular V8 family of the 1990s. But that's getting way ahead in the FE story, whose first performance application was the Fairlane's Interceptor 332ci motor.

The 4bbl 332 was rated at 265bhp, and sported a 9.5:1 comp ratio. Like its big brother the 10.2:1 comp ratio 352, both 4 bbl V8s had duals and neither utilised hydraulic valve lifters. Those with an eye to performance cast a glad one to the 352 V8, which made an even 300bhp at

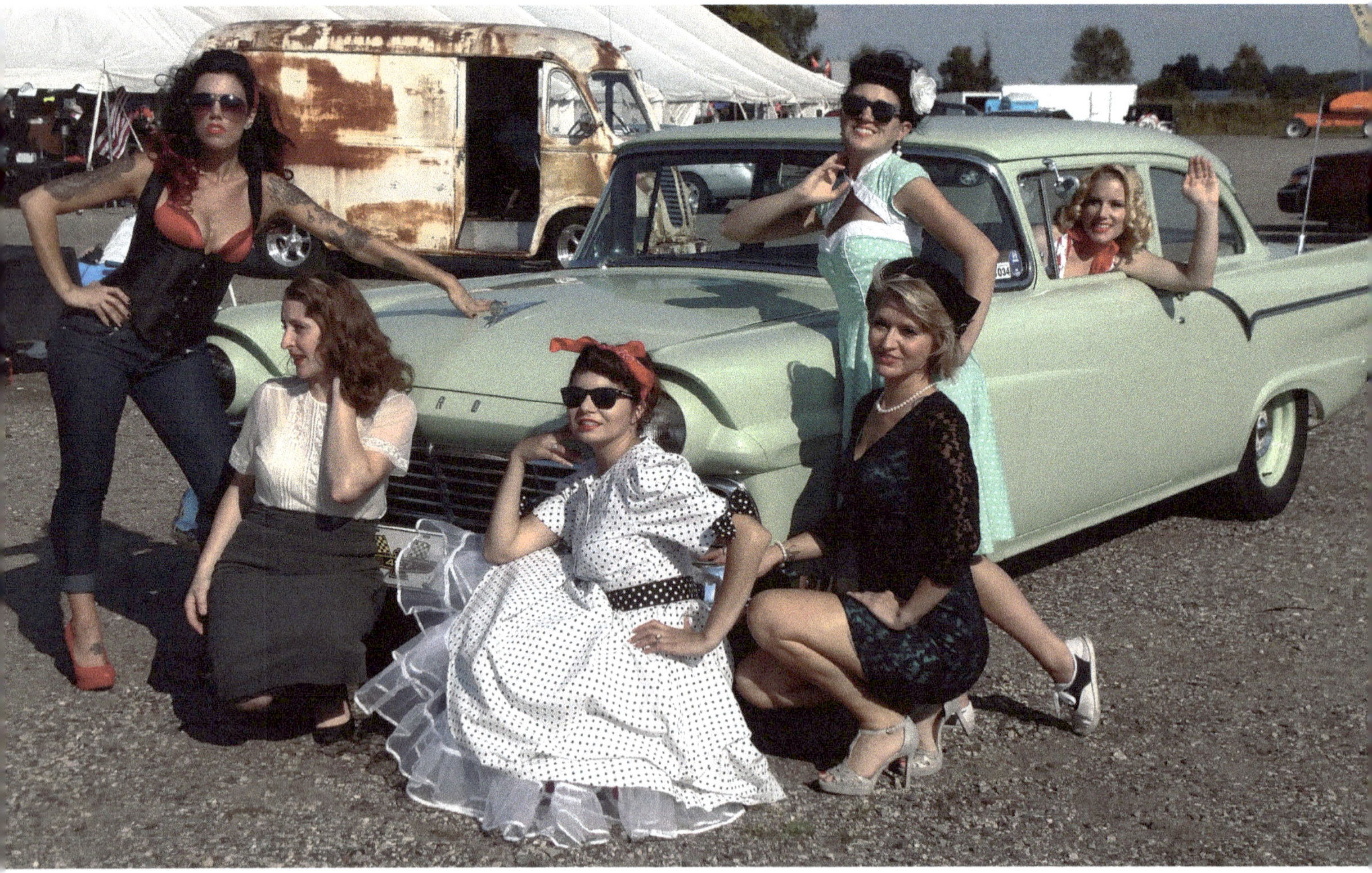

1: Hooking Up with Fairlane

4600rpm, and 395lb/ft at 2800rpm. In February 1958 *Motor Life* did a '3000-Mile Road Test' story on a Fairlane 500 four-door hardtop with 352. For 1958 MY Ford brought higher CFM Carter 4bbls to its premium fuel V8s, but the *Motor Life* car had a 2.69 econo axle. This spelt 0-60mph in 10 seconds and 14mpg overall economy.

Motor Life speculated that a normal axle ratio would lower the 0-60mph time to under 9 seconds. Attached to one's FE V8 would usually be a Ford-O-Matic or Cruise-O-Matic Ford autobox, but now Ford-O-Matic was a simplified, junior version of the upscale Cruise-O-Matic. The latter had two driving ranges, not one. For 1958 the Fairlane option sheet boasted a new 'Dual Range' auto for 332 and 352 V8 motors. With Dual Range, one could drive using normal low, intermediate and high, or stick to just intermediate and high for economy.

Apart from economy, the idea of eliminating low and taking off in second, was considered desirable for maintaining traction on slippery surfaces. *Motor*

Life's '58 Fairlane 500 352 V8 four-door hardtop had 55/45% front/rear weight distribution. This nose-heavy, cast iron V8-engined, family rear driver pattern was common from Detroit. With increasingly more powerful and heavier motors, decent winter snowbelt traction was hard to come by. The econo rear axle ratios also helped get lead sleds off the line. Some even resorted to VW Beetles, because of the

To cope with the 427 V8 motor swap, power front disk/rear drum brake combo has been fitted. The iconic Ford 9 inch differential, with Traction-Lok and 3.50 rear gears, helps transmit the 450 bhp! (Courtesy Todd Matthies)

As part of the mods necessary to cope with the 427, this '57 Custom has a 3in exhaust system and oversize 235/70/15in tires front, and 275/60/15in tires at the rear. (Courtesy Todd Matthies)

Ford Midsize Muscle – Fairlane, Torino & Ranchero

Above left: The sunvisor absence spoke to the low cost market of the '57 Ford Custom. The interior is all original, bar the addition of Ford tach, radio and new carpet. (Courtesy Todd Matthies)

Above right: The bored out 427 (4.24in bore and 450ci) has a 428 CJ crank, forged pistons, roller rocker arms, stainless valves and Comp Cams solid lifter cam with 0.616in lift and 294 degree duration. (Courtesy Todd Matthies)

Right: As a top line Fairlane 500 Club Sedan, this two-door sat on the longer 118in wheelbase. Even so, the rear drive transmission tunnel challenged the claim that domestic family cars were 6 seaters! (Courtesy Dave Miller)

rear engine weight placed over the rear traction wheels!

1958 Fairlane brought a surprising number of mechanical and cosmetic changes, given 1957 had already been a big shake up year. Keeping in vogue there was a new, optional 'Air-Suspension' system. Buyers were more concerned with ride comfort, than grease lightning acceleration in the '50s. Ford engineers even had the wherewithal to lavish a new recirculating ball steering system, in place of the previous worm and roller setup. And where would Detroit be without an annual restyle?

1958 brought a T-Bird grille and horizontal quad headlights, which fashionably spelt high-performance. After

1: Hooking Up with Fairlane

all, Corvette had them! The rear fascia was new too, Ford had dumped its famous rocket taillights. General sentiment was that Ford was over-ornamenting Fairlane to make it look like big money. A low cost Lincoln if you will. This was still a time when the family-sized car was the volume seller for US automakers. More engineering time, money and styling were devoted to such lines. The explosion in postwar consumer culture just saw geegaws and baubles added to the mix. However, there was a dark side to this 'Jukebox Fever.'

A 300 horse Fairlane was rapid, and, in four-door 500 trim hardtop guise, tipped the scales at 3850lb. And yet this mini behemoth had the same 180in² brake lining area as the much less powerful, sub-200in 1956 edition, which weighed 500lb less! There was evidence Ford, and others, were getting lost in the showmanship. At one time, changes were made to make things better, not just different. In the annual *All The World's Cars* guide of 1954, John Bentley outlined the sensible developments Ford introduced, to match the arrival of its more powerful, new OHV V8.⁽⁴⁾

Factory a/c was a rare and pricey option in the '50s and '60s. Back then, many went the aftermarket route, or a more recent retrofit in this case. (Courtesy Dave Miller)

The All New '57 Fords represented a $200 million investment on Henry's part. (Courtesy Dave Miller)

Ford Midsize Muscle – Fairlane, Torino & Ranchero

In January 1957, *Motor Life* thought its '57 Fairlane 500 four-door's 'Thunderbird Special' 245 horse 312 Y block came on cam like a Mercedes 190SL! (Courtesy Dave Miller)

Edsel, the day the clown came to town …

Amongst major chassis changes, there was adoption of balljoint front suspension, as seen previously on upscale Lincoln and Mercury. There was a new chassis frame, new rear springs, shocks, engine mounts and front stabiliser bar. The reduction in chassis lubrication points from 16 to four, and better brakes, all represented engineering improvements that only Superman's X-ray vision could detect. By the late '50s it seemed more important to look like a Lincoln, than to drive like a Lincoln. However, pride comes before an Edsel. The aspirations of marketing seemed to reach a climax with the introduction of the upscale Edsel marque. September 4 1957 was 'Edsel Day,' and everyone knew it was. TV and magazines informed the public about the new best thing since sliced bread, but the 1958 recession threw a major monkey wrench into Ford's finely engineered marketing strategy. Edsel was a range of fancier-styled, trimmed and powered Fords based on Henry's full-size family car. However, the conversation piece grille and Teletouch automatic couldn't convince the public that Edsel offered any real improvement, on the already worthy Fairlane. America's economic slowdown, and a public watching the pennies, saw to it that Dearborn lost almost $400 million on the car with that funny looking grille.[5]

Old Henry discovered the hard way in the 1958 MY, that the public preferred Doris Day to Edsel Day! By the close of 1959 model year, the Edsel marque was consigned to history. Scapegoats were sought for the project's failure. High ups closely involved with Edsel were either demoted or fired. For 1959, acknowledging economic conditions, Ford completely changed course and emphasised the value of thrift. Before FoMoCo went 'Total Performance' in the '60s, it went 'Total Economy.' It was a response to Edsel's lukewarm reception, and the success of mileage maximizers like the Rambler American, Studebaker Lark and VW Beetle.

1959 – back to economy

Ford's official 1959 press statement was 'Common sense, not excess.' The company meant it, and returned to Henry Ford's 'waste not, want not' farming roots. It had wandered too far from the five and dime. *Car Life*'s Jim Whipple commented in January 1959, on Fairlane's welcome return to simple, functional styling in 1959. However, he did miss the shorter 116in wheelbase edition, having felt it went well with Ford's 223 cube I6 and three-speed manual. Ford's '59 MY Fairlane rode solely on the longer 118in wheelbase. Ford was also looking to the stats. By the late '50s the V8 was king in the full-size family car. Even 77% of 1959 Edsel buyers specified a V8. However, what kind of V8?

In spite of all the ad copy, and car reports on the hot setups, Ford predicted 95% of family car buyers would choose the humble 292 base V8 in 1959. The hot setup was still around. That would be the 352 V8 with three-speed manual and 3.70:1 final drive, but there was little interest in such drivetrain. Tuning for thrift Ford dropped the comp ratio from 9.1 to 8.8:1. This 200 horse regular fuel 292, would go with the new, cheaper and simplified two-speed Ford-O-Matic. The three-speed Cruise-O-Matic was a premium option.

Even moving up to the 332 saw a popular set of 2-barrel carburetion, two-speed Ford-O-Matic and 2.91: final drive ratio, for easy turnpike living. The American public suddenly placed quality and good build, higher on the priority list. Ford followed the

Above: A '58 Skyliner with Interceptor FE 300 horse 352 V8. During Ford's Edsel era, more of everything was considered the right route! (Courtesy Donn Dabney www.leftcoastclassics.com)

Right: In the '50s it was ok to have a luxo ride with a cloth interior. The '58 dashboard was largely a carryover from the all-new '57 MY. (Courtesy Donn Dabney www.leftcoastclassics.com)

well made feel of Rambler, Studebaker and VW for its '59 MY. There was consensus that the '59 Fairlanes were better cars than the '58s. Fit and finish seemed improved, as were trim materials and mechanical components. *Motor Life* mentioned its 3000 mile '58 Fairlane's enamel paint easily coped with a sand blasting 70-100mph desert storm, on a trip to Southern California. Word was this enamel exterior was even better in the '59 MY.

Top: Henry's metal ragtop went by a couple of monikers, Ford Fairlane 500 Skyliner, and sometimes Skyliner Retractable Convertible. Either way, a complex beastie! (Courtesy Donn Dabney www.leftcoastclassics.com)

Right: The new FE V8 was powerful, but power in the '50s only had meaning as a complement to luxury, the latter being more important. (Courtesy Donn Dabney www.leftcoastclassics.com)

Funnily enough, the extravagant Skyliner and Air Suspension options continued into the 1959 model year. Air Suspension had been a rarely chosen '58 MY option. For '59 MY its mechanical workings were simplified and improved. It wasn't often that the British press examined American automobiles. The size and thirst of Detroit's wares made them ill suited to the road conditions of the British Isles. However, the UK's leading car journal *Autocar*, carried a report on the 1959 Fairlane sedan in its 1959 July 3rd issue. *Autocar*'s John Bolster remarked that Fairlane had firmer suspension character than the American norm.

Fairlane was now 208in long and weighed 3874lb – too big to be the 'handling' car it was in the early '50s. However, amongst American family cars it still afforded uncommonly fine controllability. *Autocar* summed up Fairlane as a luxurious touring car with infinite luggage space. Dare it be said that Fairlane's trunk could have accommodated an English Ford Popular! In contrast, American Fords had long found more comfortable homes in South Africa and Australia. Countries of right-hand drive nature, with vast distances and relatively cheap gas. Both countries had a protected car industry, with high tariffs encouraging local manufacture via CKD operations or more.

Big, tough V8 Fords were appreciated on the unsealed roads of South Africa, although by 1960 drivers there were turning to the smaller Fords of Europe, for ease of driving and economy. The Model T had visited Australia, with the wood from CKD crates serving as floorboards of completed cars! Fast forward to the '50s and Ford Australia was a CKD operation, putting together right-hand drive versions of Ford's designs from Henry's global markets. Filling the Australian big car luxury niche were locally assembled RHD Custom 300s and Fairlane 500s. The cars were put together at the Australian Sydney Ford Homebush plant.

Australian Fairlanes, Galaxies & Falcons!

Australian magazine *Wheels* journalist Doug Blain posed the question 'Are They Our Smallest Big Cars?' in the September 1959 issue article's title. By this he implied that the flashy, long, low-styled American

The new 1957-59 Ford family car chassis involved a lower floor and differential. The diff's pinion gear was very low in relation to the adjacent axle shafts compared to usual hypoid differentials. (Courtesy Walt Smith)

1: Hooking Up with Fairlane

By 1957 the fancy acrylic see-through-roofed Crown Vic Skyliner, had given way to the powered 'Retractible' hardtop Skyliner. This new variant was complemented by the conventional Sunliner ragtop shown. (Courtesy Walt Smith)

In 1958 a regular Fairlane sedan cost $2055, with the '58 Fairlane 500 conv pictured retailing for $2650. Upscale Retractible was $3163! (Courtesy Walt Smith)

Ford's Lifeguard Design safety elements, like recessed dashboard controls, were still standard or optional. However, a *Popular Mechanic*'s March 1957 survey showed only 6.2% of '57 Ford owners ordered seatbelts. Well, Henry did say safety didn't sell! (Courtesy Walt Smith)

car had reached a grand size, and didn't offer as much interior space as its exterior size suggested. The Fairlane's suspension was judged softer than in previous years. The Australian Fairlane was identical to its US counterpart, save for lagging a year or two in model updates. So the car featured in the *Wheels*' test was the 1959 shape Fairlane, not the revised '60 model.

US Fairlane would continue to be Australian assembled, until the close of 1965 Australian model year. In America the new top luxury Ford, introduced in mid 1959 model year, was the Galaxie. Unlike Edsel, Galaxie would prove to be commercially successful, and a full-size Ford legend. Australia embraced Galaxie, and for a number of years it became Australia's favorite big American car, albeit satisfying a very small part of the Aussie luxury market. Once again the Australian Galaxie was its US counterpart in RHD guise.

The Fairlane nameplate returned to Australia in 1967. This time the model was of Australian design, and was sized slightly smaller than a US intermediate. This car was positioned between the Ford Falcon and the Galaxie, completing Ford

Ford Midsize Muscle – Fairlane, Torino & Ranchero

Come '58 MY, and the new FE family 332 and 352 ci V8s were abound. Even with the smaller 332, owners in snowy climes were doing 2nd gear starts, to gain traction. Domestic V8s were nose-heavy! (Courtesy Walt Smith)

Australia's move to offering products better tuned to this market, away from CKD assemblers of US designs. Misgivings about the US Fairlane's size in 1959, were soon allayed by local production of the Falcon compact in 1960. Initially just a RHD version of its US counterpart, the Aussie Falcon diverged from its US template as the years went by.

The fully Australian designed and manufactured Falcon and Fairlane became local icons, lasting decades beyond both nameplates being laid to rest in America. By 1970 the 351-engined Australian Fairlane was obviously intended to take over from the increasingly unprofitable, and ill-suited to the market, RHD version of the Galaxie 390.

It soon did, but back in 1960 the chief concern with the Fairlane was lack of power. With fuel in Australia being more expensive than in America, and high octane gas being unavailable, motor choice was limited to a 7.4:1 comp version of the 332, making 204bhp gross.

For the Australian Victorian police force using the Fairlane four-door as a cop car, this made the sedan somewhat of a lead sled. The fuzz worked with Ford Australia to soup up the sedan. The engineers increased the compression ratio to 8.9:1 and played with carb settings, taking output to 220 horses. Essentially this was the US '59 MY Fairlane 332 spec. This motor/model when done for the police was dubbed 'Interceptor.' The same tag was applied to the hotter version of the 170ci six-cylinder Australian Falcon created for the police force, a version which also became incorporated into the normal model range.

The Aussie police 332 became the standard powerplant in 1960 Australian Fairlanes, just before higher octane gas became available to the wider public. The 1960 MY Fairlanes looked just like their 1959 US counterparts, complete with 'Stars In The Night' effect chrome grille decorations. The 1961 MY Aussie Fairlane continued with the 1959 US styling, but incorporated some cosmetic items from the 1960 US Fairlane. The 1960 style wheels/hubcaps and 1960 'chainmail' grille insert decorations were adopted. It was normal for CKD operations to take on such alterations in piecemeal fashion. This didn't just apply to Ford.

Fairlane – bigger in 1960!

It was onerous, financially and planning wise, to adopt Detroit's frequent annual changes. So, overseas operations let changes build up before major local relaunches. In America, Fairlane rolled on to something fresh for the '60 MY. The wraparound windscreen was gone, and

Left: "Don't let the stars get in your eyes, don't let the moon break your heart" sang Perry Como! Unless, it was the 'Stars In The Night' chrome grille of '59 Fairlane. A Fairlane 500 Skyliner is at hand. Right: McNamara's statisticians predicted 95% would select the 2bbl 292 base V8, just like on this '59 Skyliner. A 200 horse regular fuel motor; snug enough for Jack Benny! (Courtesy www.almeidasclassiccars.com)

1: Hooking Up with Fairlane

Left: Skyliner's automated top boasted ten power relays, ten limit switches, eight circuit breakers, four lock motors, three drive motors, 610ft of wiring – and a partridge in a pear tree!
Right: Skyliner and Air Suspension were complicated and expensive, but both were still around in post recession '59 MY. The latter both simplified and refined further. (Courtesy www.almeidasclassiccars.com)

Skyliner never officially went Down Under, but the Aussie police did use CKD '59 Fairlanes as pursuit vehicles! (Courtesy www.almeidasclassiccars.com)

Left: Ford's pioneering auto safety work continued with fully padded armrests, and rear child-proof door locks available. Plush interiors meant Fairlane and other family cars were moving away from the low cost field tag by the late '50s.
Right: Although Ford's family car was getting big, *Autocar*'s John Bolster felt '59 Fairlane's firmer than Detroit average suspension made it America's best full-size handler. (Courtesy www.almeidasclassiccars.com)

there was a new 'raised eyebrow' quad round headlamp visage. It was a sleeker, more modern look for sure. Galaxie shared this styling and body, with expected exterior embellishments and uptrimmed interior. The full-size Ford had become bigger, now on a 119in wheelbase with overall length of 213.6in for a two-door sedan.

Full-size Ford could be a better deal because Ford had a compact, and would soon have a new intermediate, to cater for size classes. Fairlane's sleek looking new hood made a crossflow radiator with auxiliary top up tank necessary. The tall base 223ci six even had to have its air cleaner mounted beside the engine, instead of the normal over the carb placement. Ford engineers made it all work, using a 90 degree elbow connection. Although longer and heavier at 3540lb the new two-door could still get by on the base six. The 223 145 horse/three-speed manual power team equaled 0-60mph in 16.5 seconds and 14mpg city/19mpg highway economy.

25

Ford Midsize Muscle – Fairlane, Torino & Ranchero

Representing Ford's long law enforcement vehicle supply involvement, this 1960 Fairlane 500 sedan is a faithful replica of the cop cars that used to protect and serve. (Courtesy Michael Calhoon www.mjcclassiccars.com)

Post Edsel, Ford got sensible. So it was that this ride got the 200bhp, regular fuel, 2bbl 292 with 8.8:1 CR. (Courtesy Michael Calhoon www.mjcclassiccars.com)

The floor mat is factory original, but the blue vinyl upholstery is new. Outlets of the aftermarket Vintage Air a/c are at the dash ends. (Courtesy Michael Calhoon www.mjcclassiccars.com)

With optional overdrive this Fairlane could challenge the economy of a Vee Dub, whilst offering much greater comfort and speed. The even traction 52/48% weight distribution was enough to put a smile on the dials of snowbelt traveling salesmen. Kicking off the '60s was an ultra-sensible, pre-Beatles conservative time. No doubt Henry was taking heed of the Rambler's puritanical ways. Robert McNamara was in charge of Ford by now, which meant Edsel out, Falcon compact and safety in. Which probably explained why Ralph Nader was knocking on Corvair's door in the '60s.

Reading the thrifty mood of the times, McNamara's belt-tightening saw 'reduced' horsepower ratings through the entire regular Ford engine line for 1961 MY. There was emphasis on convenience and economy for '61. Being sensible meant more rigid side panels for full-size '61 Fords. Lincoln had gone unibody in 1958; resonance and vibration studies concerning Thunderbird and Lincoln unibodies had positive flow-ons to the low-cost line. The Cruise-O-Matic now featured the refinement of vacuum throttle valve controls; it no longer used a mechanical shift linkage.

Lest one feared Henry was becoming a trifle dull, the full-size Fairlane received an almost complete restyle for '61 MY. Appearance changes, often annual, were a commercial necessity in the competitive North American car market. Styling sold cars. The 1960 roof was harmoniously combined with a sleek new body, reminiscent of a '59 Caddy. The difference was that Ford's look was more subtle, avoided the 'Mile-High' tailfin billboards, and, dare it be said ... the Fairlane/Galaxie looked better?! The front grille/headlight treatment was very '59 Caddy. Ford took things forward with a novel 'grille at both ends' look.

Was Fairlane coming or going? With a grille at both ends, it was hard to tell. However, when it was going, it was going more quickly. Still on a 119in wheelbase, in 1961 Ford made its full-size smaller on the outside. A most unusual Detroit development! Length was down from 213.7in to 209.9in and width decreased from 81.5in to 79.9in. Height stayed the same at 55in, with front and rear track constant at 61in and 60in respectively. Smaller meant less baggage, and even the revised Cruise-O-Matic was 25lb trimmer. It all promised a return to Ford's fine full-size handling reputation.

1: Hooking Up with Fairlane

The hot 390!
There was also a new 390 top dog motor option. The 135 horse 223 I6 still kicked off the full-size range, next was the 292 V8 with 8.8:1 comp and 175 horses. Second from top was the trusty 352 with 8.9:1 comp, making 220 ponies and 336lb/ft using 2-barrel carburetion. Then came the new 390 V8. As a 4bbl 9.6:1 motor, bet the house on a genuine 300bhp and 427lb/ft. The 390 was a bored and stroked 352. Bore was up from 4in to 4.05in and stroke moved northwards from 3.5in to 3.78in. There was also the refinement of an aluminum front timing chain cover, promising less weight and minimized oil leakage.

Team this with the latest three-speed Cruise-O-Matic, and one had a power team even Rolls-Royce would have been envious of! However, positive crankcase ventilation, was an emissions warning of darker things to come. Unburned hydrocarbons from the combustion chambers were directed to the crankcase and back to the intake manifold. Of more imminent concern, was the arrival of more zotts under the hood. On the 1961 and 1962 full-size Fords, it was possible to get a higher performance 390 V8.

This hi po edition featured an aluminum intake manifold for the 4bbl carb, cast iron header type exhaust manifold, solid lifter valve train and 10.6:1 comp ratio. Of course if 375 horses didn't interest performance fiends, triple 2-barrel carburetion on a special intake manifold could be added to the hi po 390. This equipment took power to 401bhp at 6000rpm and 430lb/ft at 3500rpm. Such additional parts were to be installed by your friendly dealer. The triple 2bbl carbs and associated aluminum intake manifold were merely trunk delivered in plastic wrap!

Henry was saying that if you wanted more than 375 horses, then on your own head be it! The factory wasn't going to fit it. It should be noted that this was still a speed limited time. The generally agreed Big 4 anti racing pact, meant no super hot motor outside a full-size. The mighty Ford Thunderbolt, and buying homologation hop up parts related to SCCA Trans Am racing, were still some years away. In 1961 the public, and a minority at that, were into banker's hot rods. These were full-size sleds fitted with the hottest motor

Fairlane got a sleeker front fascia for '60 MY, replete with chainmail grille décor. The sleek hood meant a new crossflow radiator and auxiliary tank. Complementing the era-correct roof siren and dual spotlights is a passenger-side grille stoplight! (Courtesy Michael Calhoon www.mjcclassiccars.com)

The original AM radio has been converted to AM/FM operation. Power disk brakes now help arrest this cop car's forward motion! One would normally have had to wait until '67 MY to get Fairlane disks. (Courtesy Michael Calhoon www.mjcclassiccars.com)

Even fancier gadgets and trim distinguished Galaxie from Fairlane in the pre '62 shared six-seater body, full-size days. Fairlane went midsize thereafter. (Courtesy Michael Calhoon www.mjcclassiccars.com)

Ford Midsize Muscle – Fairlane, Torino & Ranchero

The period-correct CB radio and dual whip antenna allowed Smokey to keep tabs whilst in hot pursuit! This Fairlane bodystyle was even CKD assembled by Ford South Africa to avoid high import duties. (Courtesy Michael Calhoon www.mjcclassiccars.com)

available. Heavy-duty (HD) suspension and special brake drum linings, usually reserved for cop cars, were added. It took a determined soul, a helpful dealer, and money to create such dream cars. However, no formal stand-alone muscle car models existed yet.

Racing was either NASCAR or grassroots drag racing supported by local dealers. The concept of using high performance to sell cars nationally, with formal ad campaigns, had yet to eventuate. What was needed was a smaller car, with a new generation of lightweight hi po V8, to get the public excited about high performance in a family ride. Soon, Fairlane would have both, but for now it was the end of an era. 1961 was the final year for full-size Fairlane, and, come 1962, Galaxie would be on its own. However, there was no waiting for Fairlane excitement to pick up!

2

Ranchero – The Tuxedo-Wearing Pickup!

For '52 MY, Gordon Buehrig designed a new line of all-steel wagons that included a two-door Ranch Wagon, shown here in 1956 form. A sales winner, Ranch Wagon gave Ford a shortcut to the Ranchero pickup. (Courtesy Dennis Crenshaw)

Car pickup history

Was it a car or a truck? That was the question everyone was asking when Ford Ranchero arrived. Public and press have been asking this very question about this kind of vehicle ever since. Ranchero entered later than other 1957 model year Fords. It did so on December 8, 1956, at the National Automobile Show, held at New York's Coliseum, and generated a tremendous amount of trade excitement. However, the concept of a car-based pickup was hardly a new one. Back in the 1920s it was common practice to turn sedans, coupes and roadsters into pickups, adding a rear bed in place of chopped off bodywork on a custom basis.

Coachbuilding was popular and easy when one had a separate chassis. Things got more formal in the 1930s with Ford. The history is cloudy, but it seems the Depression precipitated the creation of production, car-based pickups in America and Australia, around the same time.

When times were hard, farmers didn't have money for a normal car and a work vehicle, so why not combine the two in one? Thus, the Ford Model A Roadster pickup's presence was explained. In Australia a farmer's wife wrote a letter to Ford. She requested Ford build a vehicle capable of taking her and her husband to church on Sunday, and the pigs to market during the week.

Necessity being the mother of invention, Ford Australia designer Lew Bandt combined a 1932 Australian Ford Roadster, with a steel utility box. The bodywork behind the Roadster's doors was removed, and the steel box placed on the underlying chassis flush with the doors. It became a regular, and very popular production model from 1933. Australians nicknamed such car-based pickups as 'utes', with ute being short for utility; the term and vehicle would live on into the 21st century. From 1940 the ute's spare tire was carried behind the vehicle's interior seating, a

Ford Midsize Muscle – Fairlane, Torino & Ranchero

quality that was present on the 1957 Ranchero too!

Ford's Aussie ute sparked locally assembled competition from Chevy and Dodge based vehicles. However, as in America, the concept's popularity faded somewhat after the war. A more affluent society could now afford a real pickup, and a fancy wagon, and wagons were all the rage in post war America. Technical progress meant new models were 'Woodies' in name only.

Ford wagons roll!

The new wave was indicated by the 1949 Plymouth Suburban steel bodied two-door wagon. Ford replied with a highline two-door wagon of its own that same year. Once again wagon wood was now decoration, not structural. At the start of the 1950s designer Gordon Buehrig got to work on new steel bodied wagons. Historically significant for Ranchero was the two-door Ranch Wagon, done for Ford's Mainline family car series. It was essentially a converted Ford sedan delivery or panel van. Where sides were once all steel, there now lay side glass panes. Voila, a new wagon!

Even Korean War induced steel shortages, didn't stop Ford's wagons from being a commercial juggernaut. Around 116,000 units sold in 1953, almost 142,000 in 1954, and approximately half were Ranch Wagons. Indeed, Ranch Wagon popularity reversed a former trend, where now wagons boasted best resale value in the Ford line! Ford was Wagon King, making Chevy's Nomad look rather solitary! To consolidate such wagon, leisure vehicle market segment dominance, Ford management gave the green light to Ranchero.

Ford certainly had a no compromise, all new year for 1957, costing $200 million! The Ranchero and Retractible convertible were star attractions. The new models had a styling theme that would continue to 1964. Prominent designers were Bill Boyer, Damon Woods, Frank Hershey, Bob McGuire, Chuck Mashigan, AJ Middlestead and L David Ash. Ranchero profited from the glamor, because it was showcased in the 1957 Hollywood movie April Love. In this flick Pat Boone sang to Shirley Jones in a new Ranchero. It was product placement set against a Kentucky backdrop, as Ford vied with Chevrolet to secure the WASP vote!

Dina Shore was telling Americans to see the USA in a Chevrolet. Pat Boone was doing TV ads extolling the fine handling of the C1 Corvette. Ford had to afford some limelight for its products. When it came to fine-handling two-seaters, Ford had Thunderbird. In addition, Ranchero was talked up as a Thunderbird with a pickup bed! Well, it did have two doors, and was a two-seater with solid handling and a sporting nature. The Vette connection was hovering over that Kentucky bluegrass! Ranchero got sporty by way of being built on the shorter 116in Fairlane wheelbase. It was also lighter than Fairlane, due to the absence of bodywork. A quality noted by *Hot Rod* magazine in July 1957.

The stats showed that between like-engined Fairlanes and Rancheros, the latter were favored in acceleration contests. *Mechanix Illustrated*'s '57 Fairlane 500 with 2bbl 292 and Ford-O-Matic cruised to 60mph in 12.1 seconds. With the same power team *Motor Life*'s Ranchero managed the sprint in 11.3 seconds in July 1957. Ranchero tipped the scales at 3640lb and recorded 14.6mpg overall in that test. The power team in question, was the hero Thunderbird combo! Lift the

Then, as now, Ford's F-series trucks were volume sellers. However, Ranchero pickup truck was always a niche player. (Courtesy Marc Cranswick)

In the planned obsolescence heyday of '50s Detroit, Ford management couldn't have forseen a '57 Ranchero being Pro Streeted in the 21st Century! Old Fords never die, they just git it on! (Courtesy Bob Borum)

hood on Ranchero and that 212 horse 292 carried the Thunderbird script and logo on its V8 valve covers with pride!

In Uncle Tom McCahill's *Mechanix Illustrated* '57 Ford story, he noted that the '57 Fairlane 500 cornered as flat as a mailman's feet! The Ranchero was, at heart, utilising 14in wheels, and the 4in lowered center of gravity introduced on the '57 Fairlane. At the time it was normal for Ford pickups to have 15in wheels, and a lot more ground clearance. In addition, Ranchero's Ranch Wagon relation meant five rear leafs, not sedan's four, and the stiffer rear springs of Ford wagon. Weight distribution on the Ranchero V8 was 57.3/42.7%, and exterior dimensions showed Ranchero was no ordinary pickup.

Compared to a 1956 Ford pickup work horse, Ranchero was 16in lower and 18in longer. Overall Ranchero length was 203.5in, width and height were 77in and 58.7in respectively. Here was the sleek driving experience even fancily trimmed pickups, like the 1955-56 Chevrolet Cameo, couldn't provide. *Motor Life* speculated that Ranchero was probably the only truck in the world with the good driving quality afforded by Fairlane's balljoint front suspension. If fancy pickups weren't delivering, neither were conventional wagons. Wagons had become such upscale and well-trimmed middle class status symbols, one dared not use a wagon as intended anymore.

Ranchero – the glamor pickup

Into the breach stepped Ranchero. In spite of the availability of two-tone paint, this pickup could do some hauling. Ranchero was rated to carry 1190lb, and being fitted with Ranch Wagon's stiffer springs as standard, it could in theory take a heavier load than a ½-ton Ford F100. Being loaded up predictably improved Ranchero's roadability. Apart from the traction advantage of having more weight over the rear wheels, *Motor Trend*'s Walt Woron found that carrying 700lb of firewood around Apple Valley reduced oversteer and ride float.

Ranchero's bed measured 6ft by 4.5ft by 1.2ft, yielding a space capacity of $32.4ft^3$. Control from the non-power assisted worm and triple tooth gear steering wasn't too onerous. However, the 40ft turning circle was accompanied by an unwieldy '50s style 4.5 turns, lock to lock. So no need to worry about sneezing when changing lanes! The 1957 Ranchero put the driver in charge of simple, legible gas/speedo/temp instruments in a crescent display – more readable than Detroit's over-designed displays of the late '60s. Ground clearance and the car's 14in rims were the car's connection that let Ranchero down, concerning pickup duties over rough terrain.

In terms of luxury the Ranchero car connection was a good thing. Ranchero's sales distribution may have been handled by Ford's Truck Division, but how many trucks could have power brakes, power windows, power seats and a/c on the one rig?! Indeed, Ranchero could have all these items, and virtually any Fairlane car option one wished for. Ranchero answered the public's desire for nicer trucks – it was basically the brougham of trucks. Ford initiated its famous Ranchero stylized steer's head tailgate logo. There were rear fender chrome script callouts, and a tailgate handle embossed with Ford's coat of arms.

Ford designers underlined that car link, by incorporating Ford's modest and tasteful sedan tailfins. As usual in pre 1980s Detroit, how much or how little trimming, was up to the buyer. Beyond the standard Ranchero, 'Custom' brought chrome sidespear, dual sunvisors, horn ring, full custom trimmed interior door panels, upscale seats and fancy Fairlane Crown Vic wheel covers. With all the fruit, dished and vaned chrome wheel covers and wide whites, it would have been a shame to get one's Ranchero dusty! Custom's chrome work surrounded the rear cab window, with the river of brightwork flowing down to line the upper edge of the pickup bed.

Practical-minded owners avoided the wide whites and extra trimmings, and modified Ranchero for everyday utility. Having the spare wheel and toolkit placed behind the passenger seat limited the amount of luggage that could be locked up securely. Walt Woron mentioned a popular mod that many owners made:

Above: Not your father's Ranchero, nor the one Pat Boone crooned to Shirley Jones in, concerning the 1957 movie *April Love*. Two seat Ranchero had sports car connotations from day one! (Courtesy Bob Borum)

Ford utilized two-door Ranch Wagon sibling to keep down Ranchero tooling costs. Here, '57 Ranchero resides with a '57 Tudor. Henry was always careful with the pennies. (Courtesy Bob Borum)

2: Ranchero – The Tuxedo-Wearing Pickup!

it was reasonably easy to hinge part of Ranchero's pickup bed floor, and utilize the underlying wagon floor for spare tire and toolkit storage. This was indeed where the spare was kept on wagons. The only trouble was accessing aforementioned spare, when that pickup bed was already carrying a load![6]

Ranchero's pickup bed featured textured paint as standard. The aftermarket quickly hopped in with chrome bed guard rails, and cargo concealing tonneau covers. The reflective side trim seen on some 1957 and 1958 Rancheros was a dealer fitted option. Those not seeking a mountain of power could avoid the very popular T-Bird 292, and select the homely 190 horse 272 V8. To really save the pennies the 223ci 144 bhp I6 provided straight talking value, and excellent underhood service space. Perfectly adequate for riding around the Ponderosa! On an engineering level the new Ranchero embodied the useful major full-size '57 changes Ford made.

The goodness of 1957 full-size Ford engineering

Ranchero, in the tradition of car-based pickups, was a Ranch Wagon with the roof section behind the driver's cab deep-sixed, and a pickup bed placed on the station wagon floor. The underlying chassis of Ranchero, wagon and sedan, was new for '57. To achieve a sleek shape, with recessed wheels and good interior space, the frame side rails flared out in the passenger area. The reduced ground clearance of the sporty '57s involved a new driveshaft and rear axle re-design. The separate chassis side rail kicked up for rear axle clearance, that saw said axle placed 12in further back than in 1956.

This move created more rear seat accommodation, and facilitated variable rate rear springs. Rear suspension leaf springs had lengthened from 53in to 55in, from 1956 to 1957 model years. Most of the additional length was ahead of the rear axle. This enabled the forward section to be relatively stiffer than the spring section aft of the axle. The aim was reduced squat and dive, whilst avoiding the buckboard ride of sporty cars with stiff, short rear leafs. For 1957, special rubber bumpers were added to the frame's side rails, halfway between the rear leaf's front supports and the rear axle.

Once again the object was more control and less chance of bottoming out. It reduced spring deflection during a loaded ride, making a comfortable riding

Top: '57 Ranchero could have all those Fairlane options, but these power seats were retrofitted much later.
Bottom: Ranchero could call on T-Bird V8s back in the day, but this GT 40 Le Mans side oiler 427 is a bird of a completely different feather!
(Courtesy Bob Borum)

Ford Midsize Muscle – Fairlane, Torino & Ranchero

long leaf behave like a stiffer, shorter one when necessary. These changes and the 27% stiffer '57 frame were timely, since soon Ranchero would be bouncing over unsealed roads, hauling timber and other loads. Here the tough five ladder, three tubular crossmember frame, rolling on 14 x 5.5in stamped steel, five bolt rims proved handy. Ranchero and other '57 family Fords were also moving faster on average.

Compression ratios were up, and the latest two-barrel carb provided greater venturi capacity than the 1956 four-barrel! The revised intake manifold was the kind one used to only see at racetracks. Completing FoMoCo Total Performance '50s style, were the new Y type exhaust pipes for the 272/292ci V8s, which already came with that improved two-barrel. The old crossover pipe was bid adieu, and the new hardware started from the rear of both exhaust manifolds, each V8 bank, joining just ahead of the rear muffler. A three-speed manual box was standard, but those opting for Ford-O-Matic would find it H2O cooled for the first time in 1957. All the better to endure those hard 1-2 shifts at the dragstrip ¼ mile.

Gas was cheap in the '50s. Open Ranchero's left fender gas filler cap door and it didn't cost much to fill'er up for an evening's cruise. The youthful fun of impromptu traffic light drag races were aided by '57 Ford motors, with more valve area, and even an air filter that changed from oil bath to paper element type. The hot rod set also liked to play with ignition timing, and '57 Fords had a new distributor. Whereas the '56s were full vacuum, the '57s combined centrifugal and vacuum mechanism.

All changes to the good, but the one questionable mod Ford made for '57 was sheetmetal bodywork. Decades before BMW and Bangle tried flame surfacing, Ford was first with side panel sculptured styling on a low cost, mass produced car. The problem was that the technology of creating complex shapes over a large panel area, wasn't quite there in the late '50s. The result was panel weakness and early rusting. Sadly such rusting included the wonderfully custom 'frenched' headlight surrounds. In fact, 1957 family Fords got a subsequent reputation for shaky build quality, even though on the new model debut they were critically judged ok.

Uncle Tom McCahill went one further than a mere 'OK.' In his trademark expressive style he had this to say on the 1957 Fords in *Mechanix Illustrated*: "If you like it, buy it – you won't go wrong." Ranchero was certainly a '57 Ford worth buying, but as soon as such modern car-based pickups appeared, critics asked who exactly would buy them? This was a bold time in Detroit, when new concepts were tried.

Ranchero buyer profile – who was buying Ranchero now?

Corvette came out of GM's visionary Motorama shows, Ford also introduced its two-seater Thunderbird as a '50s response. Both cars didn't exactly set the sales charts alight in their early years.

Motor Trend's Walt Woron found positive public reaction when driving around in the new '57 Ranchero. Comments like "A custom pickup?" "A real beauty!" "A station wagon with the top off …" "A passenger car with a pickup bed … I like that!" In spite of such welcome reactions the exact demographic profile and volume, were uncertain. Like Corvette and T-Bird, Ranchero was a modern, volume produced vehicle without precedent in America. It soon became apparent that whilst the heavy-duty types still chose normal pickups for hard work, Mid-Westerners took a shine to the light duty, dual purpose nature of Ranchero.

The pigs to market/church on Sunday Ranchero portfolio made Ford's utility a friend to farmer and country club type alike. As Ford would later show with Mustang, the Ranchero was a classless vehicle, with enough style so it didn't look out of place in any setting. Gas service stations liked Ranchero, because the rigs looked neat next to their customer's

serviced cars. It was also a more upscale rig for their uniformed/overall wearing attendants to drive around. A good mobile advert for their business, not just another oily shade tree operation. Thus, combined with Ford's marketing hullabaloo, Ranchero managed 21,695 sales in 1957.

It was sufficient for Ford to continue Ranchero in 1958. That year, Ranchero and Fairlane took on the generally disliked '58 Thunderbird visage. Sales slowed to 9950 units. This drop was partly related to the recession, partly due to some of Ranchero's novelty value wearing off. Some of it had to do with the 1958 styling. However, Ford was getting the job done in showrooms, nearly outselling mighty butter and egg Chevrolet in 1957. With Ranchero and T-Bird, Ford had some fine moving two-seaters of its own. It seemed that not everyone believed Pat Boone's TV Chevy ad about Vette being the best handling two-seater on the market. It was the beginning of consumer awareness!

1959 – Ranchero has a rival!
Ford kept Ranchero on par with Fairlane in 1959, incorporating the whole body restyle that year. That meant 'Stars At Night' chrome grille inlay, 118in wheelbase and just one trim level. Ranchero was now using Fairlane's sole 118in wheelbase, although it previously rode on the shorter Fairlane 116in wheelbase. Observers noted the shorter 1957-58 cars rode just as well, with easier parkability! However, in 1959 it seemed Fairlane and Ranchero appreciated the no-nonsense restyle. The latter increased sales to 14,169 units. Better, but it seemed car-based pickups were niche market devices.

Ranchero's sole 1959 Custom trim opened a two-tone paint door to expected dual sunvisors, armrests, foam filled seats, cigar lighter and the usual Country Sedan Ranch Wagon accoutrements. Changing gear with the changing style implied a two-speed Ford-O-Matic for 1959. The Cruise-O-Matic was a 1959 three-speed refined development of Ford-O-Matic.

Ford went fancy for Ranchero's second year. T-Bird front clip, super fins and all the trimmings. Sadly, the '58 recession that claimed Edsel, knocked down Ranchero sales to 9950 in '58 MY. (Courtesy Mitch Hendricks)

Ford Midsize Muscle – Fairlane, Torino & Ranchero

No truck alive could match the comfort of a car-based pickup! Ranchero continued with all the luxo options one could find on an upscale Ford ... or Lincoln! (Courtesy Mitch Hendricks)

When it came to motors, one was spoilt for choice, some weren't even made by Ford! In 1957 Ranchero's T-Bird 292 made 212 bhp at 4500 rpm and 297lb/ft at 2700 rpm. However, for some this wasn't enough.

The June 1958 issue of *Hot Rod* carried the tale of the Fordillac. This was a 1957 Ranchero, converted from 292 power to accept the regal smoothness of a 1956 Cadillac 365 OHV V8 job! Continuing the tradition of inserting a high class, high powered motor into a new low cost ride. The 292 was sold to make up for the conversion cost. The Caddy 365 was bolted to a reworked '53 Cadillac application Hydra-Matic autobox. In the December 1963 issue of *Hot Rod*, the story of an owner who had fitted a Lincoln 370 V8 to his customized 1958 Ranchero was recounted. However, was there still a need for such conversions?

In 1958 Ranchero was available with Ford's biggest motor, a 10.2:1 CR four-barrel 352, making 300 horses. This motor continued as top dog on Ranchero in 1959, with some revisions like a different cam and recurved ignition advance. Compression ratio was lowered to 9.6:1, but the '59 4bbl 352 still probably had more horses in the corral. Even so the 300 horse rating remained, made at 4600 rpm, with 380lb/ft arriving at 2800 rpm. The spec sheet shenanigans were most likely from a need to honor the Detroit automaker agreed anti-racing pact, and to keep insurance premiums at bay.

In the February 1959 issue of *Hot Rod*, a Ranchero with the top T-Bird 352 was put through its paces. Fitted with three-speed Cruise-O-Matic autobox and a highway practical 2.69 rear axle ratio, the luxo rig managed 0-60mph in 9.9 seconds. Ranchero 352 crossed the ¼ mile in 17.2 seconds at 84mph. Not bad, and with a shorter rear ratio it could have done much better. Thriftier minded folk would have gone for a more low key power team. The 1959 range commenced with the trusty 223ci I6 making 145 bhp, then there was the butter and egg V8, a 292in two-barrel 200 horse form. Next up was the 225 pony 2bbl 332 V8.

Just about the only desirable feature Ranchero lacked was four on the floor. Then again, the muscle car/youth era had yet to eventuate. However, for '59 Ranchero did have a direct rival, that did offer four on the floor, not just three on the tree! The car, pickup, mini truck, you call it ... was the 1959 Chevrolet El Camino! Chevrolet, top dog in the sales race since 1937, the innovator, the big kahuna, was a bit miffed about the whole Ranchero affair. Why hadn't its brains trust suggested a car-based pickup first? Why was Henry garnering all those Ranchero sales, whilst the dealers tried to convince prospects it was wise to underseal a car a further two times post factory?!

So it was that Chevrolet embarked on two years of R&D/marketing to come up with its Ranchero rival. It was a hard road for the Bowtie Boys, because Chevrolet didn't have a two-door wagon for 1959, from which El Camino could be derived. This implied much new tooling for the El Camino body. It might have looked like a close '59 Impala relation, but was in fact largely a custom job. In the true 'waste nothing' tradition of farmer Henry Ford,

2: Ranchero – The Tuxedo-Wearing Pickup!

the Blue Oval brigade had done Ranchero on the cheap! By making the most of its two-door Ranch Wagon relation, Ranchero tooling was mainly just for the turret top, rear window and inner bed panelling.

When Henry Ford set up shop in sunny Australia, he was asked why the new factory followed the US factory style of having a roof designed to cope with heavy snow. He said it was because he didn't want to pay architects twice to come up with two different factories! Chevrolet wasn't worried about waste. Chevrolet was No 1, and figured it could amortize the mega outlay by selling over 50,000 Chevy pickups, year after year … wrong! A mixture of late '50s recession, the avante garde '59 Impala fin styling, and the novelty nature of a car-based pickup, kept 1959 El Camino sales down to 32,000 units.

The Ranchero & El Camino Comparo!

In spite of a major restyle for 1960, El Camino sales slumped to just 16,000 units. This was chump change for a Chebby, and Chevrolet pulled the plug on El Camino full-size at the end of 1960 MY. To add insult to injury, Ford outsold Chevrolet in 1960! History would show that El Camino would get reborn in 1964, reintroduced on the intermediate Chevelle platform. Time would also show that even though Ranchero and El Camino didn't set the sales charts alight, their original full-size incarnations would become popular on the cruise and custom scenes. These scenarios solely involve how cool one's ride is, or can be, and both rigs have always made the grade on that score!

As a new vehicle in 1959 there were feature differences between Ranchero and El Camino. On a practical level, Ford seemed to offer more. Ford's safety work in the '50s meant '59 Ranchero offered seatbelts and padded dash as options. Unlike El Camino, Ranchero had a triangular metal brace across the front of the pickup bed, to protect the cab from sliding loads. A 700lb load may

In these pre-Mustang, full-size Ranchero days, much was made of T-Bird V8 utilization. The combination of shorter 116in wheelbase and 300 horse 352 FE V8 was a lively one! (Courtesy Mitch Hendricks)

well have leveled Ranchero's body, but its tailgate didn't line up with the pickup bed. As was normal for car pickups, the tailgate was derived from the wagon's loading door base. However, Ranchero's open tailgate sat one inch higher than its pickup bed, whereas custom El Camino's was level.

One practical aspect that delivered a real kick in the pants to Chevrolet, was the fact that many states required El Camino owners to buy more expensive commercial license tags. The El Camino was sold and marketed through Chevy passenger car division. However, the stylish rig was officially linked to GMC Truck and Coach Division. To a muscle car fan of the late '50s – or today – what counted was what was under the hood. Unfortunately, this was one locality where the Bowtie Boys won out. Even Ford drivetrain engineers at the time admitted Chevy V8s had an edge on Henry's eight-pot motors. This quality would linger throughout the '60s.

In *Hot Rod*'s February 1959 showdown between Ranchero and El Camino with the top respective power teams, Chevrolet got home first. As nice as Ranchero's 352/Cruise-O-Matic situation was, El Camino's

Ford Midsize Muscle – Fairlane, Torino & Ranchero

Defying Detroit obsolescence, and maintaining hotrod tradition, owners held on to their full-size Rancheros. Modifying and customizing 'em as time went on. (Courtesy Mitch Hendricks)

triple deuce 348 11:1 comp mill/four-speed kept the tiger in the tank happy! That four-speed was Corvette derived, and the 348 V8 made 15 horses more than Ford's 352. Sure, the Chevy had a tighter 3.36 rear end, but even on a final drive level playing field, Ford lost this fire and brimstone contest. El Camino could draw on the peppy 283 small block with fuel-injection.

Given the El Camino's two-seater nature, that racy Vette power team was right at home in the mini rig, but who on earth would buy such a vehicle? With Detroit's multiple ordering permutations, it's conceivable no one! However, if anyone did order such a rig, it would be worth a lot because of the rare power team. That said, one didn't even have to go with injection. In March 1959, *Motor Trend* put an El Camino with mere 4bbl 283/two-speed Powerglide up against a full house Ranchero with 4bbl 352/three-speed Cruise-O-Matic. With 0-60mph El Camino won with 9.3 seconds, against Ranchero's 10.9 seconds. A performance car of the late '70s would have been glad of either result!

Being Sherlock Holmes through the Ford order blanks would have turned up a 3.70:1 final drive and three-speed manual with overdrive for Ranchero's 4bbl 352. That was as exciting as it got. *Hot Rod* did picture its test Ranchero 352 smoking an outside rear wheel in February 1959. This was mostly from opportune weight transfer and lack of traction, but Ranchero 352 was hardly underpowered. Ultimately it was Henry that had the last laugh over Chevrolet for 1960. El Camino persisted with full-size that year. McNamara's doctrine of intensive research had shown compact to be the commercial ticket for 1960.

Thus, 1959 was the last hurrah for full-size Ranchero, but its fans still enjoyed its appeal on the custom scene in the ensuing years. Ranchero was designed to be level with a load. This meant the stock unloaded ride height and wagon derived shocks/leafs, produced a sporty rake perfect for the jacked up '*American Graffiti*' era!

2: Ranchero – The Tuxedo-Wearing Pickup!

The custom scene indicated the kind of vehicle Ranchero was, and the start of how muscle cars are seen today. Even when full-size Ranchero was a current model, owners played around with bumpers, grille, hubcaps and paint to distinguish their ride from the madding crowd.

Roof chops were done, and the customized hardware utilized was drawn from Ford, Chrysler and the independents, not Chevy land! This showed a kind of marque solidarity, and the Ranchero's nature as a latter day hot rod. Even by the late '50s, modern cars were becoming difficult to customize in the manner of prewar rides, Ranchero was an exception. An exception that showed Detroit's plan of how buyers were supposed to relate to cars, wasn't going quite to plan. In the early to mid '60s *Hot Rod* magazine ran articles on some trick looking full-size Rancheros. The owners had lavished special attention on these works of art!

With Detroit's planned obsolescence people were meant to move on to the latest from the Big 4. However, these enthusiasts persevered with the discontinued full-size Ranchero as a pet project. Alluding to the niche muscle car era of the 21st century, these rides were stylized, and enjoyed by a relatively small group. How they looked was just as important as how they performed, maybe even more so. A lesson in why the 2004 GTO wasn't a sales winner. Like modern muscle car fans, these customized Ranchero owners had definite ideas on how their ride should be. Something unique from the millions issuing from the Motor City.

The tricked out '57 and '58 Rancheros featured in the December 1962 and 1963 issues of *Hot Rod*, were owned by a trucker and construction worker respectively. Men who operated a heavy-duty rig of one kind or another at work, appreciated the car-like qualities of Ranchero at leisure. It was obvious these owners didn't buy Ranchero for any kind of utilitarian task. In fact, their modifications were directed at improving the rig's aesthetic appeal. Bumper removal, lowered ride height and custom trim made these Rancheros, even less suited to ranch life.

A '59 Fairlane wagon at the 2012 Moonshine Fest. As ever, the two-door variant gave rise to the Ranchero legend. So much easier than the Chevy Impala to El Camino trip. (Courtesy Dennis Crenshaw)

Such Rancheros were selected for their individuality, not utility. In terms of the 'Hot' part of hot rod, trucker Jerry Grout fitted an Isky F300 camshaft, Thompson pistons, tri-power intake manifold for three 2bbl carbs and a Schiefer flywheel to help the 292 V8. Construction worker Daryl Emery kept the tone presidential on his customized '58 Ranchero, with a Lincoln 370ci V8. Moon Eyes decal looked upon an Isky cam, Jahns pistons and ported/polished heads. Ode for the days of cheap gas, because this Lincoln 370 V8, was topped by an Edmunds intake manifold with two 4bbl carbs!

Emery changed gear by means of a 1961 Ford transmission and Schiefer flywheel. In true Happy Days fashion, the floor shifter was topped by a pool eight ball knob. The C1 Vette chrome grille insert, only added to the late '50s flavor! So did the chopped top! The aforementioned '57 even had its tailgate welded shut, and legal limit low ride height. These rigs weren't taking any pigs to market! They were a visual message telling 'Da Man' to sit on it! Ford must have wished more people sat in a Ranchero. By the end of '59 MY 45,814 prospects had signed on the dotted line. Good enough to convince Ford to continue with Ranchero, but its research showed a smaller rig was in order. The same could be said of Fairlane.

3

Midsize Fairlane – The Right-Size Ford!

If Robert McNamara brought anything to Ford, it was the value of research when planning strategy. Whether it was the prosecution of a war, or the running of a corporation in peace time, McNamara set great store by the value of statistics, and the research that produced them. From such study informed decisions could be made. McNamara closed the chapter on Edsel; if he had been in charge of Ford earlier, Edsel may never have eventuated in the first place. The McNamara Ford years were characterized by no nonsense thinking. He even gave it a name, 'orthodox frugality.'

Ever since the Edsel debacle, Ford's consumer research program was right on the money. Turning Thunderbird into a volume selling four-seater, recognising mainstream USA's dislike of two-seaters, and that versatile import fighter called Falcon. The polar opposite of fancy Edsel, sensible Falcon would even give rise to youth market firestarter Mustang. And where would Ford be without that value added pony?

Consumer research led Ford to the conclusion that a midsize Fairlane was the right direction to take. From 1962 MY that's what emanated from the Lorain, Ohio factory, neatly completing the size line at Ford. Compact Falcon was 16in shorter, Galaxie 12.3in longer. The overbloated gashog Detroit accusation could in no way be directed at Falcon or Fairlane. Even Galaxie's base motor was still the established 223ci inline six. Fairlane rode on a 115.5in wheelbase, with overall length of 197in. Starting lineup featured two and four-door sedans. Boxy looking with a hint of Corvair, dare it be said, quad circular front headlamp fascia, stubby rear mini tailfins and pie plate taillamps. Fairlane was in a word … practical.

Fairlane engineering & specs

The lightest Fairlane could be was 2794lb, when fitted with base six and three on the tree power team. Galaxie was 209.3in long, rode on a 119in wheelbase and weighed 3877lb. Ford PR declared '62 Fairlane a return to good sense Ford

For '62 MY, Henry switched Fairlane from separate chassis full-size to unibody intermediate (midsize). In doing so, FoMoCo invented Detroit's compact II, or intermediate class! (Courtesy Bill Blew)

3: Midsize Fairlane – The Right-Size Ford!

family values. Critics felt the same way. Everyone was reminded of that butter and egg sedan delight, that was the '49 Ford. Fairlane was of similar size in all respects, bar vehicle height and headroom. It was that moderate kind of family car Ford, that everyone had been moving away from since 1950, with the exception of Rambler.

Even though Kenosha showed there was money to be made out of thrift, Dearborn felt body stamping interchangeability was a step too far. Perhaps to maintain individuality between the lines, Ford didn't do shared stampings between Falcon and Fairlane. However, they did share unit construction. Here, Ford drew upon its experience with Lincoln and Thunderbird, as well as Falcon/Comet lines. To maintain refinement, without using lots of perishable, wear-prone rubber bushings, Ford tried torque boxes on Fairlane. Four torque boxes were placed in the corners of the lower unibody structure.

The torque boxes absorbed road shock by moving slightly in the vertical plane. Apart from this, the chassis was very conservative. Front independent suspension involved single lower arm, high mount coil, swaybar and tube shocks. At the back a live axle was located by four leaf springs, and damped with tube shocks. The open tube, one piece driveshaft, with two cross-type universal joints led to a Hotchkiss type differential. The standard non-power recirculating ball steering had 4.7 turns, lock to lock.

Protecting future resale value, Ford put its contemporary, comprehensive rust protection system on Fairlane. All structural parts were galvanized. Much of the body was sprayed with special zinc-rich primer paint. The Ford engineers displayed original thinking with the Fairlane's door latches. Tong type grips closed over a rubber insulated striker pin, in what must have been an industry first! Inside, Fairlane was purely conventional, with a straightforward dash molding. However, although the three circular, hooded pods had mere speedo/gas/temp as real instruments, their simplicity and legibility put to shame the over styled dashboards of the late '60s.

On the subject of quality, Fairlanes ('63 MY on) and Ramblers of this general '60s era, plus VW Beetles, carried a two-year/24,000 mile warranty. Mercedes could only manage six months/6000 miles. Bad luck Janis Joplin! Low cost lines they might have been, but low quality they were not. As the preoccupation with consumer value waned in the wake of the late '50s recession, domestic buyers returned to their usual question, what was under the hood? For economy fiends, Fairlane's starter motor was the 170ci inline six, the engine up from Falcon's base 144ci six. However, the real buzz was about the new V8!

The star engine was the brand spanking new 221ci OHV V8! This small, compact and lightweight all cast iron motor, underlined the V8 engine format's position as numero uno in North American transportation. Ford had history in this area. Public enemy No 1, John Dillinger, wrote a letter to Ford, praising its Flathead V8, and saying what a great getaway vehicle his Ford Model A was! Guilty as

Simple instruments were limited to speedo, gas and temp. Refinement came from four corner-placed torque boxes that absorbed road shock. (Courtesy Bill Blew)

charged, it was Ford in 1932 that made the first mass produced, single casting V8 in America. Now, the fabled Flathead had an historical successor … the 1962 Windsor V8!

Displacing the same 221ci, or 3.6 liters, three decades of technical advancement were readily apparent. Using the thinwall casting process seen on the FE medium block family, the 3.6-liter Windsor weighed three-quarters of what the 3.6-liter Flathead did. This was in spite of the younger motor having twice the power of the 1930s design, and sporting an OHV cylinder arrangement! State of the art at the dawn of the '50s, even the Galaxie's base 223ci I6 weighed 60lb more than the new 221ci V8 Windsor!

There seemed no logical reason for even the thrifty soul to abstain from the smooth power pleasures of the V8 format. *Motor Trend*'s Jim Wright certainly felt so in April 1962: "The 145-hp engine was designed just for the Fairlane, and we think it will be the one that most buyers are going to want." A prediction was made that Windsor would become a hot rod favorite. This would happen, but a motor has to learn to cruise before it can run, and it was early days for the new V8. As the 221, the redline sat at a modest 5000rpm; bore was 3.5in, with stroke at 2.87in, and an 8.7:1 comp ratio. At 0.65bhp per cube the modern 221 wasn't exactly hi po, but give it time. For now, with the 3.50:1 'Performance Axle,' *Motor Trend*'s April '62 tested Fairlane 500 four-door recorded 0-60mph in 13.3 seconds, with the ¼ mile accomplished in 20.8 seconds at 70mph.

Performance reservations mentioned by *Motor Trend*'s Jim Wright didn't concern the Fairlane's lack of alacrity, more the way the performance was delivered. The test car had the two-speed Ford-O-Matic automatic, and the magazine was plain in its dislike of two-speed slushboxes like Ford-O-Matic or Powerglide by the early '60s – too few ratios, which compromised performance and economy. The view was that the 221 would shine more brightly when teamed with the standard three-speed manual. The Fairlane's 13in rims were another sore point raised.

These small wheels limited brake size to 10in drums all round. They would also make the Fairlane suspension heave the body out of ruts the small wheels fell into on unsealed roads. *Motor Trend* called 'em 'kiddie car' wheels, and suggested owners availed themselves of the 14 x 7in steel rims on the police car options list. At least Fairlane came with a five lug nut pattern as standard. Fairlane's former upscale Mercury cousin, called Meteor, had been available with a 14in rim, and shod with a 7in footprint tire.

In the old full-size days Fairlane sat on a 119in wheelbase, with cousin Mercury streaking by on a 120in wheelbase. In midsize times Meteor had shot through, with smaller Fairlane now related to Mercury Comet. Two speed Ford-O-Matic and 13in rims reminded one Fairlane was in the low cost line, but other aspects of operation displayed classless quality. A solid, rattle- and squeak-free unibody, Fairlane's chassis was neutral in behaviour; ultimately it took the understeer route when pressed. Sufficiently sound deadened, *Motor Trend* noted '62 Fairlane to be the quietest car yet tested, import or domestic, and regardless of price.

The starter '62 Fairlane motor was the 101 horse C20E 170 I6, Falcon's optional engine. By '64 MY the 200 cube I6 was an option, and a retrofit done by the original owner. (Courtesy Bill Blew)

3: Midsize Fairlane – The Right-Size Ford!

Fairlane 500 & Sports Coupe

13in rims or not, Fairlane's chassis resisted bottoming out, and for highline show choose the top '500' trim level. Fairlane 500 came with color-matched steering wheel, wall to wall carpeting and chrome embellishments. Brightwork inside, with wider profile sweepspear and rear fender bullet chrome trim outdoors. Of course, stylewise a sedan is only going to take one just so far. Fortunately, mid '62 MY Ford brought out the Fairlane Sports Coupe. This two-door bolide was basically a sportified two-door sedan. The car came with a B pillar and the humble 221. A four-speed wasn't available, but Sports Coupe was special. There had been powerful Fairlanes before 1962, but the 1962 ½ Fairlane Sports Coupe was a midsize, and it was the first family sized car Ford actively promoted under the 'enjoy it' sports banner. In essence, Ford muscle cars started with this simple Sports Coupe.

A plain vanilla flavor two-door Fairlane sedan with 170ci I6 retailed for $2345, the Sports Coupe which utilized the same body cost $2506. That $161 premium garnered one many obvious, and not so obvious, additions. On the outside more chrome, including a passenger side trunklid chrome script badge proudly stating 'Sports Coupe.' Given the B pillar's presence, it was a statement that had to be made. Lest the public miss the distinction! Underhood motorvation moved to the 221ci V8. Nice, but the Sports Coupe's interior delivered the T-Bird punch.

Bucket seats with color-matched vinyl-trimmed interior, were enough to make any prospect sign up for higher payments over a poverty six! In reality the Thunderbird style faux buckets gave the impression of comfort. From the era when a bench seat was a church pew, and a bucket was a church pew with a hole sawed out of the center, the Sports Coupe seatback offered zero contouring or padding. In August 1962 Car Life called such seats uncomfy. Even so, the journal conceded that the interior looked opulent, and that helped take one's mind off the fact 62 ½ MY Sports Coupe was a little 'all hat and no cattle.'

As a V8 model Sports Coupe got the 7in footprint 13in tires, not the I6 car's 6.50in footprint rubber, but they were 13-inchers nonetheless. The rims concealed 10 x 2.25in front drums and 10 x 1.75in rear drums – that gave a swept area of 252in², but they got the job done. Car Life reported no fade or grab, in a car with an optional V8 and weighing 3150lb. It underlined how moderately sized American cars once were, that such a weight was considered portly in 1962! Underhood the test car featured the new 260 cube version of the Windsor small block. The 260 ci V8 represented a $47.65 premium that was really worth it.

Introduced mid '62 MY to coincide with the Sports Coupe's release, the 260 'Challenger' was a 221 bored out 0.30in. Bore and stroke were now 3.80in and 2.87in respectively, compression ratio remained 8.7:1. Power rose from 143bhp at 4500rpm to 164bhp at 4400rpm. Torque improved from 217lb/ft at 2200rpm to 258lb/ft at the same revs. It certainly gave Fairlane more moxie. 0-60mph was now 12.1 seconds, with ¼ mile done in 18.9 seconds at 73mph and top speed a heady 103mph. The two-speed Ford-O-Matic dictated an upshift at 62mph, with 4900rpm on a tach Sports Coupe didn't have!

Visual distinction between Fairlane and Fairlane 500 lay with the latter's exterior brightwork. Tailfins were well out the door by 1962. (Courtesy Bill Blew)

Ford Midsize Muscle – Fairlane, Torino & Ranchero

An authentic '62 Fairlane interior, restored by owner Bill Blew of New Jersey using a 1932 Singer sewing machine. (Courtesy Bill Blew)

1963-64 revisions

1963 model year saw the arrival of the full Fairlane range. Rely on that old big Ranch Wagon no more, because Henry's Blue Oval holdall was now available in midsize! Trim levels from plain to fancy were Ranch Wagon, Custom Ranch Wagon and top shelf Squire. Plain Ranch Wagon had neat painted sidespears, Squire the expected, large exterior faux wood panels. All three featured hose out vinyl interiors, and roll down tailgate glass, with power operation of this last item being optional. Standard on all wagons were bigger brakes, 10 x 2.5in drums all around, and not standard fitment on sedan or the new hardtop. Brake swept area increased from 251.2in^2 to 314.2in^2.

With weight spread from a plain two-door to Squire involving a 422lb gain, the improved brakes were essential, so was extra engine. The 260 powered Sports Coupe could top 100mph, a 260 wagon could manage 90mph flat out. A wagon with the stock I6 was a worrying prospect. In the January 1964 issue of *Motor Trend* the journal's Technical Editor Jim Wright, praised the thrift of Fairlane six. However, overtaking with Fairlane 170 I6 was compared to the world's longest game of chicken. Even Ford engineers conceded the Fairlane six was not advisable for highway use. This suggested V8 for wagon should have been a mandatory option.

Fairlane wagon was easy on the eye, but real glamor dictated a pillarless hardtop, and Fairlane had one for '63 MY! The 1963 Fairlane 500 Sports Coupe had a windshield with more rake than its sedan counterpart. The roof was an inch lower and the pillarless coupe had a fastback rear pane. Formerly the 62 ½ MY Sports Coupe had 'Fairlane 500' script on the C pillar, now it said 'Sports Coupe.' The 'V8' chrome callout was moved from the low part of the front fender behind the wheelarch, to the leading edge of said fender, just behind the front outboard headlamp.

Substancewise, Sports Coupe power teams were 260 with two-speed Ford-O-Matic or three-speed manual with overdrive. And synchro action was only on the top two gears of the latter box. Well, at least it looked like it could move like greased lightning! In other respects 63 MY Fairlane had an upscale Galaxiesque front concave mini rectangle chrome fascia with quad circular headlamps. The tail still had the simple pie plate taillights. Overall, and in all aspects, Ford was warming to the idea of high-performance across all model lines.

Henry gets sporty!

By 1964 Falcon had completed the so called 'Great Leap Forward.' No longer just an import battling economy model, in mid '63 MY Ford introduced Falcon Sprint. Like a junior Sports Coupe, the Sprint had the ubiquitous buckets and V8 in a two-door hardtop, fastback shell. In keeping with its station in life, Falcon was limited to 260 cube motorvation in 1964. Thunderbird was becoming a reborn sportster too!

Yes, T-Bird still had 390ci power, and Lincoln luxury. However, in spite of its size and weight, with new styling and nature it was trying to get back to its sporty two

3: Midsize Fairlane – The Right-Size Ford!

seat past. With Galaxie, the banker's hot rod was still alive and well at Dearborn, with a power team lineup lovely enough to make a 1975-1990 car buyer weep! The special powerplants commenced with premium fuel 220 horse 352 V8, then a duo of 390s making 300/330bhp respectively. If these super premium gas 390s weren't enough, well, there was always the 427 V8, making 410 or 425 horsepower. The best thing? All the above Galaxie motors were available with four on da floor!

Now, that's what an objective soul would call total performance. A few seasons earlier those full-size sleds would have sported the Fairlane moniker. But not to worry, 1964's midsize was getting along just fine. To achieve the look of speed, a restyle brought lots of decorative change, not so much sheet metal change. A raised rear door section and quarter gave the impression of an air scoop. New grille, hood, side trim and front fenders were true to Detroit form of using annual refreshers to interest prospects, and move showroom stock.

1964 sedan roof, windshield and backlight were constant. The same could be said for the Fairlane fastback hardtop, but fine distinctions were abound. As with the rest of the Fairlane family, '64 Sports Coupe adopted the latest, imposing Galaxie style grille, a chrome venetian blind affair. Inside, Fairlane Sports Coupe had taken its center console from Galaxie since the start of '63 MY. Previously it had sourced the unit from the Falcon line. Going with the 1964 Fairlane console, was four on the floor transmission. This was a first for midsize Fairlane, the manual box was manufactured by Warner Gear.

On the Windsor way to the 289!

It has been said Detroit wouldn't have gotten around to four on the floor, without the influence of imported European sporty cars after the war. Beyond dispute was the flexibility a four-speed afforded, in exploiting a high output motor. The all synchro box had ratios of 2.74 (1st), 2.04 (2nd), 1.51 (3rd), and direct one to one top. That was nice close spacing for three pedal devotees, it just needed the right V8 to go with it. The Windsor small block could oblige. Starting with Fairlane in 1962, aiming to replace the Ford Y block, Windsor took its name from the Ontario engine plant it was built in.

The all cast iron small block utilized the thinwall casting technique seen on the late '50s introduced, FE series Ford medium block V8. Windsor's properties involved a separate aluminum timing chain cover, inline valves for the 90 degree OHV motor and 4.380in bore spacing. Windsor took coolant through the intake manifold via a horizontally mounted hose. A 3rd oil route passage was drilled parallel to the Windsor's tappet passages. This was to ensure the bearings received lubrication quickly.

With wedge shape combustion chambers, the Windsor small block was great on breathing air to make horsepower, it was also light and compact. The 221 V8 long engine was 24in wide, 29in long and 27.5in tall, tipping the scales at just 470lb. However, total performance didn't mean standing still, and Ford quietly introduced the 260in mid '62 MY. Then, as a regular fuel base V8, Dearborn brought 289ci V8 power to the Galaxie line in mid '63 MY, in single exhaust form. The 289 had a 4in bore and 2.87in stroke to achieve its greater displacement, but there were other reasons the hot rod crowd sat up and took notice.

Ford was getting sporty across all lines in 1964, and most obviously with the introduction of the 1964 ½ Mustang. If GTO begat the modern muscle car era, then Mustang certainly started the pony car battles. Even though Falcon, upon which Mustang was based, was limited to 260 cubes, Mustang could have a 289, a very special 289. So too could Fairlane! The motor in question was the high output K code 289. So called because of the 'K' in the VIN, this 289 was the perfect motor to let a Fairlane, or Stang, do a super ¼ mile whilst coping with corners.

In those 'ol gross rating days, when an engine was run without manifolds or ancillaries to get a flywheel rated output, the K code 289 made 271bhp at six grand and 312lb/ft at 3400rpm. A high revving unit by any standard, perfect for a four-speed. The usual tried and true methods elevated the 289 from a regular fuel 2bbl 195 horses, to this exalted rating. Try a solid lifter format, 11 to one compression ratio, sports cam, and low restriction air cleaner for the juicier four-barrel carb. As opposed to the normal 289 4bbl's 480 CFM carb, the K code 289 had a bigger, manual choke 595 CFM carb. The higher compression was helped by smaller combustion chamber heads.

The K code 289 exhaled through free flow exhaust headers, into dual exhausts. But wait, there's more, said the K-tel man! This 289 had changes to improve high rpm efficiency and durability. Apart from a dual point centrifugal advance distributor, internal block improvements saw thicker main bearing caps and balancer, plus larger diameter connecting rod bolts. A nitrided crank sporting more counterweights helped the 289 safely reach 6000rpm, as did cast spring caps and screw-in studs for the better flowing cylinder head.

K code 289 water and fuel pumps had fewer vanes, the alternator had an extra spring and the alternator pulley was of larger diameter. Leaving no stone unturned, there was even a unique K code radiator fan. All that mechanical goodness didn't come free. The regular fuel 195 horse 289 was a mere 4lb lighter than the 223 Ford six. True, that motor made only 138bhp in 1964 Galaxie guise, but the 221 V8 had been 60lb lighter!

With the extra performance upgrades K code 289 brought, add more pounds still. However, the figures showed even the regular fuel 289 powered Fairlane 500 Sports Coupe with greater zeal. *Motor Trend* tried just such a 195 horse four-speed car in January 1964. The 221 V8 was gone by the end of 1963 MY, making the 260 V8 the base for Fairlane 500 Sports Coupe. The optional 289's 195 ponies arrived at 4400rpm, with 282lb/ft of torque at 2200rpm. With two-barrel carb and standard 3.25:1 final drive, 0-60mph was clocked in 9.9 seconds. The quarter mile followed in 17.5 seconds at 78mph.

On the highway this car achieved 19.1mpg, and could touch 105mph. A solid all rounder. The base 1964 Fairlane 500 Sports Coupe 260 cost $2725.75, which included front buckets, console, heater, HD suspension and the HD brakes of 10 x 2.5in wide four wheel drums sourced from Fairlane Wagon. Optional, and very necessary, were the 14in, 7in footprint bias ply tires. As before, the 3.50 final drive was the performance axle. The 3.80 being only for the three-speed overdrive manual boxed cars. A strange omission was Ford's Equa-Lock LSD, which was much wanted to put the power down with the K code 289.

With Falcon limited to 260, Galaxie having a bevy of big blocks, and Mustang not existing, K code 289 was just for little 'ol Fairlane! For their 1964 *CAR FACTS* annual the *Popular Mechanics* crew sampled a K code 289 in a two-door, fastback Sports Coupe with four-speed. Actually, the four-speed was a mandatory option for K code motor usage at the time. With two people aboard, as was custom at the time to drive and record data, this intermediate rocketed to 60mph in 7.5 seconds. Good for the day; and the kind of scat pollution/economy afflicted domestic fans of the '70s and '80s, would have killed Lee Iacocca for!

Hot enough for *Popular Mechanics* to comment that any Fairlane with the K code 289 should have HD suspension and brakes as mandatory options.[7] Fairlane 500 Sports Coupe had these, and on a wagon it didn't matter. It would have been cool to have a four-speed K coded '64 Squire Wagon, but the 'Woody' Squire and that hot 289 couldn't be ordered on Fairlane wagon that year. In those madcap

3: Midsize Fairlane – The Right-Size Ford!

order permutation times, one could get buckets in a wagon! More practical was the third row reverse seating Fairlane wagon kinda offered. This was basically a trap door with some padding!

A lockable compartment was built into the wagon's floor. Lifting the trap door created an impromptu seatback, and Ford had optional interior matching cushions for said seatback and base. Of course, it wasn't as comfy as a real spring padded seat, the presumably child occupants would be facing rearwards and sans seatbelts! As per most cars, import and domestic, a metal ashtray was mounted on the front bench facing rear bench seated passengers. Releasing two latches dropped the rear seat almost flush, and vehicle tools were stored behind the rear seat.

With no lapbelts for any rear seating, and a cranium greeting metal ashtray facing rear wagon occupants for a whole trip, it seemed little consolation that Ford had a padded dash on the options list! Still, at this hour buyers were more interested in the 3.89 and 4.11 rear ratios that Ford offered outside the normal 2.80 to 3.80 Fairlane final drive ratios. All the better to keep that K code 289 in its rpm sweet spot! Because even a wide ratio four-speed, could knock one off the torque curve, on a crucial ¼ mile redline shift from first to second! In all this rush, the 289 was becoming legendary.

Skipping ahead to 1965 and at the behest of Lee Iacocca, Carroll Shelby's outfit gave the public a Shelby Mustang GT350 with a 306 horse 289, … still not enough? Well, by 1967 factory racing Group 2 NASCAR Mercury Cougars used 289s with a mere 10.5 CR, but also dual 4bbl Ford Autolite carburetion for 341 horses at 5800rpm and 300lb/ft at 4000rpm. A four-speed was mandatory, as was a racing license! In theory one could buy this motor on a crate basis, and fit it to the *Motor Trend* 1967 Car of the Year Cougar. 1967 was the last year before pollution controls came in. However, anyone that did would probably soon be enjoying one of those special jackets, with the straps and buttons on the back, in a nice pink hued padded cell!

Sensible enthusiasts in 1967 went to Shelby American for a Cobra Supercharger. The puffer boosted one's 289, or 260, by as much as 46% in horsepower. It was an elegant engineering solution, and optional equipment on a Shelby GT350. However, Ford's K code 289 and all the above had one problem … price! These avenues to extra go were expensive. The K code 289 was a seldom ticked order blank on a Fairlane's option sheet. This became even more so, once big displacement FE series V8s became Fairlane and Mustang options. With gas still cheap, an aversion to mechanical complexity and a liking for torque, the simple life was the favored performance route on domestics and imports.

A Thunderbolt strikes Fairlane!

It saw GM sell off their all aluminum 215ci V8 to Rover in the late '60s, and BMW chose a 2-liter mill instead of a tuned 1.6-liter to create the 2002 for North America and the world in 1968. Even puritanical Consumer Union decried the mechanical complexity of Corvair's turbo flat-six! There had to be an easier way

The 1964 Thunderbolt's purpose was to beat the Max Wedge Mopar Marvels at the strip. This it did, by combining Galaxie 427 power team with smaller Fairlane body. (Courtesy RKMotorsCharlotte.com Jeff Spiegel)

Ford Midsize Muscle – Fairlane, Torino & Ranchero

said Consumer Reports, and that way was beaucoup displacement. It created the most special Fairlane of 1964, maybe the finest Fairlane of all time, … the 1964 Fairlane Thunderbolt!

If horse racing is the sport of kings, then drag racing must be the sport of the people. Long before NASCAR Grand National and SCCA Trans Am races were reaching late '60s fever pitch, quarter mile contests throughout the country captured public imagination. Drag racing also seemed a way to get around the anti-racing pact that Big 4 management had agreed to by the late '50s. Even though the corporate types agreed not to push speed to sell cars nationally, at the local level dealers were supporting driver efforts to win on the strip. Ford wasn't doing as much winning as it would have liked.

The trouble was the lightweight, powerful unibody Max Wedge V8 motored Mopars. The full frame Galaxie 427s, in spite of lightened front ends, couldn't keep these Dodges and Plymouths in sight on the 1320ft acceleration run. However, good providence would come from Rhode Island! A dealer called Tasca Ford of East Providence shoehorned a 406 into the new intermediate sized 1962 Fairlane, at a time when the Windsor 221 was the hottest factory V8 option. This Fairlane 406 got Ford thinking the best home for their large FE V8 wasn't the full-size Galaxie lead sled, it was the smaller, lighter new midsize!

With this food for thought, Ford Special Vehicle Department (SVD) and Tasca Ford built a test mule. This rig took the form of a 1963 Fairlane 500 two-door hardtop with a 425 horse 427 V8 and four-speed power team, painted blue. The idea was putting the Galaxie's drag race combo into little 'ol church going Fairlane! No one was concerned about history in those times, so with the point proved the blue prototype was quickly crushed. Ford's next step was to get into the formal business of making a factory offered strip star. In the era of 'race what ya make,' that meant use as much hardware as you currently offer.

Due to better body rigidity and weight distribution, Ford went with the two-door sedan shape, not the fancy fastback hardtop. There were also major weight saving measures and engineering moves to make the unibody chassis stiffer, so the body wouldn't flex and drivers could get the power to the pavement. This involved square box type traction bars welded to the axle housing and extending forward to the front crossmember. Increased strength, zero body roll and more traction control! Then there was the weight saving. Although base cars utilized a Fairlane 500 trim level, you wouldn't really know it.

Henry hit the delete option so many times, it nearly turned this hot Fairlane into a Model T! Out went the radio, heater, armrests, passenger sunvisor, passenger windshield wiper, rear window crank handles/regulator mechanisms, and front bumper! The early cars had a cosmetic fiberglass front bumper. This item involved eliminating the front bottom part of the fenders, and the stone guard connecting the two fenders. The rear bumper was a stock '64 Fairlane unit. This was chosen to improve weight distribution, given that big 427 lived in the nose, and to get some traction for the rear wheels. For the same reason Ford engineers mounted a 95lb bus battery in the trunk! That said, there weren't any jacks or tire irons to be found. Weight reduction continued with no

For chassis rigidity, Ford chose the two-door sedan body, not the two-door hardtop! Traction bars were welded between axle housing and front crossmember also. (Courtesy RKMotorsCharlotte.com Jeff Spiegel)

3: Midsize Fairlane – The Right-Size Ford!

exterior reversing mirror, sound-deadening material or carpeting!

Ford 500 trim carpeting was rather heavy, so reliance was placed on rubber mats, and then there were the fiberglass body panels. At most this involved plastic hood, fenders, doors and aforementioned faux bumper. At least they didn't dent like the aluminum items used by Ford's drag race rivals.

The hood was very functional, given it was shaped to clear an air filter box mounted above the vehicle fender line. The special shape was a four leaf clover design, signifying this Fairlane would be lucky at the strip. More weight was saved through the use of plexiglas for the side windows.

Although the Fairlane drag racer had front and rear seating, the front seats were lightweight Econoline truck buckets. All the hard work saw the NHRA's 3200lb weight minimum met, just! With a full tank of gas, Ford's hero tipped the scales at 3203lb! Pushing the car along was a center oiler 427 with high riser intake manifold and dual four-barrel carburetion. CFMs varied between individual cars, but even in modern money this motor made at least 500 horses SAE net. Ford underrated it for insurance, and so as not to raise post Nader public safety concerns. The official stats were 12.7:1 comp, 425bhp at six grand and 480lb/ft at 3700rpm, but the reality was far hotter!

There were space considerations, given heretofore midsize Fairlane only had a small block V8. The 427's eight equal length exhaust headers had to be snaked through the front suspension hardware. The motor hooked up with a four-speed manual box and 4.44 rear gears, or three-speed torque converter autobox with a 4.58:1 final drive ratio. The Hurst shifter manipulated four-speed possessed an

Cold air induction for that mean 427 was delivered via trunking that started at mesh screened bezels. Fairlane's former inner lamps! (Courtesy RKMotorsCharlotte.com Jeff Spiegel)

Plastic hood, fenders, doors and front bumper, perhaps, but Ford kept the heavy stock rear bumper for better weight distribution. (Courtesy RKMotorsCharlotte.com Jeff Spiegel)

aluminum case, whereas the slushbox was a tough Lincoln unit. The Lincoln box was modified for drag racer application, featuring no kickdown, higher line pressures and a special torque converter with optimized stall rpm point.

Normally that Lincoln slushbox would be slurring its ratios in grand-daddy's luxo limo, bolted to a MEL (Mercury Edsel Lincoln) big block. Therefore, a special bell housing was required to match up this auto with the medium block FE 427. This rig was anything but a luxo limo. Cold air induction was standard, with the 427 taking air through trunking connected to mesh screened bezels, that used to be Fairlane's inner headlights! And no stock Fairlane 500 sedan came with 7in wide steel rims, or asymmetric rear springs, but this one did!

It needed them too, because one could count on this tin top to deliver mid 11s at over 120mph! A car with this kind of go, and minimal show, couldn't be called something like the Ford Violet or Daffodil. It wasn't going to shrink from anything on the road. The kid with the jacked up '57 Chevy was wise to leave this Blue Oval Bandit alone. Ford christened it the Thunderbolt, and Thunderbolt it was by name and nature. Thunderbolt's mission was twofold: win on the strip, and attract prospects to Ford showrooms. They would be impressed with Thunderbolt, and go on to buy a lovely, optioned up Fairlane 500 sedan. Which looked just like that race car, wouldn't you know?!

Marketing just encouraged the masses to speed up with the ad slogan, 'All you need to go racing is the ignition key.' To date the Thunderbolt 427's release has been the only time in history that an automaker has offered a showroom presented, turn key drag racer to the public. Perhaps not so surprising given some say Ford stands for First On Race Day! Not Henry Ford though, the man that thought the Tin Lizzie in black was all anyone would want, would have been horrified at the Thunderbolt's wanton excess. Still, this was the '60s!

Even though it was the '60s, Dearborn thought it was wise to lay down some provisos. Lest Ralph Nader got excited enough to buy a Thunderbolt, then complain to Henry about all that noise pollution. For starters Ford didn't offer any warranty on the Thunderbolt. Its power team and enhancements went so far beyond normal Fairlane parameters, any guarantee would be tempting fate. Secondly, Ford warned that Thunderbolt's specialty nature meant Dearborn's normal production vehicle panel fit and exterior appearance weren't possible. This was to stop showroom visitors asking salesmen why Thunderbolt's panels didn't line up like on a regular Fairlane.

Finally, those bastions of speed at *Hot Rod* magazine had this to say, "… not suitable for driving to and from the strip, let alone on the street in everyday use." Thunderbolt was a racing car with a license plate, and in its true domain it was a star! Thunderbolt took out the Super Stock crown in 1964, getting Ford the NHRA Manufacturer's Cup in the process. Ford's midsize rig also competed in Super Stock Automatic and the wild A/FX category. Whether you were Don 'Big Daddy' Garlits, or just a normal driving member of the public, Ford would sell a four-speed Thunderbolt to anyone with $3780.

$3980 secured a zombie shift Thunderbolt, and yes, a Thunderbolt could be ordered from any Ford dealer, even if they didn't carry one in stock. Chances are a Thunderbolt would have to be ordered in, because Ford only made 100 of the

Going fast in the '60s was easy. Simply take a full-size motor, and stick it under a midsize car's hood! Thunderbolt's four-leaf-clover hood was designed to clear the high mount air filter box. (Courtesy RKMotorsCharlotte.com Jeff Spiegel)

3: Midsize Fairlane – The Right-Size Ford!

machines, 59 automatics and 41 four-speed cars. This was the homologation number Ford had to meet to qualify the car for Super Stock competition. It was an expensive purchase, but Ford still lost 1500 to 2000 bucks on each car. However, things are only expensive if they don't work, and Thunderbolt met publicity and racing expectations. A legend was created!

In making Thunderbolt, Ford sought the services of contract car builder Dearborn Steel Tubing Co (DST). For the first 11 cars, Ford sent DST Fairlane 500 two-door sedans in hi po 289ci 271 horse K code spec. This was so the cars could start with the larger wagon brakes, and Ford's famously tough 9in differential. 500 trim it may have been, but major delete option selection pared down the pounds. The only thing Thunderbolt came with, apart from performance, was Ford's maroon like Vintage Burgundy exterior paint, and a bare bones tan vinyl interior.

These Group 1 Thunderbolts were built in October 1963. Early cars were delivered for a one buck surcharge, but pretty soon it was expected for buyers to come to Dearborn and pick up their purchase. The first 11 cars consisted of ten four-speeds and one automatic. The first nine cars were quickly sent to drag racing teams. The lone automatic was raced by Paul Harvey and sponsored by Bob Ford in Dearborn. Unfortunately, this car was subsequently destroyed in a crash.

Adhering to *Hot Rod* magazine's advice, Thunderbolt was mostly always raced. In the '60s, racing for pink slips on Woodward Avenue on a Saturday Night, was what kids did. However, Thunderbolt's specialist nature and high price, seemed to put it out of reach of high spirited youth, even though it seemed purpose built for Woodward Avenue's heyday! Ford's subsequent Group 2 and 3 Thunderbolt batches were white exterior rides, with automatics figuring greatly.

For Groups 2 and 3 Ford just sent CKD kit Fairlane 500s, to Dearborn Steel Tubing Company. 39 Group 2 Thunderbolts were made by DST between December 1963 and February 1964. There were nine four-speeds and 30 automatics made in this batch. The final Group 3 cars were constructed in 1964 between March and May. These 50 white Thunderbolts consisted of 22 four-speed machines and 28 shiftless two-doors. In spite of such similarity, there were production changes and differences between the cars. The obvious alteration was Thunderbolt's bumper.

The Thunderbolt front fiberglass faux bumper, was quickly deemed illegal by sanctioning bodies. Racers had been putting a real Fairlane bumper over the fiberglass one until race time! Ford had a solution, an aluminum version of the real 1964 Fairlane bumper. Much lighter than its steel counterpart, the aluminum copy was available over the Ford parts counter. It was automatically given to parties that had already acquired a Thunderbolt. Ford also quickly changed the air filter clearing fiberglass cloverleaf hood design, to the more common teardrop style.

Not all Thunderbolts had plastic doors, and which body panels were fiberglass depended if a Ford Factory Drag Team car was at hand. On some Fairlane Thunderbolts the side windows and backlight were all made of Plexiglas. Some cars had different style rear window retainers, some had none! However, all

Contrary to the stripper 'no passenger sunvisor' interior, Thunderbolt usually came with, this plush example lives up to the Fairlane 500 trim Thunderbolt was based on. (Courtesy RKMotorsCharlotte.com Jeff Spiegel)

Ford Midsize Muscle – Fairlane, Torino & Ranchero

cars had the normal Fairlane rocker panel area cut to aid wide slick tire clearance. A further difference between Thunderbolts concerned some coming with square or round, front-mounted tow hooks.

The company responsible for making Thunderbolt's fiberglass front fenders and hood was Plaza Fiberglass of Ontario, Canada. Ford even offered some further factory parts to help make an even lighter drag strip special. Indeed, there were some special areas Ford looked at with Thunderbolt R&D. One Thunderbolt was made with a hemi headed version of the 427, but the idea wasn't pursued. And although the two-door sedan had a more rigid body, one hardtop '64 Fairlane 500 Sports Coupe Thunderbolt was built as an experimental NASCAR racer. Beyond the 1964 Thunderbolts, two additional cars were made in 1965.

50 Mercury Cyclones with Thunderbolt hardware were also built. There were some problems with the Thunderbolt's gearboxes. The four-speed's aluminum case could crack under heavy usage. Hot-rodders swapped the casing for a cast iron equivalent. The Lincoln derived automatic also had durability issues, with many racers tossing this slushbox in favor of a four-speed. Racers made particular changes to give their Thunderbolts a durability and/or performance edge. To increase chassis rigidity, and improve power transfer to the ground, many teams went beyond the already stout traction bars included by DST.

Privateers lengthened the traction bars, sometimes even nearing the firewall area! Some teams also extended the bars towards the rear bumper. Once again the goal was to reduce bodyflex when that tuned 427 tried to deliver to the pavement. Zero roll equaled more control! Sometimes even more radical mods were tried. Thunderbolt also achieved success in Super Stock Automatic, and made out well in the altered wheelbase class known as A/FX. This hallowed forerunner to Funny Cars involved moving the rear wheels and axle forward to improve weight transfer, and traction off the line.

A/FX class saw some famous altered wheelbase Thunderbolts. There was Sidney 'Quick Draw' Foster's Thunderbolt, and the cars had unique handles too! Rattlesnake, Jerry Caminito's Holeshot, and John Donilson's The Dixie Stripper, Gas Ronda and Shazam were interesting monikers. The latter alluded to the catchphrase exclaimed by Jim Nabors' character in the popular, contemporary *Gomer Pyle* TV sitcom. Appropriate on a Thunderbolt because Pyle was a mechanic, and a mechanic would appreciate this Fairlane's engineering. Pat Gray's Thunderbolt, Whuppet, had an altered wheelbase, plus chopped aluminum bumper along with modified fenders.

It seemed the only folks that didn't like Thunderbolt were Mopar competitors and race authority types. The NHRA upped the homologation qualification number to 500 units. Ford thought that was an awful lot of showroom stockers to get shed of, and decided to call it a day. Still, the Thunderbolt symbolized just how many people worshipped at the altar of high-performance in the '60s. Thunderbolt is the only production car to date that Ford has sold in the showroom without a spare tire of any kind. People thought that was an avant garde action when DeLorean's DMC 12 came out nearly 20 years later. However, the ultimate Wacky Racer will always be the Thunderbolt!

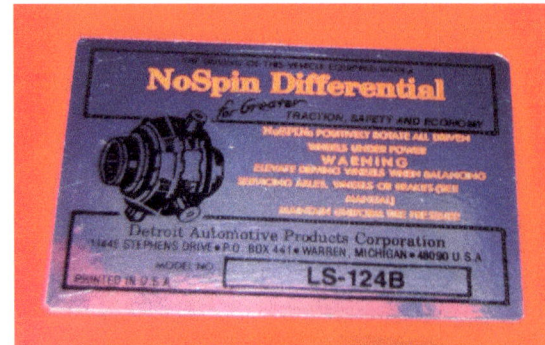

Thunderbolt's Detroit Locker LSD was iconic, albeit clunky by modern standards! (Courtesy RKMotorsCharlotte.com Jeff Spiegel)

4
Ranchero's Compact to Midsize Transition

1961-63 Rancheros were of rounded shape and compact platform. The '63 Ranchero here sports the revised fancier chrome update grille. With a no-show from El Camino, Henry had the car-based pickup segment all to himself again. (Courtesy Michael Garite)

Compact Falcon Ranchero

If Henry Ford rolled in his grave at the wanton excess of Thunderbolt, he would have been right at home on the farm with compact sized Falcon Ranchero. Not to mention the ideas that created it. The compact Falcon had been a huge success for Ford. If safety didn't sell, Ford quickly found out that thrift did. At least it did for a narrow range of time between the demise of lavish Edsel, and the 'Option To The Max' Mustang, which ironically was humble Falcon based. For now, 1961 MY, it was the Ranchero that was Falcon based, and that embodied the economy-minded, Romneyesque thinking of Ford's boss Robert McNamara.

Ranchero was on hiatus during 1960 model year, a time when revised El Camino sales crumbled into the dust. Ranchero returned as 'Falcon Ranchero,' and the economy/savings route was certainly the better idea Ford put on wheels. The most upscale thing about Falcon Ranchero's 1961 ad was its artwork. It was common for artists doing these ads, on domestic and imported cars, to use some creative license and make smaller cars look larger, longer and sleeker. The banner, on the other hand, said 'Ford Trucks Cost Less,' Ford also said Falcon Ranchero was America's sportiest and most economical pickup truck.

As per Ford's conventional pickup range, Falcon Ranchero was available with a factory designed fiberglass camper body. Ford advertising wasted no time reminding prospects the plastic body was low cost. The Falcon Ranchero ad also promised up to 30mpg, and up to a 15% insurance premium saving, compared to regular pickups. Ford, in its advertising, also quoted the purchase price saving to be $231, compared to the cheapest normal truck-based pickup. With a starting sticker of $1862, Falcon Ranchero was appreciably cheaper than conventional pickups, and the last of Ford's '59 full-size Rancheros.

Ford Midsize Muscle – Fairlane, Torino & Ranchero

This Ranchero has a Comet dash cluster as a custom touch. Making a '60 MY debut, Comet was Falcon's upscale Mercury cousin. On Henry's ranch, Falcon, Ranchero and short Comet all rode on a 109.5in wheelbase. (Courtesy Michael Garite)

This Falcon Ranchero has a C4 autobox, and '68 bench seat from compact cousin Mustang. Even with Falcon Ranchero, the spare continued behind the passenger seat. (Courtesy Michael Garite)

Compared to the previous full-size glamor rig, Falcon Ranchero was like a trusty little workhorse. Here its car-like Falcon driving properties seemed to have more utility for small business owners than for luxury buyers looking for something novel. The cost savings started with a mini mill that Ford introduced with the compact Falcon. The lightweight 144ci inline OHV six, was more compact apt than the hefty 223 I6 seen in full-size Fords. Bore and stroke were 3.5in and 2.5in respectively, comp ratio was a regular fuel-suited 8.7:1, and gas was sipped through a 1bbl carb. The 144 made 90 horses at 4200rpm and 138lb/ft at 2000rpm.

With optional two-speed Ford-O-Matic autobox, Falcon Ranchero zipped to 60mph in a leisurely 18.2 seconds, according to *Motor Life* in June 1960. One could get a three on the tree manual box, but the automatic suited the florists, plumbers and timber collecting carpenters that Ford's 'economy makes dollars and sense' ads were directed at. 1962 MY saw the larger 170 cube six join the power team combos, but once again, most farms don't have drag strips. Falcon Ranchero got back to the 1930s idea of a car-based pickup in size, affordability and utility.

Ranchero length had shrunk from 1959's 208in to a much easier to handle 180in, with weight at just 2436lb, but not all dimensions were smaller. The pickup compartment was 71.6 x 14.6 x 55.6in, giving a greater space stat than in the 1959 full-size Ranchero. Box volume was up from 27ft^3 to 31.6 ft^3!

However, as a concession to Ranchero's smaller body and engine, payload capacity had dropped from 1100lb to 800lb. Another key difference was the change from body on a frame construction to Falcon's unibody style. There was a whole lot less shake, rattle and roll, not to mention squeaks, going on with Ranchero in 1961!

In other respects Falcon Ranchero's engineering was less surprising. As before Ford commenced with a station wagon model, and substituted a pickup bed in place of the normal rear seating and trunk. For durability, and to keep an even keel when toting a load, stiffer wagon type shocks and leaf springs were used.

Also used were the Falcon wagon's larger brakes, 3.89 rear ratio, plus larger differential housing. In keeping with Ford standards of good rust-proofing, underbody brackets and panels were zinc coated at the factory. For even more value, Ford claimed its stock aluminized muffler lasted up to three times longer than standard rival steel units.

Ford engineered Mini-Ranchero for light rugged duty. There were publicity shots of Falcon Ranchero tackling a kingsize camper van body accessory, and handling

4: Ranchero's Compact to Midsize Transition

As a long time customizer favorite, it's apt this Ranchero has a custom Electra 'Rat Fink' bike! A tribute to legendary customizer and artist Ed 'Big Daddy' Roth. (Courtesy Michael Garite)

loose terrain. However, one didn't have to be a miserly puritan or madcap rancher to get a kick out of Ranchero. One could probably option up a truck with white walls, dress up hubcaps and color contrasting roof, but the pigs would still be taken to market in a pig rig dressed up in Sunday best suit. These luxuries were more at home on car-like Ranchero. Little Ranchero ran through 1961-63 with rounded bodystyle that made it look like a small four seat T bird! However, big changes were in store for '64 MY.

1964 – the V8 returns!

In 1964 Falcon Ranchero embraced the squared-up 'Razor Edge' look of '64 Falcon. This encompassed the big chrome, reverse slope segmented grille which was, in a word, imposing. McNamara had left Ford by this hour to run America's defense: no wonder Ford now had a compact small kids could mistake for a Galaxie! Making sure the form had substance, Ford's 260 V8 was across-the-Falcon-board available in '64, bar Club Wagon and Station Bus. It was a fun motor that had first Falcon appeared in the sporty, mid '63 MY Sprint fastback. However, one could now get 260 power in Ranchero: the first time the pickup had seen eight cylinders since 1959!

Consumer Union economy fiends could still seek solace in the revised 85 horse 144 and 101bhp 170 cube straight sixes, but that 260 V8 was the hedonist ticket. 164bhp at 4400rpm and 258lb/ft at 2200rpm on two-barrel carburetion was the kind of 'motorvation' formerly found on weighty Fairlane 500 Sports Coupe. However, in Ranchero V8, the only load to haul was the one placed in the pickup's bed! Choose a V8 in a Falcon variant, and an all-synchromesh three-speed manual was included as standard. 170ci six and V8 motors could also be teamed with four on the floor. This all synchro box had ratios of 2.73 (1st), 2.04 (2nd), 1.51 (3rd), and direct one to one 1.00:1 (4th).

The '60s hi po sports era dictated four on the floor as mandatory; slushbox fans weren't so well catered for. It was a sign of Falcon's place in the Ford hierarchy that only the two-speed Ford-O-Matic torque converter box came into view.

Ford Midsize Muscle – Fairlane, Torino & Ranchero

The 170ci six was a '62 MY upgrade over very humble 144 I6. 1964 saw the return of a Ranchero V8 option for the first time since '59 MY. (Courtesy Michael Garite)

Its two ratios were 1.82:1 and 1.00:1. Ford acknowledged the frisky nature of the 260, by making all V8 engined '64 Falcon versions come with 10in drums on all four wheels, instead of the six-pot's 9in units. Good sized brakes, like one would get on a Fairlane, but something like a Falcon Ranchero V8 had its sporting limitations.

The Falcon-derived chassis for Ranchero (and Mustang) was standard family sedan FoMoCo coil over A-arm front suspension, with a leaf arm suspended live axle outback. When Lee Iacocca first approached Carroll Shelby concerning the creation of a special Mustang, the Texan replied you can't make a race horse out of a mule! Carroll Shelby did concede, and his boys at Shelby American did succeed in creating something worthy of the Kentucky Derby, a racy little number called GT350! Thus, Falcon Rancheros can be made to handle, but in stock form it had more motor than handling.

Small Ranchero continued the stowage ways of its full-size predecessor. Swiveling the passenger part of the bench seatback, gained access to the spare tire and toolkit. The new generation also continued the luxo part of Ranchero's dual purpose nature. Country club or plain country, the choice was yours. If Falcon Sprint could have buckets, so too could Ranchero! Come 1965 MY, $84.80 got one the buckets and a Deluxe Trim Pack, the latter being a mandatory option to go with said buckets. Add to this a $51.50 center console and Dearborn had delivered a plush interior fit for a king. A pity Elvis preferred Caddies!

On the outside was Ranchero's traditional tailgate longhorn head logo, optional two-tone and color contrast paint for roof, sail panel and mid-profile spear sculpture. Said sculpture was chrome trim outlined. Plain hubcaps with blackwalls, decorative hubcaps, or faux knock off hub wire covers and whitewalls accompanied two-tone paint and padded dash options.

The option limit in the '60s was only dictated by one's imagination and wallet! One 1965 option of great Ranchero interest, was the 289 V8. With vehicle weight and lavishness going up by the minute, Ford said goodbye to 260 V8 in 1964. 144 cube Rancheros were history too, so the 1965 line-up started with the 105 horse 170ci six and three-speed manual power team.

For $157 extra Falcon Ranchero came with Ford's ubiquitous two-barrel 289. The same kind of motor that nefarious types snaked into Hertz-rented Shelby Mustang GT350s, once the genuine 306 horse 289 had been purloined! The plain 2bbl's 200bhp rating was bigger than its bite. Max power came in at 4400rpm, peak torque was 282lb/ft at 2400rpm and at 3000lb in automatic trim, Ranchero could do the ¼ mile in low 18s. For '65 MY, Ford had introduced the larger 200ci development of the 170 I6, boasting seven main bearings and 120 horses. However, who could pass up that Windsor engine note, and neat 289 Vee front fender checkered flag chrome badge?

Pay a $211 surcharge, and one's 289 sported four-barrel carburetion and 225 gross ponies. In that super 1960s playground *Motor Trend*'s Bob McVay mentioned that Shelby American had go fast parts to take that even higher. However, in the July 1965 2bbl 289 Ranchero report, McVay also noted that spirited cornering saw Ranchero understeer plough straight off a dusty track!

Aside from the aforementioned simple Falcon chassis, rims and tires were 5in wide steel units, wearing 6.95in footprint, 14in tall, bias ply rubber. Thus, it was easy to overwhelm the Ranchero's handling, with enthusiastic small block V8 horsepower.

Ford's heavy-duty towing options put the small block's moxie to better use. These items involved heavy-duty versions of the radiator, rear springs, brake linings and battery. A 42 amp alternator, load leveling shocks, frame mounted load equalizing trailer hitch, and lsd helped Ranchero live up to its dual purpose 'Town & Country' billing. The optional 3.50 rear axle was also handy for hauling! It was better to enjoy Ranchero's refinements, than the pseudo two-seater sports car angle, in 1965 at least. To that end, Ford introduced a three-speed automatic to compact Ranchero for the first time in '65 MY.

Dual range Cruise-O-Matic had 2.46/1.46/1.00 for first to third, and a 2.80:1 rear end with 289 2bbl. Snick the console shifter into that first D slot, after neutral, and one got second gear starts. Useful on slippery surfaces with all that 289 torque! The next D slot saw the box

Originally this '63 Ranchero, called Rojo, was I6 motorvated. It has since had a 260 Windsor bolted to the stock two-speed Ford-O-Matic. (Courtesy Todd & Jill Reglin)

The luxury car nature of Ranchero continued into the compact era. Optional Ranchero Deluxe Buckets could outplush almost any '80s luxo car! (Courtesy Todd & Jill Reglin)

Ford Midsize Muscle – Fairlane, Torino & Ranchero

go through all three speeds normally, nice for Woodward Avenue holeshots! Ever since Ranchero was reborn as a compact, it sat on a Falcon 109.5in wheelbase, 1965 was no exception. However, the market was changing. Buyers were looking for more refinement and sophistication.

1966-67 Ranchero – compact or midsize?

The official word from Ford Product Planning, was that changes were needed to satisfy a more competitive market. Reading between the lines, Ford obviously had the success of the intermediate Chevelle-based 1964 El Camino on its worried mind. With McNamara thrift a bygone age, Ford redeveloped Falcon off of a shared Fairlane platform. This naturally encompassed Ranchero, meaning bigger things for Falcon and Henry's pickup for '66 MY. Falcon moved up from its original 109.5in wheelbase to 110.9in. For Ranchero the new number was 113in, while Fairlane stayed on 116in.

In this reordered hierarchy, Comet was placed between Ranchero and Fairlane. Ranchero was also moving away from compact life, although technically it was still in the Falcon line. The Falcon Ranchero name was no longer used. There were no external Falcon badges, and Ranchero was sizing towards Fairlane. In 1965 Ranchero length/width/height dimensions were 181.6in/71.6in/55.2in, for '66 MY the respective numbers were 197.5in/74.7in/56.2in. With the same 289 and Cruise-O-Matic power team, weight remained around the 3000lb level.

Ford played around with engine availability to reflect the new status quo. Falcon was now limited to the 200 horse two-barrel 289, not 1965's 289 4bbl. Ranchero continued with the 225 horse four-barrel 289, whilst Fairlane's new zenith was the 390 V8. In a sign of the platform sharing of decades to come, 1966 Ranchero had a Falcon face, on a shared unibody Fairlane chassis that had the bigger car's refinements. For styling in spite of a Falcon front fascia, the Ranchero featured a Thunderbird roofline and long hood Mustang look, to go with the pickup's larger dimensions.

1966 Ranchero had greater passenger compartment bulkhead stiffening. Plus, there was that road shock-absorbing torque box design, seen on unibody Fairlane, and engine bay catwalks on either side of the motor to boost body

With Mustang yet to come, and T-Bird a four place chariot, Falcon Ranchero was the sportiest ride Henry offered in 1963! In its third model year, Ranchero was moving away from McNamara thrift. On the eve of a factory V8, by 1967 Ranchero was midsize! (Courtesy Todd & Jill Reglin)

4: Ranchero's Compact to Midsize Transition

rigidity. Like the Ford Product Planner said, it was a more grown up Ranchero. At the front it was the usual Ford A arm set up, with coil and MacPherson strut on top of upper A arm. However, the front roll center of the front suspension was now raised, and there was a new anti kickback steering linkage.

Outback were now five leafs, where there had been four, with said leafs wrapped in butyl rubber. A normal Falcon 0.65in swaybar was present, but the Falcon connection had people thinking the Ranchero HD suspension hardware, were actually Fairlane GT components. Ford didn't describe them as such, but economies of scale suggested otherwise. The HD option did raise 1966 Ranchero's payload from 850lb to 1250lb. A good number to go with the top 4bbl 289. This motor continued to mosey along with 10:1 compression and 266 degrees of duration on the intake and exhaust sides.

There were good things to find, and more signs Ranchero was becoming its own model. The longhorn badge motif was now on the sail panels, the restyled body featured more modern-looking curved window glass panes, although vent wings were retained. Inside, the continuing Deluxe Trim Pack had the plushness of Custom deep loop pile carpeting. The Cruise-O-Matic shift quadrant was illuminated red for second gear start mode, green for all ratio mode, a little too brightly according to *Car Craft*'s July 1966 article. In a word, blinding! The test car had the canted T bar Sports Shift automatic console, so one could pretend they were piloting a Fairlane GT/A down the ¼ mile!

Ranchero Custom trim ran to $136, with the optional console an asymmetric, rounded affair by 1966. The cars submitted to magazines had all the fruit, naturally to show Ranchero in its best light. Engineering wise, Ranchero was still a wagon shorn of its aft greenhouse. Under the rear cargo floor lay the footwell for third row wagon seating. However, in the 1966-67 era, 3rd gen Ranchero built

at Lorain, Ohio, the footwell was filled with a gas tank. Wagons had their tanks placed in the rear fender panel. A base '66 Ranchero cost a mere $2299, but with the top 289, power brakes/steering, radio etc, the price climbed to over $3100 on the way to auto nirvana. Here one would pick up a Falcon Custom Ranchero, as some still called it. However, for 1967, say hello to Fairlane Ranchero!

Upscale to Fairlane Ranchero

By moving to a shared Falcon/Fairlane chassis in 1966, Ranchero pickup box capacity increased again, to 39ft^3. However, dual purpose meant Ranchero couldn't live by utility alone. The idea of a compact Falcon front on a bigger rig, didn't sit well with some folks. Ed Skelton, an electrical contractor from Charlotte, North Carolina decided to right what was wrong with Ranchero. His story was covered in the September 1966 issue of *Hot Rod*. Skelton simply bought a brand new 1966 Ranchero, and added the appropriate parts from the FoMoCo catalogue. Back in the V8 rear drive days, this could be done!

Taking advantage of the Falcon/Fairlane unibody, he replaced the Falcon front

Windsor 260 made 164bhp (gross) on debut in the '62½ Fairlanes. With tuned 260, smaller Falcon Ranchero was the real Ford 'Sports Coupe!' (Courtesy Todd & Jill Reglin)

Ford Midsize Muscle – Fairlane, Torino & Ranchero

As a '65 ride, this marks the end of Falcon Ranchero. 1961-65 era pickups rode on a 109.5in wheelbase, and here length was 181.6in. (Courtesy Fred Strom)

Originally a Kansas delivery, this '65 Ranchero came with 200 horse 2bbl 289/three-speed manual power team, with stock 2.80 rear gears. The V8 was a desirable $157 option. (Courtesy Fred Strom)

with a 1966 Fairlane front fascia. Feeling that a 'Big Rig' should be powered by a Big Block, a 427 motor was dropped into the custom Ranchero's engine bay. 1966 was the first time Fairlane had seen the FE series V8 since full-size pre-1962 days, so why not Ranchero? Skelton's custom Ranchero was like a '66 Fairlane GT/A 390, but with a lot more go! To cope with the performance, a 428 Police Interceptor C6 automatic (Part No C60P 7000-H) was bolted to the 427. Faster shifts came courtesy of a GT/A sourced automatic valve body, the brain of an autobox.

31 spline Thunderbird axles helped reliably transfer drive to the rear wheels. The 1966 Thunderbird hardware carried the part number C65W 4200-H, associated with Ford's biggest passenger car line 9⅜in ring gear and Equal-Loc lsd. Competition racing hardware one could purchase over the counter in the good 'ol days! Highlighting Ranchero's Fairlane engineering connection, this project car used a 390 V8 1966 Fairlane wagon driveshaft. The driveshaft carried part number C60Z 4602-S, and fitted between the automatic and rear axle on the 1966 Ranchero sans modification.

The whole affair slowed down better than stock, because Skelton replaced the front drums with Mustang factory catalogue Funny Car disk brakes. In 1966, Mustang was available with front disks, but Ranchero and Fairlane were limited to four wheel drums. Given the Funny Car disks had the same bearing area as Falcon (upon which Mustang was based), and since Falcon and Fairlane had shared platform in 1966-67, the brake substitution worked out fine. New refinements that a normal '66 Ranchero could have anyway, were the first time Falcon option power brakes, and foot operated parking brake.

Mr Skelton's custom '66 Ranchero 427 looked like a '66 Fairlane GT/A pickup, except it went harder and stopped better. Great minds must have thought alike, because for 1967 model year Dearborn launched Fairlane Ranchero, and factory introduced the cosmetic, engine and braking upgrades of Ed Skelton! So it was that factory Ranchero adopted Fairlane's face. A fashionable high, wide and square rigged look, with vertically stacked pairs of circular headlamps. It was the kind of appearance seen on Pontiac GTO, Mercedes S class and American Motors Rebel/Ambassador.

Loadwise, Fairlane Ranchero continued with the ease of a torsion bar actuated tailgate. That said, even though Ranchero and Falcon/Fairlane wagon were related, the former lacked the latter's handy two-way tailgate. A bean counter omission no doubt. Helping greatly with said load, was the newly available 390 V8. This optional Thunderbird-sourced motor came in 2bbl form, costing $74.30, or 4bbl trim with $150.10 surcharge on Fairlane. This roughly accorded with Detroit industry practice of a buck for every extra cube, and $50 from 2bbl to 4bbl, but the power return per dollar wasn't all it might have been from Ford.

2bbl 390 made 270bhp at 4400rpm and 403lb/ft at 2600rpm on a 9.5:1 comp ratio. For the 4bbl edition equivalent the stats were 320 horses at 4800rpm and

4: Ranchero's Compact to Midsize Transition

427lb/ft at 3200rpm using a premium fuel hungry 10.5:1 comp ratio. Concerning Fairlane Ranchero, the 2bbl 289 wasn't available, neither was the 4bbl 390. The 2bbl 390 was a $104 option. With this motor, Ranchero could do 17 second ¼ miles, and offer superior real-world fuel economy, compared to an 18 second 2bbl 289 Fairlane. Ranchero's traditional lower weight meant it offered better braking and acceleration, versus normal Fairlane counterparts.

Ranchero's trim levels roughly corresponded with those of Fairlane's base, 500, 500 XL, with the $2474.40 Ranchero 500 Deluxe matching the buckets, vinyl and console of a Fairlane 500 XL very evenly. The budget minded could specify a 200ci I6 Ranchero, but the plush personal car interior was hard to pass up, as was that 390 V8! Safety was something one didn't have to pass up, it was being federaly mandated. Getting ready for 1967, the '66 Ranchero had a 'Fasten Seatbelt' light under the dash, and lapbelts that weren't easy to use in terms of getting jumbled up, and limiting the movement of a belted driver.

If this, and finding it hard to reach dashboard controls wearing a belt, were a concern, it didn't just affect Fords. 1967 federal requirements involved a dual circuit braking system, with dual chambered master cylinder, collapsible energy absorbing steering column, with padded steering wheel hub, soft interior trim, four-way hazard flasher lights and provision of shoulder belt anchors. To look after pedestrians, '67 Fairlane featured padded windshield pillars. Inside, the three spoke steering wheel had a '67 only style, of very noticeable center crash pad. This protruded beyond the wheel's flexible rim. The non-hostile interior contrasted greatly with Edsel of a decade earlier. Ralph Nader could have no qualms about Fairlane Ranchero!

Nader may even have been seduced by Ranchero's charming comfort, available with all the usual Fairlane luxo options. Performance, or engine response to be

Above: '65s had a softer touch to the '64 'Razor Edge' look. A junkyard Ranchero Deluxe ($84.80 option) bestowed trim pieces on what was a plain Ranchero.
Left: Custom touches include moving the column shift to the floor, and adding a Hurst shifter. An ergonomic wonder more suited to a car-based than a truck-based pickup! (Courtesy Fred Strom)

Bone stock 289, except for the dress-up chrome air cleaner. 4bbl 289 was a 225bhp option, but K code 289 was reserved for Fairlane and Mustang. (Courtesy Fred Strom)

Ford Midsize Muscle – Fairlane, Torino & Ranchero

Ranchero Deluxe genuine buckets, center console, and chrome strips were rare upgrades on the base Ranchero 289. (Courtesy Fred Strom)

precise, was a concern. California led the way on air pollution laws, and even before the 1968 federal coming of smog gear, Golden State Fords gave a taste of the sour future. The word was 'Thermactor.' *Car Life*'s February 1966 report on a 289 4bbl Ranchero said it all, 'Like a California Albatross strung by a fanbelt to the engine's neck.'

This 289 4bbl carried the same 225 horse rating, as 49 state Ranchero 289s, but something wasn't right. Don't blame the cam – intake and exhaust duration were still 266 degrees, but Californian Rancheros, and other affected Fords, turned in slightly slower ¼ mile figures. Thermactor didn't involve the thermal reactor pollution gear seen on '70s imported cars. The name concerned the method of raising combustion temperature, to achieve a more thorough burn, thereby reducing pollutants. It involved that dreaded device, that bastion of back pressure, called the smog pump!

A belt driven air pump, working off the engine, added air to the exhaust side. This was combined with lean carb settings and ignition retarded by six degrees. The objective was to raise combustion chamber temp, so that fewer hydrocarbons exited the tailpipe. Some at the time, and since, have questioned whether a high compression, high efficiency premium fuel motor sans smog gear, doesn't burn cleaner than such emissionized engines. Beyond question were the rising driveability quirks and poor response/gas mileage of the smoggers. Ranchero buyers, and others, started reaching for larger engine options like the 390 to compensate for performance woes. That said, the regular Fairlane range showed the 390 to be a mixed blessing.

The 1966 Ranchero represented a transitional phase for the car-based pickup, from compact to intermediate platform. It was the final year for the 'Falcon Ranchero' tag. This '66 has a 302/AOD automatic power team upgrade. (Courtesy Dennis Crenshaw)

62

5

Fairlane Becomes a Muscle Car 1965-69

Fairlane – Ford's overlooked gem!
You have to feel sorry for Fairlane as an industry innovator that got overlooked. The late '50s and early '60s recession gave rise to the US compact, and a desire for smaller family cars. Unibody Fairlane became a trailblazer in 1962 as a second generation compact, or intermediate to use contemporary industry parlance. Apart from size, Fairlane brought many useful things to family car life. For one, a new generation lightweight V8 called Windsor. It satisfied the rising family demand for V8 power and smoothness, minus the big inch thirst and weight. The hi po 289 figured in Fairlane before Mustang.

Then, there was suspension, with Fairlane bringing Lincoln Continental drag strut front suspension to the low cost line. For NVH chassis refinement, Fairlane's unibody construction with computer optimized torque boxes, were an elegant counterpoint to anyone that reckoned the '50s tri year Chebbies were the zenith of a fine riding and handling car! You want more? Apart from Ford's galvanized underbody structural members, there was multi-rail roof construction. Plus, rigid backbone driveshaft tunnel and spring tower structure.

Fairlane V8s, by far the most popular since no one wanted a poverty six, had a removable carrier type rear axle. This was quieter in operation and stronger, but a bit more expensive to fix, versus the unit on 170/200ci I6 Fairlanes. So there was no need to spring for dealer done underseal on the solid, worthy and good handling Fairlane. However, by the mid '60s, being tough wasn't enough. Apart from playing second fiddle to popular upstart Mustang, Fairlane had to contend with quasi sibling Mercury Comet.

After the full-size Merc Meteor days, Fairlane had to deal with an increasingly popular and fashionable Comet. A posh Falcon at the '60s dawn, the public took a shine to Merc Comet Cyclone. A sporty two-door hardtop with buckets, tach and padded dash, that made poor Fairlane look like a wallflower at a spring dance!

Marketing gave Mustang and Comet the nod, which meant a convertible option that homely Fairlane didn't have in the post-1961 era. Thus, roll on 1965 model year and Fairlane was billed and sold as a sedate sedan. Even worse, poor Fairlane was duking it out with four badge engineered GM A bodies, which Fairlane intermediate inspired!

GM quickly wooed buyers with more power and luxury in its inters, which put even more pressure on the increasingly dour Fairlane. Ford cruised family Fairlane into '65 MY with a restyle of a bulky, square type nature. 1963 had been the tailfin's final hurrah, '64 Fairlanes had a purposeful pie plate practicality, but '65 MY saw a bank vault like blandness. Fairlane was awfully squared up that year, with a tank like body that looked like it had received a visit from an aluminum siding salesman! Even that former bolide, the Fairlane 500 Sports Coupe, was looking more mainstream than meatloaf!

If the Sports Coupe's hardtop rear window had some rake to it, it was hard to discern. The 289 checkered flag callout badge still lived on the lower front fender behind the wheel well, but the base 200 horse two-barrel edition/Cruise-O-Matic power team delivered ho hum acceleration. Zero to sixty in 12 seconds with high 17s in the ¼. MPGs in the high teens qualified it as a frugal bank vault though.

Tick the 4bbl 289 order blank, and one's two-door hardtop, sedan or wagon, put out 225 gross ponies on a ten to one comp ratio, but no more. The old 271 horse K code 289 had gone AWOL, whilst Fairlane was becoming a solid citizen for '65 MY. Formerly a Fairlane exclusive, this hi po motor now resided in Henry's Mustang stable. No K code, no ragtop, but yes to engineering refinements.

Ford's once well known good handling family car was absent, as Fairlane adopted a fashionably soft ride for '65 MY in keeping with its new quiet, unsporting nature. *Car Life* declared said ride akin to a child's carnival 'flying

Ford Midsize Muscle – Fairlane, Torino & Ranchero

After the sober '65s, and getting upstaged by Comet, the view from '66 Fairlane was rosier, as Ford made midsize the new full-size. (Courtesy Brian Cline)

elephant' ride in March 1965. Well, not everyone could be a tiger in the mid '60s! Fairlane left that sobriquet to V8 English Alpines and Wide Track Pontiacs, whilst adopting 88lb of sound deadening, so Andy William's radio rendition of *Moon River*, would retain its high fidelity. Fairlane power steering was quicker, the former linkage boosted system, giving way to Galaxie's fully immersed hydraulic pump apparatus.

Standard V8 sedan and hardtop 14-inchers came with a 6.95in tire footprint, but one could specify optional Fairlane wagon sourced Goodyears of 7.35-14in nature. This footwear reduced tire squeal during spirited cornering. For more than this, Ford fans had to wait for 1966 and a Fairlane makeover that brought big inch power!

1966 makeover!

The most obvious change for '66 MY was Fairlane's more upright, square rigged styling – very fashionable for the era, and unmistakeable for a Pontiac and American Motors intermediate. That which was horizontal had become vertical. Ford's stylists had rotated '65's taillights upwards. The same applied to the former dual circular lamps, which now adopted a vertical Mercedes stack, years before Granada had passed Iacocca's lips.

The Squire wagon and ragtop variants were back for 1966, the latter offering major innovation. Personal cars and sports cars had put convertibles in the suburban status symbol shade recently. Fairlane convertible tried to make ragtop life easier. The large glass rear window was divided by a silicon rubber hinge. This horizontal hinge allowed the top to be folded minus unzipping the back window. The system was developed by Corning Glass, with the company notching up a *Motor Trend* Special Achievement Award for its efforts!

As ever with domestic cars, interest and emphasis was on what lay underhood, as well as appearance. To match show with go, 1966 was the first year the FE series medium/big block became available in the intermediate sized Fairlane. Previously all inter Fairlanes used Windsor small block power. With the base two-barrel 390 making the same power as the Fairlane discontinued K-code 289, there was little need for such solid lifter small blocks, in theory. Ford introduced a raft of 390 upgrades, befitting its midsize Fairlane debut.

All Fairlane 390s of '66 MY came with lighter pistons and pins, to enable the motor to rev more easily and safely. A new design oil pan and baffle system protected the big end bearings from oil starvation during heavy cornering. For maximum efficiency the size of the new intake manifold's passage was worked out optimally by computer. There was a new camshaft with higher lift and increased overlap, plus new valve springs for higher rpm operation. Not forgetting a less restrictive air cleaner.

Fairlane GT – Ford's supercar

In the style stakes the latest 390 pep pill was of little help. Fairlane's formal sedate styling was holding sales back, and dealers complained about the absence of a fastback. It seemed a hardtop with a raked rear window just wasn't going to

5: Fairlane Becomes a Muscle Car 1965-69

1965 was the final year before Ford's family-natured Fairlane made the move to a sportier life. (Courtesy Ford Canada)

cut it. 1965 was the final hurrah for the Sports Coupe, as Ford moved on to more exciting packs. 1966 saw luxury XL and, more importantly from the sports angle, GT. This was the stand-alone performance Ford that fans had been waiting for, in a midsize. Its inspiration was all too clear: the Pontiac GTO.

Just as Mustang got everyone to take the pony ride, GTO sparked the hot intermediate stampede. Available in quasi hardtop fastback, and convertible, Fairlane GT and its zombie shift GT/A counterpart, it had the visual hi po get up. A wheelwell-to-wheelwell lower body profile decal stripe, and faux V8 intake trumpet louvers. Said louvers carried '390' script at the leading edge, representing GT's sole engine choice. Inside were the expected buckets, console shift, and wood-rimmed, three-spoke tiller, plus tach. In the tradition of supplementing family car instrumentation, the tach, like the GT, was stand-alone.

Available separately, a circular tach gauge with Cobra emblem, made by Rotunda Division, sat atop the dash. Special GT suspension revived Fairlane's once great handling reputation. A normal Fairlane hardtop had front and rear spring rates of 75lb/in and 82lb/in respectively. Ford's prototype Fairlane GT/A had rates increased to 109lb/in and 132lb/in respectively. Steel 14 x 6in rims shod with Firestone Super Sports rubber were also part of the plan. These nylon two-ply bias belted tires were speed rated to 125 continuous mph, and were highly regarded at a time when enthusiasts were starting to look to radials for the best overall performance.

The stock 0.65in front swaybar of the Falcon/Fairlane 1966 common ground era was replaced by a beefier 0.85in unit. A very necessary change, given the weight difference between Windsor and FE 390 V8. For all the changes, Fairlane GT sported the Detroit normal front independent A arm, MacPherson strut, five leaf live axle sprung rear end. Series production GTs and GT/As came with softer front springing of 119lb/in, but the rear leafs were firmer at 146lb/ft. Production rims were only 5.5in wide.

Originally GT was to have 10 x 2.5in drums all around. In reality it was 10 x 2.5in front and 10 x 2.0in rear. This dropped swept area from 314 to 282.6in^2, but no one complained about Fairlane GT's stoppers in the ¼ mile era! All fine and dandy, but what about that 'GO' angle after the 'WHOA?' Regular 1966 Fairlane 390s put out 270 and 315 horses, in 2bbl and 4bbl trim, respectively. This was more power than the 390 had in full-size '65 MY, as well as 5% more economical. However, Dearborn delivered a special 390 underhood, with each and every GT suffixed car.

For GT and GT/A hardtop and ragtop, there was only one choice. Unusual, given GTO and rivals provided a few order blanks to tick. At Ford it was a 335 horse 10.5:1 comp 390 four-barrel, where max power came in at 4600rpm. Not that high a rpm, for a tractable motor with 427lb/ft at 2800rpm. This hydraulic lifter motor had 270 degree duration on the intake and exhaust side, with 40 degrees of overlap. The special 390 was connected to a dual 2in exhaust system, had Autolite BF-32 sparkplugs and no Thermactor in California, which must have heartened some.

Bizarrely, GT and GT/A's 4bbl carb device, marked it as a 'high-performance' motor, therefore above and beyond Thermactor. The theory might have been that a high-output motor was more efficient and burned cleaner. It was high output in some ways, with over 300 cubes and horses versus K code 289, but was on the mild side by muscle car standards. In the driveway bragging stakes, lifting the hood revealed low restriction air cleaner atop the big Holley, and chrome finish rocker covers as part of a GT dress up kit. An underhood viscous drive fan eked out more efficiency through less engine drain.

If the mid '60s were the 'Go' era, they were also the 'Shift' era: how one changed gear on a performance car mattered as much for style as the ¼ mile. The GT range started with a console operated three-speed manual, four on the floor was optional. However, all the publicity from Ford and attention from car magazines, was directed at the Sports Shift Cruise-O-Matic, that the GT/A's 'A' was named after. Forget about the 'leave it alone' column shift, or problematic push button types; this automatic was designed to be used.

Technical Editor John Ethridge talked about this unit, and the hot Fairlane as a whole, in the October 1965 issue of *Motor Trend*. In what sounded like a Ford editorial, the Sport Shift was advanced as the work of young Ford engineers, in favor of actively managed automatics. Fairlane executive engineer Howard Freers claimed Sports Shift was good, many four on the floor fans would now go the autobox route. It looked cool, with an angled, ergonomic T-bar handle falling to the driver's right hand.

The asymmetrical brushed aluminum console trim was handsome, and came

A special 'off the menu' Fairlane dish! Mid '66 MY in the Dearborn kitchen Henry cooked up 60 Fairlane 500 two-door hardtops, with 425 horse R code 427 V8! (Courtesy Kevin Amos)

5: Fairlane Becomes a Muscle Car 1965-69

Far left: Through its homologation special, Ford wished to qualify its R code 427/Top Loader four-speed power team for NHRA and IHRA Super Stock. (Courtesy Kevin Amos)

Left: Intended to homologate the 427/Top Loader power team, but this particular Fairlane 427 has a column shift fettled C6 auto tranny. (Courtesy Kevin Amos)

with a like-angled, brightly illuminated shift quadrant. The only non-functional aspect was that the quadrant looked a bit small, out of scale considering console and Fairlane size in general. In the heat of battle one would have to feel, rather than look for the next slot! More control meant actively selecting first or second, and the autobox would stay there to maximise acceleration, or maintain cornering line. Easy winter traction second gear starts were a boon too.

The auto shifter was connected to Ford's new C6 autobox, a heavy-duty version of the C4, which had replaced Ford-O-Matic in 1964. Given 1966 was the first year intermediate sized Fairlane got 390ci power, it was lucky C6 came out the same year. C6 offered less weight, complexity, and greater efficiency than the MX Cruise-O-Matic box Ford utilized in its larger, more powerful cars. However, it took no extra space versus MX. Based on the same layout as C4, C6 featured a Simpson planetary gearset, over 10lb of powdered metal in construction, and was the first Ford unit to use Borg Warner's flexible shiftband. The last item promising better and more durable shifting.

With all the traffic light races, pro-performance magazine tests and changing attitudes, automatics were no longer set and forget. With all those brake torqued take offs, it was reassuring Henry placed a sturdy autobox behind that 390! In terms of real estate, one's Fairlane GT or GT/A was 197in long, 74.1in wide and 54.3in tall, with the automatic GT/A weighing a normal inter 3510lb. Starting price was $2843.07, but by the time essentials like power brakes and power steering were added, plus much vaunted Sports Shift, say hello to a $3500 sticker!

Commonly specified on Fairlane GT were the 95 buck option of Mustang styled steel wheels. Back in the full-size days all the good stuff seemed T-Bird related. However, now it came off of Henry's Horse! Was Ford's family car always going to play second fiddle?! GT's body profile striping and stacked headlight look made Ford's midsize resemble a Pontiac Tempest Sprint. It was faster than that Poncho 6 cammer, but could it unseat a GTO? It seemed to depend on tuning.

The homologation mid '66 Fairlane 427 included all white exterior, fiberglass hood, and forward facing hoodscoop. It was the kinda machine some Ford fans wished the GT and GT/A were. (Courtesy Kevin Amos)

Ford Midsize Muscle – Fairlane, Torino & Ranchero

Above: After the sober '65s, Ford jazzed up Fairlane with a ragtop for '66 MY. This 1967 example sports 390 V8 and four-speed, for easy high 15s! (Courtesy Mike Mzsenyuk)

Left: On the options sheet it was denoted as '390 4V Thunderbird V8;' paying $150.10 got one 320 horse in 1967 on non GT Fairlanes. The 10.5:1 CR is stock, but the Holley carb ain't! (Courtesy Mike Mzsenyuk)

Indeed, on first acquaintance, the Fairlane GT and GT/A were reckoned to be B/SA or C/SA runners at the strip.

Motor Trend's October 1965 Fairlane GT/A advertorial, or 'Day at Dearborn,' suggested Ford had the right stuff. *Motor Trend*'s John Ethridge said Ford had worked out the cam profile just prior to *Motor Trend* arriving for Henry's 'Show & Tell.' The Fairlane GT/A did 0-60mph in 6.8 seconds, turned a 15.2 second ¼ mile at 92mph and hit an observed 125mph

5: Fairlane Becomes a Muscle Car 1965-69

at 5100rpm. The redline was stated at 5600rpm, so the journal felt north of 130mph was a given. There was a cool eye candy tire smoking start picture, and comment on the Dearborn ride/handling course that Fairlane GT/A on 6in wide rims, could match a slot car. Trouble was, this wasn't the showroom ready version of Fairlane GT/A.

Where did that tiger go?

Car Life got hold of a Fairlane GT/A for its March 1966 report. "Genuine Imitation Joins the Supercar Spectrum," was the report title. It said as much about the GT/A as magazine performance car testing in the '60s. *Car Life*'s figures were 0-60mph in 8.6 seconds, a ¼ mile of 15.4 seconds at 87mph and top speed of 115mph.

Power and torque figures were the same as *Motor Trend*'s October 1965 test, but the redline had plummeted to five grand! On top of this, *Car Life*'s GT/A had trouble making 12mpg when lightly driven on premium – disappointing, given the Pontiac Catalina family car that *Consumer Report* sampled in 1967 with premium fuel 400 and econoaxle got 20mpg plus, and still had scat a plenty! What was Henry up to?

There is no doubt the GT/A was detuned from the proto *Motor Trend* tried out earlier. However, as for real world performance, this was probably the real McCoy for everyone. Pontiac, with the help of ad man Jim Wangers, turned hot car magazine submission into a fine art. Truth to tell, *Car Life* never met a real GTO, it and others got fine tuned examples that were better than stock – to make a good impression. One time a GTO not 'prepared' by Royal Pontiac made it through to a magazine. It turned in tepid times and Mr Wangers wasn't pleased.(8)

Ford felt it had done enough, creating a 335 horse Fairlane that matched the rating of a 335bhp 389 4bbl GTO. The trouble was, the GTO range didn't stop there, many went for said Goat with triple deuce 389. This 3 x 2bbl edition had 288 degree and 302 degree duration on the

intake and exhaust sides respectively, with 63 degrees of overlap. All of which was wilder than Ford's hot 390, and yet the potential was there. Ford had marketed a 3 x 2bbl intake manifold for the FE V8 earlier, through its Parts Division. The aftermarket did offer special heads and headers for 390 in 1966, to aid breathing and exhaling.

Why didn't Ford do more? Dearborn was late to the formal muscle car race, and lavished much more attention on Mustang. Criticism was directed at GT's 390 being rather heavy, and not making the power it should, given size and weight. Thus, although Fairlane GT and GT/A were judged sound handlers, better

Above: This safety steering wheel crash pad was a 1967 only showing. That year, the feds said a collapsible energy absorbing steering column was necessary. The Hurst four-speed shifter isn't stock. (Courtesy Mike Mzsenyuk)

Left: Fairlane and Mustang may have shared hardware, but Fairlane had the upper hand in at least one area – an accommodating back seat! (Courtesy Mike Mzsenyuk)

Ford Midsize Muscle – Fairlane, Torino & Ranchero

than normal versions, that heavy motor was considered an understeer contributor. Weight distribution was 56.8/43.2% for the GT/A hardtop, and such front end bias was the reason why such a beefy front swaybar was included. No rear swaybar was present on GT or GT/A.

The situation made many scribes speculate whether Ford would have done better utilising the 289 Windsor, to create a better balanced performance car, with superior top end and frugality. The 390 was judged a luxo T-Bird motor, not much interested in venturing beyond 4500rpm. Enthusiasm over Sports Shift was muted too. Everyone liked the look of the angled, brushed aluminum shift gate, but shifting manually didn't bring the ratios requested like a good 'ol four on da floor! Changing ratio wasn't even as quick as the automatics of rivals, like Chrysler's Driver Command Torqueflite box. To avoid the lag, Fairlane fans stuck to a manual box.

As things stood, the Fairlane GT seemed like a promising first draft. The dual exhaust system sounded sweet, the Sports Shift handle felt sturdy, but was this understeerer a paper tiger next to GTO? Fairlane GT and GT/A probably approximated the performance of a non magazine submitted Goat. Evidence suggests owners were happy with their GTs, and Ford put forth a Fairlane with sport and luxury blend. Fairlane GT and GT/A came with a 'high series sound package' of 120lb worth of insulation and sound deadener material.

Ford certainly picked up on the trend where buyers wanted go, show and comfort in equal measure, as part of a stand alone model. It was becoming rarer to order a powerful midsize sans power brakes, power steering and a deluxe interior. Muscle cars were partly the new suburban status symbol. A demographic delight perhaps, but what of Ford's racing heritage? Folks tuning Flathead V8s in Model As, the dual quad and 300 horse supercharged 312s of recent vintage, not forgetting 427 motorvated dragstrip Galaxies and Fairlane inters …

Holman-Moody's spruce goose!

Ford's Total Performance campaign commenced in 1963. Using Fairlanes, Mustangs and Falcons to venture to every corner of motorsport, Henry even cooked up an OHC drag racer! However, if race and win on Sunday, sell on Monday was the plan, Dearborn had never heard of Pontiac. The GTO and ensuing relations showed how sales could be got, through hotly perceived road cars. It looked like Ford had left all its expertise and good stuff at the track. That Fairlane streeter was a trifle meek!

Things seemed bleak, but sports fans were heartened to see Holman-Moody try and turn Henry's frown upside down! Race experts that put Fairlane on the NASCAR grid, Holman-Moody came up with a special Fairlane GT/A. A yellow fastback two-door with black stripes. One hoped Holman-Moody would turn Fairlane GT/A into a real tiger! It did so with a blueprinted 390 motor. The custom oil pan carried a Ford part number. Many of the special parts that made up this ride did have Ford part numbers. However, in reality they were specially made, and or came from the aftermarket.

As per Mercury Comet, Mercedes, GTO, et al, Ford adopted the fashionable vertical stack headlamps for 1966. (Courtesy Mike Mzsenyuk)

Above: This Sauterne Gold 1967 Fairlane 500 XL was built in Kansas City, MO on March 28th 1967. Delivered April 13th 1967, the original Parside Ford Sales (Winnipeg, MB) dealer emblem is still on the trunk lid! (Courtesy Ted Nourse)

The H-M 390 sported dual points ignition and modified distributor with 15 degrees of advance at 7500rpm, an optimistic 390 figure. Ye olde 406 tri-power V8 had donated springs and dampers shimmed to 4800rpm, to get that Fairlane GT 390 motor to the redline on time! The 335 horse edition came with a 600 CFM Holley four-barrel, the regular 390 Quad possessed a mere 430 CFM stat. Dual cast iron headers, a lightweight engine-cooling fan clutch and chromed low restriction air cleaner came along for the ride too.

Beyond this, H-M added a FoMoCo fiberglass radiator fan shroud, but didn't

This beast packs a 450bhp 347 stroker with aluminum heads, Holley 650 DP, MSD distributor, wires and coil. The fuel pump is by Edelbrock. (Courtesy Ted Nourse)

Ford Midsize Muscle – Fairlane, Torino & Ranchero

'Project Scarelane' has a Crites' 427R code hood, but original trim Ivy Gold interior. (Courtesy Ted Nourse)

Originally with a 2bbl 289, C4 auto and 2.79 rear gears. However, with mods, the first Wheeler Racing (Blaine, MN) dyno run of the Patriot Performance (Georgia) built 347 stroker rang up 453.8bhp and 414.9lb/ft. (Courtesy Ted Nourse)

state any power rating increase or said stock 335 ponies – perhaps unusual for the time, but in keeping with H-M racing experience. A lot of effort was put into handling. Kelsey Hayes Mag Star 14 x 6in magnesium steel rims gave the size Ford originally proposed for GT and GT/A. They were wrapped in the normal issue Firestone Super Sport tires. Then H-M went about subtle suspension tuning. Yes, the H-M car came with HD springs and coils, but the front swaybar and rear HD springs were special order items beyond GT stock fare.

The H-M car had a custom, handmade front swaybar, even though said item carried FoMoCo part no C60Z-5482-A. The other H-M car hardware had FoMoCo part numbers assigned. However, using such numbers over the Ford parts counter, would probably have yielded no results. As it stood, sturdier brackets for mounting aforementioned swaybar carried part no C4HM-5486-1. Staying with the front, ultra stiff shocks were C60Z-18124-C, and stiffer springs were C1-MM-5310-K. Out back HD shocks had part number C60Z-18-25-C, with tough Galaxie axle housing carrying a 3.70 final drive ratio and part no B7A-4209-A.

The one-off car H-M made had a Detroit Automotive lsd with 4.11:1 rear axle. Like the normal GT/A, H-M skipped a rear swaybar. However, also like the stock car, the H-M GT/A was a first rate handler, if a trifle understeer prone. Decoration wise expect the usual GT/A stripes, plaques and 390 hood script callouts. Stopping the beast were large and finned four-wheel drums. Drums were a drag racer favorite, since they created less aerodynamic drag than disk brakes.

H-M followed Ford's lead in not installing traction bars. This oversight limited ¼ mile performance, due to axle wind up. As things stood the April 1966 Cars Road Test divulged figures of 0-60mph in 7.1 seconds, ¼ mile in 14.5 seconds at 99mph and nearly 115mph. All on Sunoco 260 hi test. This was decidedly swifter than a stock GT/A, but traction problems saw the ¼ mile bettered by GTO and Olds 442, in this magazine's experience.

Price was looking like $4500 for the H-M fettled GT/A. This was a steep price, given that overall the machine provided just slightly superior performance to a stock Olds 442. The unspoken thought in many race fan minds was whether H-M GT/A, or any GT/A, was worth it? In the competitive melee that was the mid to late '60s muscle car wars, Fairlane GT and GT/A didn't seem to have the fan base of GTO, Olds 442, Chevelle SS or Mopar marvels. However, the facts suggest Fairlane was a diamond in the rough.

Just the facts, ma'am …

In 1966, *Car and Driver*, the journal that famed GTO by comparing it with its Modena namesake, had GTO and Fairlane GT/A in its data comparison tables for 'Sports Sedans (Over 300 cubic inches).' The Pontiac panel can be found in the *Car and Driver Yearbook* (1966), the GT/A panel in the April 1966 issue. On test were GTO convertible with four-speed and 360 horse triple deuce 389. Fairlane GT/A had its sole 335bhp 390 4bbl choice, and weighed 3605lb versus the GTO's 3620lb. Both had identical 0-60mph times of 7.5 seconds.

GT/A hit 80mph faster, in 12.3 seconds versus GTO's tardy 13.2 seconds. However, GTO topped out at 130mph, GT/A at a lower 125mph, but, with Fairlane, one avoided manual labor and had a better chance of stopping. Fairlane GT/A had four-wheel 10in drums, GTO merely 9.5in drums x4. GTO's stock stoppers were known for being limited, given vehicle size and weight. Pontiac was known for being 'wide track' at 58in front and 59in rear. However, Fairlane GT/A, with no such fanfare, possessed front and rear track of 58in.

In '60s advertising the substance got overlooked, with all that concentration on the form. Sadly GT/A got overlooked, while GTO became the stuff of urban myth and legend. Ford had a super white hot Fairlane in 1966, but it was pretty much under the radar. In the tradition of 1964 Thunderbolt, Ford issued forth 60 very special Fairlane 500 two-doors in mid 1966. Ford did have a 410 horse Q code 4bbl 427 at the time, but these low volume run hardtops came with 425bhp! These dual quad R code 427 machines, could have the cogs stirred by a sturdy four on the floor Top Loader manual box.

Just the thing to catch a wide track tiger by the tail, one would think. Unfortunately, this car showed Ford's mentality of Total Performance, mainly for the track. Its sworn purpose was to qualify its tough power team for NHRA and IHRA drag strip duty. With less fanfare than earlier Thunderbolt, these Fairlanes were the supercar with no name! That said, the all white exterior, fiberglass hood, and forward facing hoodscoop promised heavenly performance. But, once again, just for the pros, not the general hoi polloi. Joe Q Public only had his eye on 1967 MY Fairlane revisions.

Stylewise there wasn't much to report. One could tell the '67s from the '66s courtesy of three aforementioned vertical grille stakes, placed in the middle and outer thirds. Then there were the '67 federal related safety changes seen on Ranchero too. These included the '67 MY only prominent crash pad safety steering wheel. A very important active safety improvement one couldn't see was the intermediate size car availability of disk brakes. Disk brakes offered more consistent, fade free, straight line stops. On a 1950s Citroën DS there was a disk brake at each corner, on domestic cars they were hard to find.

A lot of emphasis in American performance was on acceleration, with cheap gas, but even on a sporty 1966

Left: Ford's sports shift console automatic was part of the 1966 GT/A's headline act. However, it was a little fiddly in practice. (Courtesy Ted Nourse)

Right: The 'Project Scarelane' Fairlane was built up by Rich Wait of the Hot Rod Factory (East Bethel, MN www.hotrodfactory.net), with much owner input. (Courtesy Ted Nourse)

Ford Midsize Muscle – Fairlane, Torino & Ranchero

At first an export to Winnipeg, MB, this Fairlane 500 XL was a clean three owner car with 72,000 miles on the odometer before major mods commenced in the 2000s! (Courtesy Ted Nourse)

In the early 2000s owner Ted Nourse experienced brake lock up and swerving to avoid a highway fender bender. Nourse then realized it was time to deep six the stock four-wheel drums! (Courtesy Ted Nourse)

Fairlane GT/A there was just no choice concerning stopping. Finned drums and metallic linings were the best even Holman-Moody would fit. Industry stats showed only around 3% of domestics had disks in 1966. Most of those would have been the standard four-wheel disks seen on 1965 and later Vettes, and the front Kelsey-Hayes disk brake option available on Mustang. Going into 1967, Ford was the biggest installer, followed by Chrysler, GM and AMC.(9)

It wasn't much fun being pitched all over the place, until you hit something, in a hot Chevelle with four-wheel drums. However, major change was afoot with Ford at the forefront. Speculation was that Ford would be going all out in 1968, with 30% of its rides featuring front disks. It was expected to be a major part of its power brake option, on all but its smallest models. On 1967 Fairlane power drums were a $42.29 option, power front disks cost $85. This latter option was standard on Fairlane GT and GT/A. On the front were 11.375 x 2.07in disks, rearward were the usual 10 x 2.5in drums.

How quickly one's Ford stopped the first time depended on Fairlane body type and equipment. Lighter cars stopped in a shorter distance, with drums beating disks. For controllability and consistency disks won out. In June 1967, *Motor Trend* declared disk brake Fairlane stops from 60mph, to be as straight as the hero in a Roy Rogers western! Just as well, because Ford had upwardly revised regular fuel 2bbl 390 and premium gas 4bbl 390, to 275 and 320 horses respectively. With all that power, one could add a few options to the payment plan.

Power steering was $84.47, Select Shift Cruise-O-Matic was a princely $220.17. Ford's 'Sports Shift' three-speed auto was more widely available on 1967 models. Popular AM radio was $57.51, with newly emerging 8-track Stereosonic tape system retailing at $128.49. Ford's very effective Selectaire Conditioner was a huge 356.09 bucks. Often the single most expensive option on any car, a/c, still wasn't commonly found, even on domestics in 1967. In colder parts of the country, it was normal to see quite luxurious cars with many options, except a/c.

Items like optional engines, limited slip differentials and special tires cost far less, explaining their popularity. The 4bbl 390 T-Bird V8 was a mere $150.10, LSD $37.20 and 7.75 x 14-4PR WSW rubber $48.35. All that helped enthusiasts keep a Fairlane under control, a very important goal in racing. For 1965 MY Fairlane's wheelbase increased one ½in to 116in, by repositioning the rear axle on its springs. This was partly for marketing, let it be known Fairlane was a genuine intermediate (midsize), and partly for racing. Ford moved to intermediates and Fairlane, when NASCAR rule changes occurred.

Hooker headers and Flowmaster 40 mufflers play a sweet tune! (Courtesy Ted Nourse)

5: Fairlane Becomes a Muscle Car 1965-69

Onto the ovals – 1967 Daytona 500

The 1967 Daytona 500 was certainly one for the racing scrapbook. The race was won by legendary driver Mario Andretti, in a Ford Fairlane, with Holman-Moody. Today, reputation of such notables would make that result seem a foregone conclusion, but at the time it was a real surprise. Andretti, 27 years old at the time, was contract sent by Ford to accompany Holman-Moody No 1 driver Fred Lorenzen. As part of Holman-Moody's famous Ford, NASCAR and Fairlane connection, well known engine builder Waddell Wilson and chassis expert Jake Elder were aboard.

Mario Andretti requested an unusual race car setup from team engineers. He wanted the car set up real loose, so that the Fairlane racer could go from the bottom of a corner on entry, to the outside of the oval wall on exit. The result was a dangerous looking maneuver of two power slides per lap! Everyone thought it was just a matter of time before Andretti got seriously hung up, but he didn't. Andretti dominated the race, and won it in spite of his team.

Although Andretti has never confirmed it, it is suspected that his suspiciously long final pitstop was an attempt by Holman-Moody and Ford to put number one team driver Fred Lorenzen on top.

The history books will always show the 1967 Daytona 500 was Mario Andretti's sole NASCAR Sprint Cup win, from just 14 career NASCAR starts. He went on to become 1978 Formula One World Champion driving a Ford Cosworth DFV V8 powered Lotus, for team boss Colin Chapman.

Those stylish '68s!

While Mario Andretti was slipping and sliding at Daytona, Ford was fettling Fairlane for major 1968 model year changes. The new body, or bodies, were obvious. Gone was the headlight stacked high, wide and handsome look. In came a fashionable, lower, sleeker, sportified appearance. A full width, recessed grille, with pairs of round horizontally placed headlamps.

1968 Fairlane accommodated federal side marker lighting laws, in a typically integrated domestic manner. That meant parking lights that wrapped around the front fenders. Small rear fender side markers let folks know one was around at the tail end. Taillights were vertical rectangles, with reversing lights placed in the middle.

With bodystyles one could have the usual suspects: four-door sedan, formal two-door hardtop, convertible and wagon. Two- and four-door 1968 Fairlanes continued on 1967's 116in wheelbase. Fairlane sedan was 201in in length, wagon 203.9in, with weight range for the '68s in the 2932-3514lb ballpark. Fairlane was bigger and heavier this year in keeping with intermediate rivals, but Fairlane wagon continued with the 113in wheelbase. A legacy of the Falcon, Fairlane and Ranchero shared platform approach instituted in 1966.

In the 1966-70 era, Falcon wagon, Ranchero and Fairlane wagon were close cousins under the sheetmetal, and rode on the aforementioned 113in wheelbase. However, in the late '60s, prime ponycar and muscle car era, all attention was on Ford's new fastback. FoMoCo speak saw this fancy two-door denoted 'SportsRoof,' although this moniker was only formally used from 1970 MY onwards. There was Mustang fastback, which was loved by all and sundry, but Fairlane fastback posed the problem. How to get a good looking shape out of a big fastback? American Motors had such troubles with Marlin.

It was the problem of melding a big car front with a fastback. For the most part Fairlane did OK, but early SportsRoofs were more macho than beautiful. Apart from a slightly concave tail panel, there was that rear expansive sloping glass pane. Ford fastback wasn't alone in the limited and distorted rear visibility such windows offered. They also required frequent cleaning from moisture and dust, in a time before rear wash/wiper systems. To maintain rear driver vision the rear window went long, eating into trunklid size.

Ford Midsize Muscle – Fairlane, Torino & Ranchero

Aside from a small trunklid, fastback also suffered from a high loadsill, whereas formal hardtop had a loadsill almost at bumper level. Fastback owners had to clear a 33.8in high panel. Then there were the C pillar blind spots, common to all sporty cars. However, in the Age of Aquarius such practical trivialities meant nothing. This was the year Mr McQueen redefined cool with a turtleneck and a fastback, not a hat and horse! People were looking forward, not back. A sensible strategy given the rocket power domestic V8s were putting out!

Was it a coincidence an intermediate fastback looked just right with a surfboard mounted on its roof? Perhaps that's why Henry called it SportsRoof?! Maybe this was the new kinda family car, perfect for California dreaming. If California wasn't already the Mecca for sporty personal car sun worshippers, it soon would be. Marketing wanted us to believe we were all just one ashram away from utopia, and Fairlane SportsRoof was it!

As was fashionable at the time, Fairlane hardtop and SportsRoof did without wind noise provoking vent wings. So did Ford's latest intermediate convertible: it was thought unnecessary, given modern flow through dash vents, but Fairlane sedan and wagon kept them. These were the utilitarian family mainstays. In the absence of a/c, domestic car flow through ventilation wasn't that cool, so four-door sedan and wagon profited by retaining said quarter panes. At the time one could save 1-2mpg overall in a family car by not using a/c. Thus, vent wings were money makers.

Wagon was probably the most overlooked Fairlane variant, yet that's where the magic resided. Can you say 'Magic Doorgate?' This was Ford's three-way tailgate of convenience. Specifiable with rear powered glass window. Optional rear facing third row seating, boosted the occupant count to eight. Dealers seeking to value add, reminded prospects about the optional chrome roof rack! Looking at Fairlane four-door sedan and wagon, one could see reasons to avoid full-size Galaxie, namely size and price. Fairlane sedan was 12.3in shorter than Galaxie, on a wheelbase curtailed by 3in. This used to be the full-size car of yore, making Fairlane the right size Ford, again, for '68 MY!

Ford was building that new '68 Fairlane in all kinds of places. At factories in Atlanta, Georgia; Lorain, Ohio; Chicago, Illinois; Canada's Oakville Ontario plant, and in Argentina! South American production took place at the General Pacheco plant. As happened with American cars made under license in other countries, such markets often hung onto a design. Less inclined to annual US obsolescence, the Argentine 1968-69 style Ford midsize continued in production, improved along the way, until 1981! By that hour some Stateside enthusiasts, sick of I4 econoboxes, were wishing Ford USA had shown such persistence.

Back in 1968 America, the Fairlane range kicked off as expected. Base Fairlane came with Ford's econo 200 cube six, and bodystyles involving two-door hardtop, four-door sedan and wagon. The well known 'Ranch Wagon' nameplate had been consigned to history, soon to be joined by Ford's 289 motor. The trusty 2bbl 200 horse 289 was being phased out during '68 MY Fairlane's run, in favor of the latest development in the Windsor small block story, the 210bhp (gross) 302ci V8. The 5.0 started as a humble two-barrel optional Fairlane motor in '68. It was actually 4.9 liters, and would go on to power countless plastic bodykit clad Foxstangs, driven by young street racers who liked to wear their hats back to front in the '90s!

Fairlane visits Turin! Hello Torino!

Upscale of base was the usual Fairlane 500. Once more, two-door hardtop, four-door sedan and wagon choices existed, as well as Fairlane fastback and convertible. Then came a new luxury trim level called Torino! In the mid to late '60s, jet travel to the Mediterranean spoke of affluence and glamor. Ford Europe was making the

5: Fairlane Becomes a Muscle Car 1965-69

move to nameplates like Fiesta, Capri and Granada. Suddenly Fairlane seemed very homely and staid, so for upscale Fairlane, Ford named its new variant after Italy's equivalent to Detroit!

Three coins in Henry's fountain

Torino was a name originally intended for Mustang. Here, Fairlane Torino spoke of the fancy, well-trimmed plushness buyers were expecting from modern personal cars. One could have a Fairlane Torino in two-door hardtop, four-door sedan and Squire 'Woody' editions, the last with Detroit America's expected simulated wood paneled exterior. However, Torino brought trim trinkets aplenty for interior and exterior, luxuriate in full color-keyed, deep pile carpeting and all vinyl trim. In March 1968 *Car Life* wryly observed that such vinyl trim, safety padded dash and all the fed mandated suduko puzzle lap and shoulder safety belts, made Torino's interior resemble a suburban padded jungle gym!

Poor, humble cloth was now ever so lowball. Something for base models with 200ci I6s and three on the tree. In the classic era, vinyl was well done, could be wiped and looked like leather, which used to be rare and a very expensive option. In modern times leather is practically standard, and looks like cheap vinyl! In the '68 Fairlane range Comfort Weave was an optional interior upholstery. It was a breathing vinyl that sought to overcome that clammy feeling in humid places like Florida. Nothing righteous about feeling sweaty in a Ford midsize!

To keep glare from Floridian sun at bay, Torino came with standard tinted glass. There were also standard era trinkets like faux interior dash wood, to remind one of the TV set at home, electric clock, Torino moldings and medallions. Exterior decorations brought Torino C pillar crests and deluxe wheel covers. It could be said Torino was better value than cheaper Fairlanes. Ordinarily, the stock motor was the 115 horse poverty six, with one optioning to a V8 with the $2579.87 hardtop. Torino came standard with the new 210bhp 302 V8, all the aforementioned kit for a hardtop retail price of $2933.97.

The whole was cheaper than the sum of the options! Naturally in such increasingly sporty times, when companies were even designing fastback vacuum cleaners for the little lady, there was a GT variant. Say GT and one immediately thought sports/luxury. That was Torino GT down to a fine tee! In Detroitese, sporty Fairlane Torino GT happened in two-door hardtop, SportsRoof and ragtop editions. Being a GT of fancy nature dashboard center console, front buckets and special name plaques were a given.

There was a GT plaque rightwards of the glovebox on the dashboard's lower edge. A 'Grand Touring' plaque existed on the GT's interior door card. On the outside there was a mid grille 'GT' insignia belt buckle, Argent-styled rims with GT lettering, plus body decals/striping. On hardtop a neat lower third body profile band, on fastback and convertible something more elaborate. A joined upper body profile contour and mid body stripe, had a C portion starting at the front fender side markers. It was like an asymmetric tuning fork lying down, but Torino GT never slept!

Ford explained the situation in its brochure, "Torino moves like an Olympic sprinter, holds on curves like part of the pavement." All Torinos did come with the sprightly 302 starter V8, and if one specified the $30.64 GT handling pack, the brochure blurb seemed for real. The pack included $39.11 radial tires as a mandatory option. As previously with Fairlane HD suspension, the stock 0.65in front swaybar was replaced with a 0.85in unit. The usual firmer spring and shocks completed things. Then there were the F70-14 Firestone Super Sport Wide Ovals. A limited-slip differential was $41.60.

Torino GTs came with the GT suspension plus Wide Ovals, and what a balanced performer Torino could be! Fitted with 302 V8 the 3500lb intermediate had 57/43%

weight distribution. Standard gearbox was the three-speed manual, Cruise-O-Matic auto and four-speed manual box optional. four-speed cars had staggered shocks, where the right rear shock was located ahead of the rear axle, with the left one placed behind said axle. This was to curb axle tramp on hard acceleration. One might also have considered the optional $65.77 power front disk brakes.

Ford was recognised as offering excellent front disks. These 11.3-inchers were non-energizing ventilated units, clamped by single piston, floating callipers. Versus non-power drums *Motor Trend* found they cut braking distance from 175ft to 155ft for 60mph stops. This was when testing a Torino 390 GT in December 1967. They also brought the bonus of reduced fading and swerving, both problems when drums heated up. So tick the correct option boxes, and Torino GT provided sound control. Steering was via recirculating ball, with parallelogram linkage geometry, cross links and idler arm.

The steering system was common between Fairlane variants, including Torino. The power setup had a 21.6:1 ratio and manageable 3.5 turns, lock to lock. For non-power steering make that a 29.4:1 ratio, with an unwieldy 5.25 turns, lock to lock. Even with stock 14 x 5.5in Argent rims and optional Super Sport Wide Ovals, the non-boosted steering was light on the move. However, it was tiring in urban driving, or on mountain roads where changes of direction were frequent.

There was no fast manual ratio in this intermediate neck of the woods, so most went for power steering and brakes, putting up with the reduced feel such Detroit conveniences involved. Ford was a lot quicker to copy the Mercedes grille, than Mercedes' power steering feel! Torino GT brought a lot of good roadable refinements, but it should be remembered they were attached to a chassis that made a '62 debut; that is, front independent short long arm MacPherson drag strut suspension, coils mounted on the upper arm, plus front swaybar. The usual live axle with multileafs and telescopic shocks, lived out back.

A smooth road handler to be sure, but watch out for bumps off the glass smooth freeways. That said, testers were impressed with GT's ride/handling compromise, and regarded Torino's GT handling pack a boon for active safety. The same could be said for Fairlane/Torino's new 1968 four-dial face dashboard. This latest energy absorbing, padded safety dash, had four circular pods placed right in front of the driver/racer! They were common to Fairlane and Torino variants alike, but varying in the info said pods carried. In the embattled domestic family car buyer's quest to get full, legible instrumentation, 1968 Fairlane represented progress.

The first from the left of the equal sized pods possessed fuel gauge and temperature overheat light; second from left was the 120mph speedo; third was battery charge and oil pressure lights, with the fourth having a fuel blank. An optional rev counter could live in the third gauge. A circular, non-novelty tach that was contained in the actual dashboard, it was a domestic car revelation! Upscale Ford intermediates saw a clock in the fourth pod. Not as many idiot lights as some, but there were some design snafus. Pods and their markings were a bit small and therefore hard to discern.

The optional tach was obscured by the driver's right hand. Whilst the gas gauge was in pod one, the optional low fuel warning light was in pod four! However, one could dig the optional 'door ajar' warning light, and feel good about being in the loop about most of one's Fairlane/Torino vital stats. Overall, one could describe Fairlane/Torino as functional, with the right options. A high floor and low roof, due to Formal Hardtop and SportsRoof style, meant ingress and egress weren't that hot, even compared to fellow domestics.

The new Volvo 144 offered a boxy body, four-wheel disk brakes and orthopaedic, lumbar adjustable seats. However, a strip speedo, even harder to read, no flow

5: Fairlane Becomes a Muscle Car 1965-69

through ventilation and dog slow four-cylinder performance, were reminders of the compromises car buyers had to make in the '60s. In an overall objective sense, the Fairlane/Torino buyer could feel pleased, and when it came to talking turkey, Ford's midsize was quite a deal. There was a lot of extra fruit included with the move from $2579.87 Fairlane two-door hardtop V8, to $2933.97 Torino hardtop, but it seemed like Henry was just giving it away with GT.

Torino trumps Henry's pony!

Torino GT hardtop was $2909.37, with the fastback SportsRoof an absolute steal at $2884.04! F70-14 Wide Ovals were $50.13 on Fairlane, but $64.43 on a 289 Mustang. Out of all this it seemed that only a 427 Stang could work out cheaper than Ford's midsize with the same motor, theoretically. Dealers and buyers didn't take long to get wise to the situation, resulting in Torino poaching sales from Mustang in quite a few parts of the country. It turned out Henry was crazy … like a fox! Mustang was a cheaper, smaller compact, but it was 'the' hot seller for Ford. Thus, Dearborn exploited the situation by pricing up the little car's options.

Ford's brains trust also knew something the general public didn't, pony car sales had already reached their zenith. The only way, or so it seemed between 1968 and 1972, was down. So Ford was looking for the next sales star. People in the industry felt it was the upscale intermediate class. The 1968 sales numbers seemed to lend credence to this belief. Out of 371,787 Fairlanes sold, 172,083 were Torino types. Fancy features like inner door panel courtesy lights on the latter seemed to do the trick. It seemed to play into the value added hearts of Ford management!

Something too about midsize being the new full-size family car. Four-door and hardtop sales were the most popular, with sales of the latter more than doubling to 44,683. Folks were loving Formal Hardtop, especially in Torino trim. Fairlane wasn't the 'getting by on Ranch Wagon' range it used to be. New Fairlane/Torino were commercial and critical successes. *Motor Trend*, in its advertorial vein stated "It's a lot more than a name. It's quite a car." Following from this 1967 declaration of love, *Road Test* brought everyone back down to earth in March 1968. Its article title put the question, "Torino – Has Ford really got a better idea?"

Putting some zotts under da hood! 302 & 428 V8s

Road Test ended its assessment acknowledging Torino's virtues, but saying Ford's 'all-new Torino' claim was slightly far fetched. The magazine felt it was neither

This 1969 Mercury Cyclone GT has period correct hood locks, but the top decal stripes aren't quite factory! This upscale Torino cousin has the right 390 V8. (Courtesy Stephen Barber)

Ford Midsize Muscle – Fairlane, Torino & Ranchero

On top of the stock 390 is a '69 Police Interceptor 428 intake manifold, plus associated 715 CFM Holley. MSD electronic ignition came along for the ride! (Courtesy Stephen Barber)

all that new, nor that special. However, at that hour folks were more into performance than the *Consumer Reports* angle, and Ford was finally bringing its Total Performance to a showroom near you! The aforementioned 302 was the everyday Clark Kent grocery getter V8, not the speed demon it had to become in the '80s, once all the big motors had gone post fuel crisis. Like 'ol 289, the 302 had a 4in bore, but possessed a larger 3in stroke in this latest Windsor incarnation.

There were improvements to 390 V8 as well. 1968 brought new high-performance valve springs and dampers to this FE motor, with longer lasting components giving the 390 higher rev capability. For refinement there was a new front end accessory drive package. This was so all hardware, like power steering pump, alternator, a/c compressor, etc, and associated belts, ran smoother. For power, 302 made 210 ponies, 2bbl 390 was re-rated to 265 horse, with both these 2bbl motors running regular fuel. Then came the semi performance 4bbl 390, drinking premium on a 10.5:1 compression ratio to make 315bhp at 4600rpm.

The 4bbl 390 came with an appealing sounding 427lb/ft at 2800rpm. Holley carb had 1.44in primaries and 1.56in secondaries, with 390 exhaust system being a 2-incher of duals format. If anything, it seemed like Ford was getting more honest with its power ratings, since this was pretty much 1966/67's GT/GTA motor. Same 10.5:1 comp, 427lb/ft, 1.56in secondaries, 2in exhaust and even 270 degree cam intake duration. However, the 1966 version was rated at 335 horse, and the 1968 edition had a 290 degree exhaust cam duration.

Car Life's March 1968 test of a Torino GT 390 four-barrel fastback turned in figures of 0-60mph in 7.7 seconds, ¼ mile in 15.8 seconds, 111mph top speed and 13.5mpg. This was quicker acceleration than achieved by the same journal in March 1966, with the higher rated GT/A. Both Cruise-O-Matic, non-power steering cars, although the '68 fastback skipped on power brakes too. The 1968 390 car also had Thermactor air pump emissions control, which *Car Life*'s 1966 GT/A did not. Emissions were tighter in 1968, the first year when smog pumps were seen nationwide. In the case of '68 Fairlane and others, a fast idling speed was another common trick to please the feds.

In spite of smog controls, the 390 seemed peppier outright in 1968. The power re-ratings reflected the fact Ford and others didn't want to wave a red flag to insurance companies. A big inch motor, four throat carb, and coupe bodystyle were enough for insurance companies to slap on a high premium, before one cruised up to that first stop light drag race. The days of boasting about high outputs in ad copy were over. *Car Life* was critical of its 390 fastback. The journal felt 302 was the number for gas mileage, with 427 the right size Ford for the dragstrip. The 390 was dismissed as too understeer-inducing heavy, and not powerful enough for the cubes. According to *Car Life*, FE 390 was in no man's land between 302 and 427!

The fabled 427 was a planned $622.97 option, rated at 390 horses with a 'Cobra' nametag. It included chromed and hardened exhaust valves, high-performance valve springs and dampers,

5: Fairlane Becomes a Muscle Car 1965-69

and cross-bolted main bearing caps. It was an option that would have included HD suspension, HD cooling system, HD alternator and battery. Fairlane's $65.77 front power disks would have been an additional cost, and mandatory option. There were also some definite ideas on the finished Fairlane. It was only going to be a Cruise-O-Matic, 3.25 final drive ratio ride. With a 390 car 2.75 rear axle ratio was standard, 3.00 and 3.25 ratios optional according to *Car Craft*'s March 1968 issue.

As with other hot Detroit cars with top performance power team, air-conditioning was a no show. The two-door Formal Hardtop body alone was reserved for the 427. However, as per the best laid plans of mice and Ford men, the 427 option didn't transpire. Strike action delayed the introduction of both the 427 and fastback bodyshape. By the time Ford's SportsRoof appeared, the Fairlane looked to the 428 for hi po action! Choosing to get the 428 up to speed instead, Ford's reasons were twofold. Have a more inexpensive engine for the budget supercar ranks, and NASCAR homologation purposes.

On any given Sunday – racing V8 parts

In March 1968 *Motor Trend* described 302 and 428 high-performance engines that FoMoCo was going to introduce in spring that year. The magazine noted that Ford was overcoming the disconnect between its racing expertise, and not having good hardware for street racers.

This Cyclone's rebuilt C6 has 2400rpm stall converter. The rear end has a Ford 9in, 4.11 gears and Detroit Locker LSD. So it hooks up just right for holeshots! (Courtesy Stephen Barber)

Although it always hoped buyers of such components would try out their steeds legally in the safe and controlled confines of a drag strip, or road circuit track day. Ford had lots of 302 goodies for Mustang and Torino devotees, with the new base Windsor being homologated for Trans Am Group II sedan racing. Thus, Ford offered an engineer-observed 302 making 240 horse at five grand, and 310lb/ft at 3000rpm.

Comp ratios were 10.5 to one, with the 302 ingesting fuel and air via two four-barrel carbs on a dual plane aluminum intake manifold, and don't forget the tunnel port heads! Then came the parts' counter options of domed 12.5:1 comp full trunk pistons and metal combustion seals, welded steel tubular headers and high riser 4bbl intake manifold, along with shaft-mounted rockers, forged steel crank and transistorized ignition. If this wasn't enough, try uprated connecting bolts and a solid lifter conversion to ensure longevity and high rpm ability.

All these parts were necessary and worked great in Trans Am battles, but on the street their value was questionable. In a race car one is always on the high side of the tach; on the street it's torque that gets one moving. People discovered this with the Mustang Boss 302 and Camaro Z/28 homologation specials. They embodied many of the go-faster parts, but their 0-60mph times were less than stellar. True, the Boss 302 did have intake ports that could admit a beer bottle, and sounded great, but these 5-liter engines didn't much care for life under 3000rpm.

With the technology of the day there was no replacement for displacement, which was where that 428 came in. Initial magazine info put this motor at 335 horses, arriving at 5600rpm, and a mighty 445lb/ft at 3400rpm. Bore of 4.13in and stroke of 3.98in got the size, and the cast iron heads and headers were no surprise. Initial specs were 10.7 CR, 2.06in intake valves/1.625in exhaust valves, and hydraulic lifters. Then came all that good homologation stuff, and lightweight valves, with sodium-filled stems on the exhaust side to dispel heat.

The 428 would normally arrive with a cast iron intake manifold for a 710 CFM Holley four-barrel to sit on. This stock manifold was a cast iron version of the aluminum unit found in the police 'Interceptor' package. The stock item could be swapped for ones that could take 3xtwo-barrel carburetion, or 2 x 4bbl. These respective triple deuce and dual quad intake manifolds were resurrected from ye olde 406 days of yore.

Carroll Shelby liked the idea of the dual quad 428. Powerful and cheaper than a 427, it became the GT 500's base motor. In 1967 one was looking at 355 horses at 5400rpm and 420lb/ft at 3200rpm on a 10.5:1 comp from Shelby American. To its 428 the company added oval, finned aluminum open element air cleaner and cast aluminum valve covers. On Ford's 428 special parts list were 427 headers, 427 tunnel port heads, 427 mechanical lifters and super high lift cams. 1.76:1 rocker arm ratio could run shotgun on a hypothetical Fairlane/Torino ride.

The fly in the ointment was that all the 427 parts weren't easily adaptable to 428. For example, the tunnel port heads saw exhaust valve interference with the combustion chamber wall. Yes, 427 cross bolted mains could be put on a 428, but, like all the above adaptations, not easily at the Ford factory. It just took too much hand fettling to get the parts to fit.[10] How far the 428 could go depended on you and the parts counter; the factory would only go just so far. Ford also had a better oil pump for the 428, with extended reach for more pressure.

How far would the dedicated enthusiast go, even if they could? The 428's deep sump oil pan looked familiar – it was the part Holman-Moody designed for its one-off 1966 GT/A. With it fitted, *CARS* stated, in April 1966, that one would be lucky to deal with suburban driveways. Something to consider was the dual quad carb's maximum flow rate of 1800 CFM. To take full advantage of this would require a

5: Fairlane Becomes a Muscle Car 1965-69

seriously big cam, a drag strip and state of tune requiring enough Sunoco 260/ aviation gas to fuel a Boeing 707, or hyperactive ride on lawnmower! Still, it's the thought that counts, and Ford was running the lightbulb "Ford … has a better idea" ad slogan by the late '60s.

Before pollution controls and gas mileage took center stage, what worried many was engine breathing. For domestic V8s there were the twin evils of production core shift and OHV pushrods to overcome. So, employ tunnel port heads! A mainstay performance enhancer of the time, it involved steel tube inserts for the pushrods. As per rivals, Ford had bolt-on tunnel port kits for small block Windsor and medium/big block FE series V8s. It routed the pushrod through the aforementioned special shaft, in the center of the intake port.

There were no tunnel port 428 motors inserted in Fairlane Torino Cobras direct from the factory. Not that a normal 428 powered car's performance was exactly wanting. Indeed, it seems the press were spoilt by the high general performance of the era, provided by Ford and rivals. As such, even complaints concerning 390 V8, seem rather churlish. Production examples showed Ford's credo of budget supercar speed, by warming up the 428. Thus, from the factory expect 10.6:1 comp pistons, HD big bolt conrods and tri-metal bearings. No solid lifter motor, just the practicality of smooth idling hydraulic action. However, new style larger port heads, with bigger 2.09in intake and 1.66in exhaust valves, were factory fitted to what was unkindly considered 'the sedate 428.'

Sedate or no, at $306 the Cobra Jet 428 option was under half the price of the proposed 427. It did only have a mere cast iron facsimile of the Police Interceptor aluminum intake manifold, but it also had a 735 CFM Holley 4bbl upgrade over the plebeian 600 CFM 4bbl Holley that came with that allegedly tardy 390 GT. Cobra Jet 428 seemed value for money, but proved a rare option in 1968. It made its debut on April 1, 1968, as a mid '68 MY device. Ram Air cold air hoodscoop and air cleaner assembly were available as parts, according to a June 1968 *Car and Driver* report on David Pearson's NASCAR Torino, and Torino Cobra Jet 428 factory model.

Owners with this hot setup served notice to fellow road users, courtesy of red and chrome 428 front fender rectangular badges. They were located just behind the parking lights, and such callouts carried a lot more weight with the street crowd than a Windsor number. The Big Inch had reached Ford intermediate, and it happened on Formal Hardtop and SportsRoof fastback. Style and public interest dictated that most journals tested that fastback, which enabled a ride 201.1in long, 74.5in wide and 53.5in tall.

In the March 1968 issue, *Car Craft*'s 390 powered GT fastback with optional Cruise-O-Matic tipped the scales at 3610lb. This rig managed a 14.85 second ¼ mile at 99.5mph. At Carlsbad Raceway a 428 engined car was sampled too. On stock Wide Ovals and no LSD, this bolide did a 14.23 second pass at 104.54mph. None too shabby, and without the fuss of a four-speed. In the evolution of midsize Fairlane, 1967 was the first year for big block (390), and 1968 was the first for the 428. Introducing the 428 necessitated a realignment of the exhaust on the left side, between header and muffler.

With 428, Henry was telling the public Ford still stood for First On Race Day! GTO, the tiger that started the modern intermediate race, was stuck on 400ci power. To get a 428 in a Goat required a trip to specialist dealer Royal Pontiac for a Bobcat! Leave that rooftop shouting to Jim Wangers, Ford was keeping its light under a bushel. Ram Air or no, Henry said his 428 made a mere 335 horses, the same rating as the humbler 390 GT, the same rating the Fairlane GT/A carried in 1966! No doubt the 428 had more moxie than either the 1966 or '68 390. No doubt either, that in budget supercar mode, Ford's Cobra was trying to avoid the wrath of the Allstate man!

Ford Midsize Muscle – Fairlane, Torino & Ranchero

Torino paces the field!

A high insurance premium was like throwing cold water on the proverbial camp fire – so modesty it was, except for the Indy 500! The honor came Mustang's way on 1964 debut, now it was Torino's turn in '68. It certainly didn't hurt sales for the new Torino, and the halo glow of the Brickyard was far greater than the mere 709 Torino pace cars built. Most came off the line in April, some in May and one even on race day, May 30 1968. The version chosen was the 1968 Torino GT Convertible. Truth to tell, only 5310 1968 Torino GT ragtops were built, and ragtops were getting as popular as fedoras! However, no one was going to rain on Henry's parade, or that of his grandson.

Come race day the pace car was driven by William Clay Ford Sr, Henry Ford's grandson and owner of the Detroit Lions. Well, this pace car was one Detroit Lion that really roared! A cool cat with the 390 horse 427 option that Torino never got! There were also two 428 and one 390 motivated machine on deck. Celebration festival cars were all 302/C4 automatic power team editions. Looks-wise, pace cars were in possession of a white exterior and blue two-tone interior.

Torino GT's exterior graphics were adapted, with the GT's asymmetric 'Tuning Fork' profile decal, pinstriped with red. On the front fenders were the words 'Official Pace Car,' completely in black capitals. Mid Tuning Fork, on the door's upper part, was 'Torino' in capital, silver-gray letters outlined in red. Under the Tuning Fork, on the lower part of the door, '52nd Annual Indianapolis 500 Mile Race May 30, 1968' appeared in smaller black capitals. The cars rode around on Firestone F70-14 Super Sport Wide Ovals covering the ubiquitous American Racing Torq rims.

Most pace cars bought by the public (approx 90%), and Torinos for that matter, came with the humble base 302 V8/C4 auto power team. As per normal Big 4 limited edition fare, dealers would buy cars in, and option 'em up into a pace car. Such machines didn't roll out of the factory looking like this. In terms of authenticity, look for an original window sticker and build sheet, pace cars also came with a five or six digit DSO door tag, indicating a special order car. The cooking power team reflected the bare bones nature of the cars that dealers usually ordered for pace car transformation.

The argument was that cars would be difficult to sell, if too loaded up. Add a 390/Cruise-O-Matic power team, power accessories, a/c, etc, to an already decaled pace car, and watch that showroom dust accumulate! Prospects would say the ride had a lot of stuff they didn't need. Indeed, many special cars from the '60s and '70s were notoriously slow sellers, even though valuable collector machines today. Pace cars, AMXs, Superbirds and Super Duty Trans Ams did their best job as showroom eye candy. They brought folks into the dealership, who then signed up for a plain brown envelope with column shift, 'Love Bench' and whitewalls.

On the ovals – NASCAR 1968!

Chances are those middle of the road steady gents would drive home, turn on the TV and watch the real heavy hitters duke it out in NASCAR. Whereupon the comment would often be made in living rooms across the country, 'Look honey, he's racing our car!' They actually were, in those production car based, homologate what you raced days. There was a greater connection between road car and race car, than a mere nameplate and familiar looking silhouette. What's more, Ford was at the action forefront, making the most of NASCAR's intermediate focus. Incorporating Fairlane/Torino into that Total Performance program.

Torino and cousin Mercury Cougar tussled with the Mopar Hemi crowd. GM was sitting out this dance. It was worried about how any homologation special would breach federal safety standards. Plus, by 1969, in Pontiac and Chevrolet it had the number three and number one sales brands in the country, respectively, so it just didn't care! For sporty, Chevrolet

5: Fairlane Becomes a Muscle Car 1965-69

had Corvette, plus the increasingly popular SCCA Trans Am series, at any rate.

The 1968 arrival of the Fairlane/Torino SportsRoof fastback was most fortuitous, because that's the model that would do the Grand National rounds! The kind of car raced was typified by the Torino SportsRoof utilized by A J Foyt – a stock car that the Jack Bowsher racing team received from Holman-Moody in kit form. H-M was closely associated with Blue Oval racing exploits, and its hardware carried the famous 'Competition Proven' decal. Torino fastback's rear glass pane was big at around 20ft^2. However, given the angle and usual 2in high aluminum rear spoiler, rearwards visibility was poor.

To keep tabs on what was going on back there necessitated a full bar, five-sectioned, rear view mirror. Torino racer sported the production car's upright grille, but with wire mesh dirt grille protector. For aerodynamics, three of the four headlamps were blocked off. The remaining lamp was an aperture to admit cool intake air for the motor. Said air went through an 800 CFM Holley 4bbl carb and high riser aluminum intake manifold to feed Ford's respected 10.9:1 427! This was connected to a Ford Top-Loader four-speed, manipulated by a Hurst shifter. Out back were Detroit Locker LSD and 3.70 rear gears.

Racing items to be expected were transistorized ignition, differential oil cooler, and dry sump lubrication. For racing, ride height had to be as low as possible, and the dry sump was placed in the center of what would normally be the rear passenger compartment. The 22-gallon Goodyear fuel cell lived in the trunk. NASCAR racers kept tabs on their ride, using a full row of horizontally placed circular analogue gauges. No clock, or idiot lights like a normal family car! Foyt's Ford used Grey Rock drum brakes all around, with Holman-Moody 15 x 8in front and 15 x 8.2in rear rims, wrapped in small white-lettered Goodyear Stock Car Specials.

With racers assembled it was off to the track, where Fords and Cale Yarborough's lone Mercury Cyclone dominated the super speedways. Ford won in nine of 12 major races on the big tracks. As an historical aside, the January 21 *Motor Trend* 500 held at Riverside International Raceway, was the first event where protective driver window sidescreens appeared. They would become mandatory in 1970. Ominous for the championship, on May 11, 1968, racer and businessman David Pearson won the Rebel 400 held at Darlington Raceway. It was his first super speedway win since 1961.

Pearson was racing for Holman-Moody Ford, and for this win made use of a power to weight rulebook loophole. Using a little 396 FE motor, his Torino fastback netted a 293lb weight saving. This burnt off the heavier opposition. At Daytona International Speedway, Cale Yarborough's Merc Cyclone won both the Daytona 500 and Firecracker 400. The Wood Brothers Mercury team he raced with, had full Ford backing. It also enjoyed a three year sponsorship deal from 60 Minute Cleaners, and race cars run on sponsor dollars as well as they do race fuel!

At the October 20 National 500, Charlie Glotzbach got his first career victory at Charlotte Motor Speedway, underlining how well Ford was doing – it was only the second super speedway Dodge win of the season! In the final reckoning it was Mr Pearson that took out what would be his second NASCAR Grand National Championship. To achieve this, David Pearson had a mighty tussle with Bobby Isaac for much of the season. With 16 wins, Pearson's tally tied with that of other NASCAR legend Richard Petty. However, under NASCAR rules Pearson's track type victories carried more points, securing him the title.

Going into '69 MY with Fairlane Terrors!

Acknowledging that Ford was the hot ticket, Richard Petty put aside his historical Plymouth achievements, and announced he would be joining Henry's farm for '69 racing season. It was quite

Ford Midsize Muscle – Fairlane, Torino & Ranchero

a blow for the Mopar Mob, its hero had flown the coop! Ford was also putting the sizzle into its road cars for '69 MY, even though bodystyles were basically a carryover from 1968. The Fairlane range was moving upscale, with more prominent center division grille bar, and more formal, squarer taillights. All models higher than base Fairlane had an aluminum dividing trim bar across the rear fascia. This between the taillights trim, was in line with the SportsRoof's reversing lamps.

Coming attractions – 1970 – the new 335 engine family

However, trim changes aside, the silhouettes were like '68 MY, underhood the substance had moved on. Base motor was a larger 250 cube version of Ford's 200ci six. This was useful because the starter engine on heavier wagon was still a six, and combined with three-speed 'on da tree' manual, this gave family haulers owned by gas misers a fighting chance on inclines! More exciting was Ford's new 1970 Torino medium displacement 351 Cleveland. Like the 250 six it reflected the heavier nature of the family intermediate, and bridged the chasm between Windsor and FE V8s.

That Cleveland moniker came from the Cleveland located factory the motor was mostly made in. The 335 family designation was a displacement number, believed to be taken from a particular marine application of the engine. Indeed marine usage set the design nature of Cleveland. The design brief was for a V8 where water didn't pass through the inlet manifold, and no requirement for a separate camshaft timing cover. Thus, in

A 1969 Mercury Cyclone 428 Cobra Jet is at hand! In the late '60s the Montego name supplanted Comet, in the same way Torino took over from Fairlane. Cyclone was the super sports Merc variant through 1971 MY. (Courtesy Roger Pirtle)

5: Fairlane Becomes a Muscle Car 1965-69

terms of coolant routing, the Cleveland had a dry manifold, with the coolant hose connecting vertically to the block, above the cam timing chain cover.

The name is Cobra!

The 335 series was bigger externally than Windsor, but smaller than FE V8. It had the same bore spacing and cylinder head bolt pattern as Windsor, but Cleveland utilized smaller 14mm sparkplugs. 335 series rocker covers had eight securing bolts, compared to Windsor's six. Over time Cleveland has received criticism concerning oil lubrication shortfall, but it has only been a worry in very high-performance applications. Cleveland featured large main bearing caps, with some high-performance editions having four bolt mains. Only the 300 horse hi po 4bbl 351 Clevelands possessed 'Polyangle' canted valves, with this four venturi variant having much larger ports and valves, plus a quench type combustion chamber.

For 1969 showrooms, Ford had the 351W (Windsor). This neat, middle of the road V8 made 250 gross ponies in two-barrel form, 290in four throat spec. However, serious performance interest lay in Fairlane Torino Cobra. With Mustang, Ford was leading the pack, but with Fairlane/Torino it was more playing catch up. In this case the target was that hot, cheap stripper called Plymouth Road Runner. And if Plymouth could comically use Looney Tunes' Road Runner 'Beep! Beep!' decals, well, snake charmer Iacocca could always call on Henry's Cobra! Cobra was indeed the name, although the car was referred to in various ways.

In 1969, the magazine *High-Performance Cars* called Cobra and Torino GT 'Fairlane Terrors!' When entered in NASCAR the fastbacks were named Torino Cobras, whereas most Ford literature usually just called them Cobras. In January 1969 *Car Life* magazine denoted 'em Fairlane Cobra! However, whatever the tag, this was one snake with venom and a 1969 list price of $3139. In all the Cobra hysteria of the late '60s, Mr Shelby applied the serpent too. There was also the De Tomaso Mangusta. The Mangusta was a mid engine Ford 289 powered, low volume Italian sports car. The Mangusta, or Mongoose in English, eats Cobras in the wild …

The Merc Cyclone and Torino Cobra may have been in the 'Budget Supercar' category, but there was nothing downscale about their interiors. Buyers were moving away from that plain Jane Road Runner look! (Courtesy Roger Pirtle)

Ford's Fairlane Cobra was much cheaper than Shelby's AC Cobra and Mustangs. Given the Road Runner stripper segment, one noticed what wasn't there, more than what was. To keep price down, Ford's midsize Cobra didn't come with buckets, hoodscoop, clock, rev counter or power front disks. Equip the Cobra sensibly and its price was more like four grand. However, even at base price, Ford included worthwhile hardware, like 335 horse 428 motor, four on the floor, Competition Suspension, Wide Oval F70 14 in bias belted kidney punchers, and a funny front fender Cobra decal!

Ford's Competition Suspension involved the usual HD shocks and springs, with rear shocks in staggered formation on four-speed cars to combat axle hop and brake tramp. Also functional were racer style hood locking pins, and an optional trunk mounted battery. This latter item was optional on any Torino or Cobra variant, helping to combat nose heavy weight distribution on FE engined cars. On a 1969 Cobra 428 that weight distribution was 56.9/43.1% front/rear. The HD battery had a special venting system, to get rid of battery fumes.

Visually all Cobras announced their presence with a horizontal bar grille, made of extruded aluminum and painted non-gloss 'Racing Black.' Cobra's front fender cartoon decal consisted of an angry, fanged Cobra running on two Wide Oval tires, with flames issuing rearwards. This decal gave way to an actual badge with serpent atop 'Cobra' script badge, no Wide Ovals. For '69 MY Ford Fairlane variants continued with the four circular pod dashboard, but reversed dial face/numeral marking colors. In 1968 it was light markings on a dark dial face, in 1969 it was the other way around.

The latest style was brushed aluminum outer circle, white inner circle and black markings. Style aside, Cobra's budget performance raison d'etre, implied Fairlane 500 trim level, plus Fairlane 500 body code. It let Cobra concentrate on what mattered in the Total Performance Ford era, that entailed standard 80 amp HD battery, 3.25:1 open differential, HD cooling system hardware, 55 amp alternator, chrome dress up valve covers and dual exhaust system. Ram Air 428 Cobra Jet brought a shorter 3.50:1 open differential, and functional hoodscoop.

One's elapsed time would improve if the motor inhaled cool, dense outside air, instead of hot underhood air. Ford's hood inhaler was a meshed, forward facing fiberglass scoop. This aperture led to an underside with vacuum solenoid actuated flap, surrounded by rubber gasket lined air filter housing, that sealed to the underhood. Tramp on the loud pedal and the flap would open to admit sweet cool air, lowering the quarter mile time. Other Big 4 ram air setups worked like this, with mild variations. To legally exploit a Cobra's performance required a trip to the dragstrip, or an illegal one to Woodward Avenue. Either way Ford had you covered, if the Super Cobra Jet 'Drag Pack' was specified.

Inspired by the hot street car trend, and yearly improvements by Big 4 rivals to create the Top Street Dog, the strip oriented Drag Pack brought Ford's best ¼ mile goodies under the one option umbrella, for the seriously committed. One could order it with the Q code 428 4bbl motor, or the R code Ram Air 428 4bbl Cobra Jet motor. Therefore, it was possible to order the Drag Pack on a non-Ram Air car, a Cobra sans hoodscoop! To maximize one's machine, starting with cold air induction was advisable. Super Cobra Jet cars possessed cast pistons, nodular controlled cast iron crank casting. Castings were coded 1UA or 1UAB, with external weight on the snout behind the balancer. Le Mans spec 427 type capscrew connecting rods and engine oil cooler were your dragstrip insurance policy!

For a Drag Pack Cobra's rear end it could have been Ford's legendarily tough 9in differential, with 3.91 rear axle ratio and Traction-Lok LSD. Alternatively, extremely dedicated souls could have a 4.30 ratio rear end with Detroit Locker LSD. Ford stood alone in offering engine oil cooler and Detroit Locker LSD on a muscle car. For all this, Ford's 428 rated horsepower never went above the 335 pony mark, not even on Ram Air Drag Pack cars. Ford didn't fear the reaper, but it did fear the Allstate insurance man, so Henry pretended his best 428 was no hotter than 1966's best 390!

Identifying a Dearborn mover and shaker, just look to the standard Cobra's front fender 428 chrome and red badge callout. This item was absent on Ram Air Cobra Jet cars. To avoid badge overkill Ram Air cars had just a 428 badge and cursive 'Cobra Jet' script on the hoodscoop's profile. There were turn signal indicators at the rear of said scoop. Functional Ram Air was priced at $133.44, and showed the compromise nature of late '60s performance. Working on intake manifold vacuum change, tromping the gas pedal saw a vacuum control valve open the fresh air flap. However, the rest of the time one's 428 was inhaling warm underhood air! Ford IMCO and

5: Fairlane Becomes a Muscle Car 1965-69

Thermactor smog gear came along for the ride too!

The regular air filter snorkel ended within the engine bay, and ingesting such warm air helped pass emissions. Going the other way the 390 horse 427 V8 option may indeed have pre-empted in 1968 MY due to strike action. However, it was available in 1969 MY, albeit in very small numbers. Boasting NASCAR homologation block, cross bolted mains and 4bbl Holley, it was an option few knew about at the time. Most were well served and satisfied with the 428. To show the uniqueness of Cobra variants, such cars had no Fairlane or Torino interior or exterior ID badging.

In terms of exhaling, Cobra's dual exhaust system had branched headers, two reverse flow mufflers, and mid and tail exhaust diameter of 2.25in and 2in, respectively. Key options like Traction-Lok LSD, power steering and power disk brakes were priced at $63.51, $100.26 and $64.77, respectively, in 1969. With power steering, lock to lock turns were reduced to 3.5 – unfortunately, so too was steering feel, in typical Detroit manner. Even so, Cobra's chassis represented a good ride/handling compromise. Fine distinctions were revealed by badge engineered cousin the Mercury Cyclone, showing less lean

In outright terms, Ford powerplants were a mite down on Chevy counterparts. However, smooth, tractable power was a given. As per Torino cousins, the 428 CJ in this Merc, meant 335 ponies at 5200 rpm. (Courtesy Roger Pirtle)

Merc fans said goodbye to Cyclone at the end of 1971. By 1972, Montego was caught up in the Ford midsize re-shuffle. Montego GT was a kissing cousin of Gran Torino SportsRoof. (Courtesy Roger Pirtle)

Ford Midsize Muscle – Fairlane, Torino & Ranchero

with its optional handling pack. On Cobra, standard Competition Suspension meant 0.85in front swaybar, with 137lb/in front spring stiffness, and 145lb/in leaf springs out back.

Brakes were the familiar, if specified, 11.3 x 2.07in front power disks, and 10 x 2.5in rear drums. A key element of the 1969 Cobra chassis, an element much would be seen of on hot cars into the '70s, was the Goodyear Polyglas tire. Not a radial tire, but a bias belted unit of the kind domestic performance car fans were familiar with. 'Polyglas' was a US registered trademark of Goodyear, #859,703, and the name suggested the tire's constructional properties. Fiberglass belts surrounded a strong polyester cord body. In acceleration/heavy braking, this was intended to hold tread grooves open, for less squirm and improved traction, plus braking.

The Polyglas' polyester sidewalls were aimed at creating stability on a heavy car, sans very high tire pressures. The Polyglas was made in South Africa too, where local production started in 1970. For the South African market the tire was called Decathlon, and nylon was used for sidewall construction, not polyester. Either way, the intention was to get the benefits of a radial, firm road grip and long tread life, in a bias belted tire. US Goodyear ads ran a compare test of two identical cars. One shod with a rival tire, one with Polyglas. Stopping from 45mph to standstill on wet macadam, the stopping distances were 226ft versus 194ft in Polyglas' favor.

Like Goodyear said, "Buy Goodyear Polyglas tires for traction. You'll see why they're on so many 1970 cars." Ford and others were transitioning away from the Firestone Wide Oval. Not so many were moving from Road Runner or Super Bee to Cobra, but perhaps they should have been? With Road Runner budget, performance equaled a front bench and full instrumentation. On Cobra it was less instruments and a slightly plusher environment. *Supercars* magazine described the '69 Cobra Jet SportsRoof styling as "completely out to lunch." Not one staff member liked the styling, feeling a Mustang fastback look just wasn't harmonius on a larger midsize. Guess they would have gone for the Formal Hardtop.

Grand touring – Torino style!

Supercars' non- Ram Air '69 Cobra Jet machine, with 3.91 rear gears and Traction-Lok did 0-60mph in 7 seconds, with the ¼ mile in 13.94 seconds at 101.7mph, topped out at 120mph. It delivered 8mpg city, 13mpg highway. This made the California style Mustang Mach 1 side reversing mirrors very apt! Spinning those Ford 12 slotter Argent rims was a pleasurable pastime, but most were satisfied with merely the style. Ford had been re-orienting its midsize of late, to suit changed market tastes. The upscale 500 XL of 1967 had given way to 1968's up imaged Torino, boasting luxo accoutrements like chrome moldings and vinyl roof.

Sportswise Fairlane GT was replaced with Torino GT, but by 1969 it was a different kind of GT. The super sports side of things was now occupied by Cobra, with GT more luxo sports, personal car in that order. Torino GT for '69 had revised grille divider bars, with its GT emblem moved from central belt buckle location, to lower left grille corner. Unlike Cobra, one could order GT in Formal Hardtop, SportsRoof and ragtop! However, base power team was the 302 2bbl V8 and three-speed manual box. From here on up were the 2bbl and 4bbl 351s, quad throat 390 and the two 428s.

In Fairlane/Torino of 1969, four on the floor started with 351 V8. However, even on base 302 Torino GT the forward facing fiberglass hoodscoop was standard equipment. In a bizarre state of ordering, this non-functional item with rear trim signal indicators, was optional on base Cobra! It was a device that could be functional on Ram Air Cobra Jet. GT had Argent styled rims, chrome trim rings and GT hubcaps. It also stuck with Firestone

5: Fairlane Becomes a Muscle Car 1965-69

Wide Ovals, whilst Cobra had moved onto Goodyear Polyglas. In more mix and match GT and Cobra could have the same single piston, floating caliper front power disks.

The same went for Ford's LSD Traction-Lok differential, it could appear on Cobra and GT. Promising greater chance of transferring power to the ground, by locking the rear wheels together under high torque. Performance anomalies continued in that GT came with Ford's 'quasi buckets' standard, whereas Cobra had a bench. GT had racy profile decals, but Cobra came plain. Cobra did have a 428 as base motor, and this couldn't be teamed with the all synchro three-speed manual, only the four-speed and Select Shift C6 autobox. The difference between GT and Cobra, was that the former mostly wore its performance on the outside. However, that suited many folks just fine.

The business of selling Ford's midsize

A 302 powered GT was the perfect antidote to soaring insurance premiums, and rising base stickers. Want a high-performance chariot? Just fake it! Even compared to 1968 the market was changing. After the 'all new' '68s, Ford Fairlane/Torino's 1969 total was down to 129,054. However, Torino GT had emerged as a commercial star, being the single most popular variant at 81,822 units. A sign of the popular sports/luxo midsize personal car category to come. More than this, family car buyers continued to vote midsize over full-size as a default choice. Industry totals put the smaller size category, not far behind the once dominant full-size six seaters!

There was no shame in being called Fairlane on plainer, non-Torino, family examples. That said, even these had trimmings to elevate 'em above mere wallflower status. Fairlane 500 had bright wheel opening moldings, full length door bottom level chrome strip and full-width bright molding rear fascia treatment. Inside there were expected federal safety touches. Seatback locks for front folding seats on two-door variants, dull finishes on metallic surfaces, seatbelt usage warning light in one dash pod even! Two to ten second intermittent windshield wiper sweep was for safety, as were padded interior surfaces. Ford also continued with soft green night interior dash lighting.

The industry had also reached a decision, that power brake options should apply to front disk specified family machinery. Lest the power vacuum booster lull drivers into a false sense of security concerning lock up on four-wheel drums. As ever, Henry was right about safety not selling. The government made safety equipment a non-profit automotive item, so companies couldn't make $$$ off 'em, as per other speed and luxo features. Mr. Average cared not for all this, he was more into Fairlane's 'full-size car like' comfy ride. With a wheelbase around 4in longer than the average intermediate, Fairlane didn't bother occupants with the road beneath them!

It showed the performance diversity Ford, and others, were building into their family car ranges. A Cobra man worked a standard four-speed with 11.5in diameter single dry plate clutch, encased in a bell housing of high-strength malleable cast iron with built in scatter-shield. Whereas Fairlane 500 man cast an appreciative eye over the faux mahogany panels laid into

In the 'race what you made' era, the 428 CJ amassed kudos from drag racing and NASCAR. It needed premium gas, though, due to a 10.6:1 CR. (Courtesy Roger Pirtle)

Ford Midsize Muscle – Fairlane, Torino & Ranchero

Fairlane's door trims and dashboard, not to mention the high pile vinyl/rayon blend carpeting. Something for the street racer, and the family guy. It was something one wouldn't find in the front drive Taurus range, 15 or so years hence.

The Cobra name came from Carroll Shelby's AC and Ford V8 amalgam. Perhaps it's unfair to compare this era of animal intensity, with the cyber slickness of later Taurus SHO balanced speed? However, the comparison highlights the uniqueness of the respective times. In the mix and match late '60s, Ford's excellent Selectaire HVAC could be enjoyed on a Torino GT with one of the milder V8s. Air-conditioning was usually unavailable on top horsepower Detroit motors. Selectaire on a vent wing free SportsRoof, Formal Hardtop or convertible promised a civilized, wind noise free interior and rear axle ratio of at least 3.00:1.

Where would one buy such a car? Ralph Williams might have sold you one. In 1969 Williams owned the World's biggest Ford dealership! The emporium was located in the San Fernando Valley of California. Williams was 39 at the time and worth $60 million. He believed in the high volume automotive supermarket concept, lots of TV advertising and used his celebrity super salesman status with appearances on such shows as the very popular *Laugh-In*. Naturally any appearance on TV, was like an advert for his mega lot. Know Williams, know the dealership. To achieve this commercial result in the 1950s would have required a corporation, in the '60s an individual could be a corporation![11]

Williams was very much an entrepreneur of his time. The business wouldn't have worked without freer social attitudes to consumerism, and lots of color TVs across the land. The same might have been said about *Laugh-In*! It was probably no coincidence that John Z DeLorean came to the fore during this time, pushing Pontiac to number three in the sales race. The public seemed increasingly willing to place their trust in an individual's reputation, whereas before only a company would do. However, even in the Age of Aquarius, Ralph Williams came up against the old school Detroit.

He encountered the disconnect between factory and dealer. Ford, like rivals, didn't wish to listen to dealers. We make 'em, you sell 'em. It was a one way conversation. This was related to the second age old Detroit puzzle. How to make money on small, cheap cars? The solution according to corporate bosses, was to load them up with options. That was Ford's intention with the Falcon successor called Maverick. However, as Williams kept trying to tell Ford, it already had small cars loaded with options. Twenty years later the Big 3 sidestepped the small car low profit margin, by going the SUV route. Forty years later many dealers were left high and dry during the Global Financial Crisis (GFC) with excess, factory dictated stock.

With GFC, dealers were told excess stock was their problem. The Big 3 had also overseen too many dealers open too close to each other, burger chain franchise style. As a result, some very old, family run dealers were forced to close. In the business of selling cars, the only thing that had changed, was the model year.

Walk into William's dealership, or any Ford outlet, and the base sticker for a 1969 Fairlane 500 was $2845. With essentials added like 351-W 2bbl V8 ($58), Cruise-O-Matic ($200), power steering ($100), power disk brakes ($65), AM radio ($61) and a/c ($380), and the price climbed to nearly four grand. The road to hell is paved with great options.

1969 – A safer NASCAR series

Soon, some Ford dealers would even supply a NASCAR racer, or at least a Torino that looked like one. On the speedways of the nation, 1969 was similar to 1968. Ford and Dodge continued to lead the way. Ford and Mercury were dominant at the start of the season. On the big tracks, those equal to or greater than 300 miles, Henry went on a 13 race winning streak! Ford claimed the top five places at

5: Fairlane Becomes a Muscle Car 1965-69

Atlanta, the first four slots at Michigan and managed 1st and 2nd finishes in eight of the 13 aforementioned victories.

The one key conquest sale Ford made in 1969, was getting Richard Petty. The NASCAR king scored only one super speedway win in 1968, using a Plymouth Road Runner. Chrysler wouldn't let Petty drive the more aerodynamic Dodge Charger 500. Thus, in a shock move, Richard Petty left for Ford in 1969! The February 1969 *Motor Trend* 500, held at Riverside, represented Petty's first Ford start. He won the race, 25 seconds ahead of AJ Foyt, who was also flying Henry's flag.

On February 23 at the Daytona 500, Lee Roy Yarbrough used his team back-up car to pass Charlie Glotzbach on the final lap to win! On March 30 at the Atlanta 500 Cale Yarborough dominated in his Mercury. He led for 308 of the 334 lap race, held at Atlanta International Raceway. The race saw the debut of the Ford Blue Crescent Boss 429 motor. 1969 was a year of engineering change for the Ford Torino racer, of competitive necessity and rulebook developments.

Torino Talladega

The 1968 Torino fastback body wasn't exactly bad aerowise, but was behind the slippery ways of Dodge Charger 500. This caused Torino to lose a little on top speed, even though it had been successful in races, with that mighty 427. Ford put its chariot in the wind tunnel, and found the nose to be the drag culprit. The designers extended the front fenders 5in, drooped them and added flush mount grille. The front bumper was replaced with the rear bumper, which was cut and shaped to fit the body closely.

Ford also played fast and loose with the rulebook. The Blue Oval Boys got around the minimum height rule by rolling the rocker panels an inch higher, so the Torino could sit an inch lower. Roger Penske wasn't the only one with an unfair advantage! Added to this was the 'Gurney Flap' originating with racer Dan Gurney, it provided more downforce with minimal additional drag.

Motorwise, Ford was forced to dump the NASCAR banned SOHC 427 in 1965. Authorities took exception to Ford's high riser FE V8s, saying they didn't fit under stock hoods. Ford countered with medium riser intake fettled OHV FE 427s, which did fit. Now Henry's henchmen moved on to their new 429, which would make its way underhood into top Fords soon.

The proof of the pudding is in the tasting, and on April 27, 1969, Richard Petty won the Virginia 400, with some driver aid from James Hylton, at Martinsville Speedway in a Torino Talladega. Named after Alabama's new super speedway, Talladega moved Ford onto an aero par with Dodge Charger 500, and provided a future road going collectible for muscle car fans. In the production car based homologation NASCAR era, the public would be getting a Torino Talladega resembling the one Richard Petty raced.

That said, Joe Q Public would only be entitled to the Cobra's 428, not the 429, since the homologation for body and motor were separate. However, the Boss 429 with dry sump lubrication did find its way under the hoods of some Mustangs. This was so Henry wouldn't get embarrassed by Camaro ZL1 in the pony car bragging stakes. Standard power team concerning the Talladega that could be purchased from the friendly Ford dealer, was the 428 Cobra Jet/C6 auto combo. Most of the 754 units made were such autobox rides. The SportsRoof body was mandatory, and exterior color choices were limited to Wimbledon White, Royal Maroon or Presidential Blue. Flat black hoods and special belt line pinstripe outside, cloth and vinyl bench seating inside, plus, a Fairlane 500 body code shared with '69 Cobra. No options were permitted!

Regular Fairlane fastback was 201.1in long in 1969, but Talladega with its special droop snoot took that out to 206in, so happy parking! In any case, Ford had easily met the 500 unit homologation requirements, sanctioning Talladega's usage. On July 6 1969, Mr Petty won the Mason-Dixon 300 by six laps at the new Dover Downs International Speedway. Torino Talladega's FoMoCo partner in crime on the high speed ovals was the Mercury Cyclone Spoiler. Richard Petty's 100th NASCAR Grand National victory was notched up in a Ford! This happened on August 22 1969 at Bowman Gray Stadium, when Petty took out the Winston-Salem 250.

The Ford fest continued with Cale Yarborough winning the inaugural Motor State 500 at Michigan International Speedway in a Mercury Cyclone. Fords came 2nd and 3rd, with another Mercury 4th. Lee Roy Yarbrough won the Firecracker Medal Of Honor 400 at Daytona Beach FL in a Ford. Yarbrough's switch to Torino was by FoMoCo decision. Former Mercury team-mate Cale Yarborough's Mercury Cyclone retired at the same event with a broken valve. However, it wasn't going all FoMoCo's way.

On September 14 at the Talladega 500, non-championship contender Richard Brickhouse took the winged Dodge Daytona to victory in the inaugural Talladega 500, held at the new Alabama International Motor Speedway. The event was notable for a Dodge that took aero to the next level, and for a driver boycott that involved nearly all top NASCAR racers. It represented the first official NASCAR driver boycott, and concerned the rough track at Talladega. Many drivers wanted to wait for safer tires, better attuned to the track. However, NASCAR officials weren't having it, and said no to the drivers.

On the subject of safety, NASCAR drivers had a secret August Ann Arbor meeting, where they formed the Professional Drivers Association (PDA). The Talladega race boycott was called by PDA president Richard Petty. Eventually the top drivers returned in the final months of the 1969 racing season, amid tension. Petty may be considered a NASCAR legend, but fans weren't happy about the driver's strike. One spectator threw a beer can at Petty's car during the Old Dominion 500, which actually struck the car's windshield!

At the same time across the Atlantic, a body of drivers led by Jackie Stewart tried to make Formula One racing safer. Opposition from race organizers was faced once again. The attitude of many track owners, officials and fans, was that danger was just part of racing. There were few calls to eliminate unnecessary circuit risks. The aero work done by the Mopar fraternity, certainly helped stick their cars more securely to the track at high speed. However, those aero add ons were considered by many to be less than lovely.

Ford didn't lose a super speedway race until September. However, David Pearson driving a Ford, still secured his third NASCAR Grand National Championship. Pearson took the title 11 wins to Richard Petty's ten. Petty's title hopes were dashed by missing two races, due to a May 1969 crash at Asheville Speedway, where he suffered broken ribs. Petty or Pearson, it seemed Ford and Torino were NASCAR Kings!

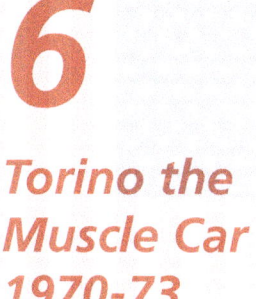

6
Torino the Muscle Car 1970-73

1970 – Year of the intermediate!
All the time, intermediate, or midsize, cars were getting to be the new family car vanilla flavor. Chicken or egg, whichever side the motivation was coming from, Ford was ready. Did inter popularity increase because buyers switched preferences, or because the Big 3 had made their full-size cars too big, and were now actively pushing midsize? Probably some of both, and it made the very new 1970 Coke bottle-shape Torino, courtesy of Ford stylist Bill Shenk, crucial for Henry. Dearborn had its statements ready, to let press and public know Torino was the one for America's driveway and highway!

In the lead up to model release John Naughton, General Manager of FoMoCo's Ford Division that would make Torino, predicted that 1970 would see inters catch or even pass full-size car sales. He said, "This may be the year of the intermediates." Indeed, for Ford Torino was the new Mustang. Given it originated the pony car phenomenon and Mustang was still the golden child, Ford wouldn't admit it, but the pony car segment had passed its sales peak. GM was using its new 1970 ½ F body, not as an outright death sales blow, but as a stepping stone.

Pony cars would now lure younger prospects into showrooms. These buyers would then trade up to a loaded inter or full-size, which was where the real money was at. Ponies were a means to a corporate end; no longer Iacocca's end game. No wonder one Ford executive, when commenting on '70 Torino, said "We've put a lot of eggs in this one basket." On the new 351 Cleveland V8, a Ford engineer informed *Road Test* magazine in December 1969, "When the 351 is well broken in and in tune, it will burn the wheels right out from under you."

Designing & engineering a sales winner
It was clear Ford was holding nothing back with this mighty midsize. Actions speak louder than words, and fortunately for Ford the sales numbers backed up Dearborn's confidence and investment in Torino. The Fairlane family contributed a huge 407,493 units to Ford's tally: 230,411 of those were value added Torinos. The goal had been to make Ford brand number one in car sales for the first time since 1959, and styling would play its part. More curvy, swoopy and looking like a family car born of the muscle car era, *Motor Trend* picked Torino as its Car Of The Year 1970, and suggested the two-door hardtop fastback SportsRoof variant might even be too racy-looking for a supercar!

Even the regular two-door hardtop looked sufficiently fastback and supercar worthy – who would need a Mustang

A 1970 Torino GT ragtop. The first of two model years featuring the final Ford midsize convertible. (Courtesy David Conn)

The very similar looking '71s marked the end of ragtop availability. Changing market tastes, the rise of a/c, and the spectre of proposed federal roll over tests, sealed the convertible's fate. (Courtesy David Conn)

Ford Midsize Muscle – Fairlane, Torino & Ranchero

now?! A new bodystyle that underlined 'Style' for 1970 was the four-door hardtop. No doubt Fairlane/Torino's pointed prow visage advanced a more aggressive attitude for Ford midsize. The tagline for SportsRoof was "Shaped by the wind." Ford certainly worked in a new rear window slope, and raked Torino's windshield back a further six degrees. That said, the wagon models received less stylistic attention, and came out looking squarish next to 'Mod Squad' Torino sedans and hardtops.

Inside, Ford was more generous sharing out the style. For '70 Fairlane/Torino received a new dash molding. It was a modern one piece design, with instrument-containing hooded binnacle directly in front of the driver. Gone were 69's circular dials, at the top was the then fashionable 120mph strip speedo. Gas gauge, odometer and temp gauge were directly below. To the left of these items was either a clock, or Carousel tachometer. The latter was optional on V8s, and was of a 49 buck, 8000rpm, horizontal tumbler nature. Ford made up the rest with idiot lights. The HVAC panel was on the right of the temp gauge.

The only voice saying full instrumentation was the sales brochure, but at least it looked cool! Keeping its occupants cool and refreshed was Ford USA's newly developed DirectAire vent system – an optional setup, taking lessons from Henry's Ford of England operation. With draft free, face level vents on either side of the steering column, it was touted by *Motor Trend* as offering the best free flow in Detroit.

DirectAire was good at a time when one had to order a/c to drive comfortably with windows closed in a domestic car sans vent wings. Normal flow through ventilation was poor. Complaints versus arch rival Chevy, was that Ford's inter didn't come with face level vents and inertia reel front seatbelts standard, in Chevelle versus Fairlane. Indeed, even Ford's 'Rim-Blow' steering wheel horn was an option, in an interior where Ford tried to work ergonomic magic on its two-door rides. In SportsRoof, the rear quasi bench was lowered to improve headroom over the '69s, but this made taking a seat tougher.

Ford added its 'Clamshell' highback buckets to sporty Torinos in 1970. These items had been introduced on 1969 Mustang. Said buckets were placed on slightly curved tracks, again trying to liberate more rear interior space. But however poor the interior accommodation was in Ford midsize, it could only be worse in Mustang! For all the gee whizness of '70 Fairlane/Torino, it was still a very conventional car, similar in layout to all Fairlane inters since 1962. That meant a steel unibody clothing a rear drive, leaf sprung axled family car.

Front suspension was still independent, MacPherson strut short/long arm with coil. However, versus 1969, front swaybar diameter was up from 0.72in to 0.75in. There was engineer recognition that the new Torinos would be carrying more weight up front, in terms of larger average engine size/sheet metal. 1969 to 1970 weight would be up approximately 102lb. Therefore, 1970 Torino, when specified with a/c, had #1925 front coils with 295lb spring rate. The part number had been 1850 with a 275lb rate in 1969. In spite of increases, the typical mid displacement

With the 351C/auto power team that most Ford execs thought folks would option, this convertible is a luxo cruiser. (Courtesy David Conn)

6: Torino the Muscle Car 1970-73

Torino V8 now had better weight distribution of 55/45% versus 1969's 56/44%.

Typically the Torino would be working its suspension through Firestone F78-14 in bias ply Wide Ovals, on a 5in wide steel rim. As part of Torino's continual upscale push, its suspension for '70 MY was tuned to take the harshness of bias ply tires. Sports orientated Torinos made use of Goodyear's Polyglas tire. The Ford midsize $65 power front disk brake option, was the same 11.3in vent disk floating calliper front, 10in drum rear system. However, even though price stayed the same versus 1969, the diameter of the rear cast flared and finned drums decreased from 2.5 to 2in.

Fairlane/Torino's 105 buck power steering option had good feel, and was precise, by domestic standards, but was a trifle slow and unwieldy. Not bad at 3.5 turns lock to lock, but the big 42.75ft turning circle was large for a rear driver. Even though all power steer cars came with this recirculating ball system, featuring an unsporting 20.64:1 steering ratio, the top Cobra cars were felt to be able to change direction quickly. On more sedate variants, a typical mid spec two-door hardtop, the ride/handling compromise was considered good. Shocks had been revalved to match Torino's new 1in longer 117in wheelbase.

Standard brakes on Fairlane/Torino were still four wheel drums, 10 x 2.5in front and 10 x 2in rear. Optional HD suspension on non-sporty models cost $23, and involved front and rear spring rates of 91lb/in and 102lb/in respectively, whilst using the stock 0.75in front swaybar. However, being Detroit, The Motor City, major interest was in what lay underhood. The long and short of it was a base 155bhp 250ci inline six and a 375 horse 429 V8. Indeed, Ford's midsize was wider for '70 MY to accommodate said canted valve 429 motor.

Sensible souls would have accepted the 220bhp 302 Windsor, standard on upscale Torinos, but new kid on the Ford interblock was the 351 Cleveland (351-C). Whereas Windsor small blocks mostly issued from a Canadian Ford plant, the Cleveland was made at a huge, very modern, highly automated add on to the Cleveland, Ohio plant. The 351-C represented a $100 million investment by Ford, in what it felt most folks would want in their upscale inter. With bore and stroke at 4.02in and 3.50in respectively, good breathing was a 351-C design goal. With Ford 'Free Flow' heads it offered the biggest valves of any volume produced V8, bigger intake and exhaust ports.

On the subject of breathing easy, the top $93 option 4bbl Cleveland had a premium fuel hungry 11:1 comp ratio, and heads inspired by Ford's Boss 302. Indeed, 351-C 4V mimicked Chevrolet's 'Porcupine' head design. Valves were canted in two planes, which allowed larger intake and exhaust passages, along with large oval ports. A header type exhaust manifold with large oval ports went on to a dual exhaust conclusion. The four-barrel motor utilized an Autolite carb with 1.56in primaries and 1.69in secondaries. The 2bbl 351 Cleveland didn't have canted valves. Running on regular, with 9.5:1 CR, it was rated at 250bhp at 4600rpm and 355lb/ft at 2600rpm.

The humble 2V Cleveland shared its power rating and VIN code with the 2V 351 Windsor, but featured benefits in common with its hi po bro! That is, stronger valve train, shorter/stronger pushrods, wider stamped steel rocker arms and stiffer valve springs. The bottom end had new wider main bearing caps with ½in bolts. The hi po 351-C 4V possessed a 600 CFM carb, and made 300 gross ponies at 5400rpm, along with 380lb/ft at 3400rpm. It featured a medium lift cam of 268 degree intake and 280 degree exhaust duration.

The 351-C 4V motor had an air cleaner decal callout, stating "Ford 351-4V premium fuel." This was true, and an 11 to one comp with 300 ponies was a little unusual for a motor that could live under a family car's hood. The fact

Ford Midsize Muscle – Fairlane, Torino & Ranchero

the family Ford needed the same diet as a L88 427 Vette, indicated Ford's Total Performance had truly reached suburban garages, with practicality. The Cleveland's other design goal was compact exterior dimensions, allowing easier underhood service work. Not having to undo a motor mount to change a sparkplug! This was a problem on inters with big blocks, and would become a '70s problem on some subcompacts with small blocks.

Ford's extra ponies were necessary, because midsize was getting bigger. Two-door SportsRoof was now a '69 Torino Talladega matching 206.2in long! Compared to 1969, Ford's muscle car fastback track had appreciated from 58.8in front/58.5in rear to 60.5in front/60in rear. The load lugging wagon was 209in long, even though it lived on a shorter 114in wheelbase. Widths for four-door, two-door and wagon bodies were 76.4in, 76.8in and 75.4in respectively. Base curb weight was up from 1969's 3232lb to 1970's 3335lb. Nothing to worry a 21st century SUV, but frightening for VW Bug road users!

Then again, believe Ford's publicity and Torino could ergonomically accommodate all body types, from that little old lady from Pasadena, to basketball player Wilt Chamberlain. No need for Mr Chamberlain to scrunch up in a Bug, like in that humorous VW ad. In truth, Ford's midsize had practical problems, related to Fairlane's new found overt style. On SportsRoof the raked windshield, high sides and sloping rear glass made it hard to see out, and parking difficult. The new '70 midsize fell into the category of big on the outside, not so spacious inside. In spite of SportsRoof's 206.2in length, front driver legroom was tight and made working the clutch difficult.

Indeed, on sporty four-speed cars, the anti-theft measures Ford built in meant one had to put the stick in reverse to get the ignition key out. Removing the key was a chore because key positions weren't marked clearly. The trying experience *Car Life* had with its Torino 351 GT in February 1970, caused the journal to speculate that the end of Ford four-speeds might be nigh. Fortunately, claims of said death were greatly exaggerated! The only Ford midsize with stock four-speed was Cobra, and there was always that convenient $200 optional Select Shift Cruise-O-Matic autobox.

In the 'bigger was better' era, popular ponies Mustang, Firebird and Javelin, had, or would puff out with, larger, more extravagant sheetmetal. The respective model years were 1968, 1969 and 1971. Fairlane/Torino played that partly marketing inspired game too. The only thing that seemed longer than the car's length, was the model range.

Fairlane gallops past Mustang!

2.2in wider for '70 MY and 5.1in longer, 14 different models classed in four distinct groups. However, the length increase was from the radiator forward, and the 14 models were all based on the one Ford midsize! That said, specify a model as one liked, and no two were the same. There was also a world of difference between a 155bhp six-cylinder Fairlane Falcon two-door sedan, and 375 horse Super Cobra Jet SportsRoof. They certainly drove differently! Detroit's option sheets were as long as ever, but Ford's star Mustang was ailing.

The Mustang name goes back much further than 1964. By 1530 there were so many runaway horses, that Mexican cattlemen called 'em Mustangs! The name Mustang was derived from medieval Spanish, where the word mestengo meant stray.[12] Fast forward to 1970, and Mustang sales had certainly gone astray. According to *Motor Trend*'s October 1971 article, titled "The Last Roundup," Mustang sales in 1970 had fallen to under 165,000 units. For 1970 Ford was pushing Torino and de-emphasizing Fairlane.

Fairlane, as a nameplate, kicked off the 1970 Ford midsize range as the Fairlane 500. This was joined mid model year (January 1 1970) by a low cost, entry level Falcon version. Ford had discontinued its seminal compact at the close of '69 MY. It

6: Torino the Muscle Car 1970-73

wouldn't have been able to meet pending fed regs, and Ford was busy with its compact successor, the snazzy Maverick. Maverick shared its tartan trim upholstery with the starter Torino. Even sans tartan, Fairlane was gaining on Mustang. In 1970 110,029 people bought Fairlanes, 67,053 bought lowball Fairlane Falcons. The latter notched up a goodly number of sales, for just a one half MY appearance.

Ford had played the innovation game well. First with Thunderbird, then Ranchero, Falcon Compact, Mustang and Bronco SUV. Now, as Mustang ran out of steam, Henry's midsize came to the rescue. Fairlane Falcon was a real austerity special, available in two-door and four-door sedan, plus wagon editions. With 250ci I6, rubber floormats, three on the tree manual, pillared roof, and no DirectAire ventilation, Falcon wasn't going to make neighbors green with envy. The six banger wasn't going to test the stock front 10 x 2.5in/rear 10 x 2in non power drums, but the wagon variant's weight just might.

Move up to the normality of a Fairlane 500 to enjoy nicer trim, and greater body format choice. Two-door hardtop in addition to Falcon's two/four-door sedan and wagon. Then it was time for upscale Torino's two/four-door hardtop, four-door sedan and wagon – the four-door hardtop was new for '70 MY. Ford had been pricing midsize competitively versus Mustang since 1968. It's not certain whether Henry was anticipating or accommodating intermediate class popularity, but either way Ford was right on the money! For value for money, Torino Brougham may have been the pick of the bunch.

The consensus was that Torino Brougham brought all of the luxury and refinement of Continental, in a much more compact package. In keeping with contemporary industry practice, Torino Brougham's suspension settings were normally chosen by computer to maximize ride/handling compromise. In trim or power accessories there was little compromise. One must have hankered for the prestige connotations of Honest Abe's namesake, to have passed on Torino Brougham's already library quiet nature. Performance was presidential too.

Brougham brought standard V8 power, in terms of Windsor 302. Supreme confidence was assured by the big 429 motor. Said big inchier was a Thunderbird exclusive in 1969. Thunderbird ads said it was a deep breathing motor, the stats bore this out: 360 horse at 4600rpm, 480lb/ft at 2800rpm on 10.5:1 CR, with a single 4bbl carb. The 429 moved a 3595lb Brougham from 0-60mph in 8.8 seconds, through the ¼ mile in 16.7 seconds at 86.1mph, as measured by *Motor Trend* in February 1970. More would have noticed the F78-14 in sourced tire smoke, and axle tramp, than Brougham 429's 115mph top speed. However, Torino Brougham was more about dignified travel.

The Comfort Weave knitted breathing vinyl could have been leather, and the Brougham wheel covers, emblems and additional sound insulation kept the ruse going. Torino Brougham's crest lived on Ford's semi-oval steering wheel, and vinyl roof C pillar trim. Brougham's circular logo was smack dab in the middle of the '70 egg crate grille. Apart from disappearing windshield wipers, Torino's optional concealed headlamps were standard on Brougham.

The concealed headlamps were a new '70 MY feature on Torino, and Ford kept faith in this troublesome gimmick, even though the rest of Detroit was getting away from it. On Torino it involved fixed pairs of round circular lights, that lived behind vacuum actuated doors that slide up and down. Go for the big motor option, and like any Torino, a 429 callout badge resided on the lowest point of the front fender, behind the front wheelwell. To save gas, improve handling and take advantage of Ford's big investment in the new Cleveland V8, one could have chosen the 351-C.

This time the callout badge said 351, and on Brougham the 4V Autolite carbed Cleveland brought duals as standard

Ford Midsize Muscle – Fairlane, Torino & Ranchero

equipment. In the December 1969 issue, *Road Test* magazine recounted its experience with a 4bbl 351-C motorvated Brougham two-door hardtop. With 0B33M100021 serial number, it was the 21st 1970 Torino off the line. Equipped with power front disks, a/c, and 375lb combined load of magazine man and Ford test driver to take figures, this was no lightweight buggy.

This mini sled did a 16.6 second ¼ mile at 78.64mph, the same time as the 429 powered Brougham two-door hardtop *Motor Trend* tried. Ford's info suggested a properly broken in 351C 4V powered midsize would do mid 15s in the low 90s! So in the Brougham at least, there seemed little point taking the big inch route. Plus, Ford set up the three-speed Cruise-O-Matic to suit the 351 Cleveland's torque characteristics, where the two were specified as a car's power team. Hinting at the mindset of the time neither *Road Test* nor *Motor Trend* mentioned fuel consumption.

Road Test also felt vinyl top, power gadgets and a/c put a car further from the typical intermediate Mr and Mrs Average might be paying off. Conclusion, the typical Ford midsize was a lightly optioned Torino two-door hardtop, with 2bbl 351C and Cruise-O-Matic. Plus, its owner was more concerned with engine pep than frugality. Apart from two-door and four-door hardtop, one could select a Brougham wagon. Whichever level of trim, Fairlane/Torino wagon could be optioned with 3 Way Magic Doorgate, power tailgate window, a rear facing third row seat and roof rack.

Functionally, and very key in pre-SUV times, one could choose the Trailer Tow Pack (TTP) rated at 3500lb. Mandatory starting point was a wagon with 351 motor, power steering and three-speed autobox. To this the TTP brought HD suspension, HD battery, HD alternator, HD cooling system and power front disks, if not already specified. From mid '70 MY, entry level Fairlane Falcon wagon joined Fairlane 500, Torino and Torino Squire wagons. Torino Squire brought faux woodgrain exterior trim and concealed headlamps, along with Brougham plushness.

Like Brougham, Torino Squire also came delivered with 2bbl 302 and power front disks as standard. As for options, all two-door Ford midsize cars could have buckets and a console. Neither item was standard GT Torino fare any more, although a showroom prospect would struggle to find a GT sans such items. Theory said vent wing cars, two/four-door sedan, and wagon, had DirectAire ventilation as an option. Two-door hardtop, SportsRoof and ragtop were supposed to have DirectAire standard.

Torino GT & Cobra muscle cars

Ford continued its Torino GT and Cobra distinctions. GT was the sports/luxo model that could have muscle, but majored on show. Cobra was the performance first stripper, that could have luxury, but turned

A '71 Torino Cobra Jet Ram Air 429, showing its optional psychedelic Laser Stripe decal at the 2012 Southern Wheels 'n' Motion car show. (Courtesy Dennis Crenshaw)

6: Torino the Muscle Car 1970-73

up with the serious hardware without buyers having to tick option boxes. Torino GT meant standard faux forward facing, broad molded hoodscoop, and 2bbl 302/three-speed manual power team. For '70 MY wheel width was an inch up.

One's GT rode on 14 x 7in steel rims wrapped with E70-14 in Goodyear Polyglas bias belted tires. The equivalent of a 195/70 14 incher. GT bodystyles encompassed SportsRoof and ragtop. The former came with horizontal black decal appliqués on either side of the trunk lock. Both came with imitation tailwidth taillights. There were lamps at either end, connected by a reflector panel. The hexagon reflector involved many small reflectors within a mesh. Apparently Ford designers were inspired by Lamborghini's Marzal showcar.

Aerodynamic bullet side mirrors were a good looking option on GT. One would be hard pressed to find a GT without 'em. Ditto the egg crate grille with concealed headlamps. It was interesting what had to be added to Torino GT, and noteworthy that buyers were often satisfied with the stock 302 Windsor. Every major magazine tested their SportsRoof GTs with the optional 300 horse 351C four-barrel.

Torino GT moseyed in at $3105, but power front disks ($65), power steering ($105), heavy-duty suspension ($23), four-speed ($194), rev counter ($49) and Traction-Lok LSD ($43) were all optional! Even F70-14 in tires were optional, although these were standard on GT Convertible. By the time all the good stuff was added, and who would get a GT sans optional buckets/console, the price was $4500 and that local Ford dealer could retire! The road to bankruptcy is paved with good options.

Tinted windows were a $40 option, undercoating for the body was optional and advisable. One option almost universally fitted were profile 'Laser Stripe' decals. These special side stripes, may have been the most spectacular decal of its type, offered on a Detroit midsize. Laser Stripe were reflective, fade-away decals with graduated color density from front to rear. Starting from GT's rear fender five faux vertical rear brake cooling vents, Laser Stripe made its mid body way to the front fender, where it surrounded the front side marker. There were GT badging above aforementioned rear brake cooling vents, plus 'G over T' medallion mid grille front badge.

Optional rear window Sport Slat venetian louvers, helped alleviate rear cabin excess sun. With '70 Torino close fitting chrome bumpers, and curved corner taillights, GT looked plenty cool. In fact, with full decal and 351 badge callout, GT looked very Cobra supercar like. In this hour of rising insurance premiums for high-performance two-doors, the Torino GT was a car in the vein of Oldsmobile's Rallye 350. Why get a 442 or Cobra, when these supercar siblings could sip gas with their 350s? Even Pontiac, modern muscle car originator, planned a hi po 350 cube version of its Goat, that didn't eventuate.

As *Motorcade* said in March 1970, the Torino GT 351C 4V was the supercar for people that didn't want a supercar! Then again, Torino GT 351C-4V wasn't exactly a paper tiger either. The optional 300 horse 4bbl Cleveland had 11 to 1 comp, and magazines liked to specify the optional four-speed to complete the test car's

With CJ 429, RA and DP (Drag Pack), this Torino GT has all the fruit! It's the Ford performance pinnacle for midsize muscle! (Courtesy Robert J Cuillerier www.facebook.com/pages/Muscle-Car-Classics-MCC/160061237435887)

Ford Midsize Muscle – Fairlane, Torino & Ranchero

power team. The optional four-speed cost $194, and came with that ergonomic, 'fits like a glove' Hurst spun aluminum 'Dog Bone' shifter handle. Hurst, the Gucci label of transmissions, also made the shifter lever, but that was it.

The actual shift linkage wasn't a Hurst affair, and thus lacked the precision that brand was known for. Still, in the muscle car era a direct 1 to 1 top non overdrive four-speed was a badge of honor. Power shifting to the 5200rpm redline allowed 351C-4V in Torino to record good, middle of the pack, performance. *Car Life*'s 1970 figures were 0-60mph in 8.2 seconds, 15.6 second ¼ mile at 89.5mph and top speed of 115mph. On the practical front the 3.25 rear axle ratio spelt 2620rpm at 60mph, and 12.8mpg average with 256 mile cruising range from the 20 gallon tank.

No Golden state Torinos had a 22 gallon tank. So overall Ford's pseudo supercar could cruise a highway, get good gas mileage for the era and dodge the supercar insurance premium bullet. Plus, on '70 Torino GT it was possible to option a functional, forward facing shaker hoodscoop. This shook when one blipped the throttle, because it was attached to the motor, not the hood! Even with HD suspension testers considered the GT's chassis too soft. Plus, even though improvement was made on weight distribution versus 1969, Torino was still a nose heavy understeerer.

All the above was considered an impediment to good braking performance. This was a pity since Torino's braking hardware was sound by domestic standards. *Car and Driver* in a December 1969 issue, blamed '70 Torino's extra girth, and forward of radiator additional length. Cobra to Cobra it noted its '69 428 machine, in a six car January 1969 comparo test, braked 30 feet shorter from 80mph!

In the mix and match Detroit golden age, it was possible to insert the 11.3:1 CR 370 horse 429 into Torino GT. *Motor Trend* sampled just such a car in February 1970, amongst the various new Torinos it was trying. The machine in question came with Select Shift autobox and Ram Air shaker

Zero to sixty in six seconds flat, mid 14s in the 1/4 @ 100mph. Or, 3.5 seconds faster to 100mph than a 2010 Dodge Charger Hemi 5.7 cop car! (Courtesy Robert J Cuillerier www.facebook.com/pages/Muscle-Car-Classics-MCC/160061237435887)

6: Torino the Muscle Car 1970-73

hoodscoop, along with 3.50:1 rear gears. Criticism concerning 351 powered Torino GTs, missed the point. The Torino range didn't end there, and the real sporty home for 429 lay in the Cobra's lair!

1970 Torino Cobra – muscle car zenith!

Unbeknownst to all, but crystal ball gazers and maybe Lee Iacocca, was that 1970 would be the high watermark for super sports performance in North America. Although smog controls were around, Detroit engineers had still managed to improve outputs with each passing model year. One would have to wait until the early 1990s to enjoy 1970 acceleration in a reasonably affordable car. It was a long time to wait for 305 horse Ram Air LT1 Trans Am, SVT Cobra and twin turbo 300ZX. By then performance had changed to encompass matters beyond the ¼ mile, but iconic terms like Ram Air and Cobra still meant something.

The base 1970 Torino Cobra had a starter sticker of $3249, and much was included. The base motor was the 10.5:1 CR 429, making 360bhp at 4600rpm and 480lb/ft at 2800rpm with single 4bbl Autolite, on premium juice. Cobra was the only Torino to come with 4 on the floor as standard equipment. However, apart from the one to one 4th, the 429's four-speed had taller ratios compared to the four-speed found with the 'small' V8s. A 351/four-speed chariot had 2.78 (1st), 1.93 (2nd) and 1.36 (3rd) ratios. A 429ci motor was paired with 2.32 (1st), 1.69 (2nd) and 1.29 ratio 3rd. Wheels were GT like 14 x 7in, but moved up from E70-14s to GT ragtop's F70-14s.

To compensate for the weighty motor, Competition Suspension was standard Cobra equipment. Front and rear spring rates were a respective, and mighty, 500lb/in and 210lb/in, with $1^{3}/_{16}$in Gabriel shocks all around. Front swaybar diameter was a beefy 0.95in, and four-speed cars came with staggered shocks, naturally. The new ultimate rim/tire combo was the optional 15 x 7in Magnum 500, wearing low profile F60-15s, still in bias belted rubber.

Cobra didn't come with buckets, console or tach, these were all options. It didn't come with GT's rear fender faux brake cooling vents. Cobra's simple grille had four circular, chrome ringed headlamps and double chrome pinstripe mid grille divider bars, running the full width face. Cobra was only available in the SportsRoof bodystyle, and had the same close fitting chrome bumpers of other '70 Torinos. The racer feel continued with functional twist, hood latches and flat black hood, just for Cobras. The latter fitted within fender and hood panel lines, and was outlined by a flat black pinstripe.

Cobra decal script and snake on rolling wheels cartoon, lived lower mid body on each front fender, behind the wheelwell, but above the 429 chrome callout badge. The same decal and cartoon combo was repeated on the passenger side of the rear fascia panel, inboard of the right taillight. Like SportsRoof GT, there were black appliqué decals on the trunk's leading edge, either side of the trunk lock. Front buckets were $133, console $54, bullet side exterior reversing mirrors $26. On a car of this size and weight, $105 power steering and 65 buck power disk brakes were essential options, that applied to GT too. On muscle car business, the Ford 429 delivered.

The normal 360 horse Cobra 429 was nice, but you could have one of those in a GT, or even a Brougham! There was the Ram Air Cobra Jet option, which ran to $229 and brought 370bhp. The extra 10 ponies were due to special heads, not the Ram Air breathing kit. There was no advertised power rating difference between Ram Air 429s and non-Ram Air 429s, or for 351s equipped or not equipped for that matter. Even so, 360bhp 429 or 370 horse 429, one was dealing with a two bolt main motor, fed by one Autolite four-barrel 700 CFM carb. Plus, 10.5:1/11.3:1 comp on 360/370 horse 429 meant premium gas, or hello Mr Misfire!

At the spiritual height of the muscle

Ford Midsize Muscle – Fairlane, Torino & Ranchero

Base '70 Torino GT was $3105, but add 155 buck DP, Laser Stripes etc, and those repayments kept on coming to nearly five grand. (Courtesy Robert J Cuillerier www.facebook.com/pages/Muscle-Car-Classics-MCC/160061237435887)

car era, the Ram Air CJ option just wasn't enough. That little old lady from Pasadena wanted more. She wanted her groceries fresh upon returning home, and 370bhp wasn't going to cut it. So Ford provided the $155 Drag Pack option. The Drag Pack option grouped together the best Ford had in hardware, to best prepare one for the 1320ft sprint. Tick the Drag Pack option box and the Torino Cobra would come with a solid lifter Boss 429 fitted with four bolt mains, and 11.3 to one CR, courtesy of impact extruded aluminum pistons.

The Drag Pack Blue Oval big block was protected by an engine oil cooler. Two steel braided lines went from a small core in front of the radiator, to an adapter placed between the oil filter and engine block. The Drag Pack Cobra Jet 429 implied an upgrade to Holley 780 CFM 4bbl carb, and standard Traction-Lok LSD with 3.91 rear axle ratio, to help channel all that horsepower through the Polyglas tires. Beyond this, ¼ mile fiends could specify an optional 'No Spin' Detroit Locker LSD with 4.30:1 final drive ratio.

The spec may have been cool, but come summer you weren't. Optional factory a/c could only be specified on Ford midsize with axle ratios up to, and including, 3.25:1. Thus, Drag Pack cars didn't have a/c. Detroit's golden era hot cars didn't have cold a/c. The Camaro Z/28 had a solid lifter 350, and couldn't have a/c until it adopted a tamer hydraulic lifter V8 in 1973 MY. Highly tuned, often cantankerous, V8s didn't take kindly to having a/c belt and compressor running off 'em. They were liable to stall when reaching a traffic light or junction!

Within the myriad ordering permutations, it was possible to get a Drag Pack car sans Ram Air. Regardless of Ram Air, Ford's top advertised power rating on Drag Pack Torino Cobra was 375 horses. These wild animals arrived at 5600rpm, with 450lb/ft made at 3400rpm. The latter figure was pretty important because a Torino Cobra without any options tipped the scales at 3935lb. Torque was key in moving all that real estate, and Cobra had it! In keeping with the mood of the hour, Ford's 1970 Cobra ad embodied Dearborn's Total Performance ethic. Titled "Torino Cobra – Striking Power!" the ad urged drivers, or racers, to "Wood it … and blow off the also rans in your class!"

Well, it was all about the sacred ¼ mile, and which drag racing class one's ride fitted into. Ford made it sound like Torino Cobra was in a class of its own. "Whenever they talk about ETs that's where you'll see Cobra Ram Air 429s – with Drag Packs – winning!" Ford couldn't resist working a blown Mustang drag racer into the illustrated ad's background. Ford's ad figures also showed the performance compromise of domestic hi po V8s. The base 10.5:1 CR 429's 360bhp came in at 4600rpm; the 370 horse edition's a less tractable 5400rpm. Torque was also reduced from the base 429's 480lb/ft to 450lb/ft. Hi Po OHV V8s made more power with a commensurate increase in valve overlap, and reduction in low speed torque.

Cobra versus Shelby Mustang et al …

Still, it was a sacrifice many on Woodward Avenue were willing to make, and possibly a worthwhile investment. The Ram Air Shaker hoodscoop mayn't have

6: Torino the Muscle Car 1970-73

brought more advertised ponies, but it certainly raises the value of the collector Cobras so equipped! The Drag Pack car's 6150rpm redline showed its high level of commitment. Then again, the opposition was stiff. Big 4 rivals came in the form of Chevy Chevelle, Plymouth Road Runner 440-6V and AMC Rebel Machine 390. *Motor Trend* filed a December 1969 report comparing 370 horse Torino Cobra 429 CJ, with the Chevy and Plymouth.

Then, and now, the big block Chevelle was regarded as the performance pinnacle. The Bowtie V8 was rated at 450bhp at 5600rpm and 500lb/ft at 3600rpm on an 11:1 CR. The spiritual muscle car King, GTO, had moved on to 455ci power for 1970, in response to heated competition. It mustered 370 horse, but the GTO's nameplate reputation preceded it as ever. Even Pontiac's Ram Air IV 400, only managed a mere 345bhp! The Road Runner's triple deuce 440 made 390 horses, with Rebel Machine on 340bhp.

Domestic power ratings, all gross flywheel readings before 1972, were sometimes inflated for advertising, sometimes underrated to keep from triggering the insurance premium radar. In Chevrolet's case overstatement. This seemed motivated by inter GM familial rivalry, and Chevrolet's ownership of No 1 position in the sales race. Normally 100 SAE net horsepower equals 115 gross ponies. However, it's generally felt a 300bhp 1960s 327 made 215 SAE net horses in today's money.

Dialling back the Chevelle's LS6 454 to a more realistic gross figure, would have put it on 370 horses. Exactly on par with the 370bhp non Drag Pack Torino Cobra *Motor Trend* group tested. It explained why the sampled Chevelle and Torino Cobra both recorded 0-60mph in 6 seconds. The realism of Ford's quoted output, and good torque, also explained why Cobra out accelerated 390 horse Road Runner in the lower speed ranges. Ford engineers worked in useful torque for its 429. Many remarked at the time and since, that Cobra came on strong and smooth, rather than explosively. It shows why Torino Cobra out accelerated Chevelle SS 454 3.5 seconds to 3.7 seconds in the 50 to 70mph passing maneuver.

Torino Cobra was swifter 0-30/0-45/0-75mph than Chevelle and Road Runner. It also carried the highest trap speed of 100.2mph on its way to a 14.5 second ¼ mile. The stats showed that torque gets one rolling, but power to weight ratio counts in the high speed ranges. Torino Cobra was the biggest and heaviest car on test, sporting a portly 4002lb test weight. Cobra was almost 10in longer than Chevelle, over an inch wider, and sat on a 5in longer wheelbase. Road Runner was closer to Cobra in size, but was also smaller in every dimension, and weighed 3935lb.

For the ¼ mile, Chevelle and Road Runner clocked best of 13.8 and 14.06 seconds respectively. Unlike the other two, Road Runner was a four-speed car with an impractically tight 4.10:1 rear end! It was remarked that Torino had the best build quality on test, was nice to live with, but its size made parking difficult. In its goal of exploiting the increasing popularity of the intermediate class, it seemed Ford had made its midsize too full-size! Torino Cobra did show consistency in magazine tests. *Car and Driver* had a Torino Cobra in its December 1969 issue too, this time

That shift may not have been where expected, but even a few SD 455 Trans Ams came with a column shift. (Courtesy Robert J Cuillerier www.facebook.com/pages/Muscle-Car-Classics-MCC/160061237435887)

Ford Midsize Muscle – Fairlane, Torino & Ranchero

By 1970, Torino had abandoned circular instruments, and that meant the infamous $49 'Carousel Tach' came aboard. (Courtesy Robert J Cuillerier www.facebook.com/pages/Muscle-Car-Classics-MCC/160061237435887)

it was a Drag Pack four-speed car, with optional 39 buck Rim Blow steering wheel!

As per theory this 3.91 rear axle ratio car didn't have a/c, but weighed an even heavier 4185lb! This 375 horse car matched *Motor Trend*'s non Drag Pack car 14.5 second ¼ mile time, but at a slower 98.5mph. It also recorded a frightening 7-10mpg range on premium fuel, necessary for the 11.3:1 comp. This implied a cruising range of 200 miles at best from the 20 gallon tank. No overdrive five-speeds on muscle cars back then! Testers of the day commented that a 3.91 rear axle ratio Drag Pack car, was a noisy device to live with on a daily driver basis.

Motor Trend's Torino Cobra originally came with 3.25:1, and a/c. *Motor Trend* gave this automatic, Ram Air non Drag Pack car a 3.50 final drive, to help it match the acceleration times of Chevelle SS 454 and Road Runner 6 Pack. In a December 1990 retrospective piece called "The Torrid Zone" in *Classic American* magazine, Tony Beadle examined a Grabber Yellow 1970 Drag Pack non Ram Air Torino Cobra with Magnum 500 rims. Being Drag Pack meant 3.91 rear gears, but soon after purchase the original Santa Fe Springs, California owner had the Ford dealer change the car to a taller 3.25:1 rear end.

Even at the age of 20 in 1990, this Torino Cobra managed an ET of 14.21 seconds at Carlsbad Raceway, reaching 103mph. Plus, the car completed 16 trouble free passes in one day. This showed that even in 1970, folks found short gearing hard to live with. Plus, sensible rear axle ratios didn't hurt acceleration too badly. The Drag Pack's optional 4.30:1 final drive, with Detroit Locker LSD, was overkill for most. This 1970 car also revealed how durable fast cars were, compared to the pollution controlled steeds of the late '70s.

It contrasted with *Road Test*'s February 1981 Turbo Trans Am Vs Camaro Z/28 encounter. Averages for the two cars were low 16s, and after six passes both were too pooped to play! It was a mild December day in Southern California, but ten years on these 4bbl V8s quickly became a drag at the strip. The coupes were loaded a/c rides, with slightly taller final drives than Torino Cobra's 3.25:1. However, the culprit was smog gear. Setting up a motor to run hot, and burn clean, with a compromise carb/two way cat setup, made 1970 look like the golden age that it was.

Motor Trend and *Car and Driver*'s Torino Cobra seemed 100% stock, but it was customary for cars submitted to magazines to be 'breathed on.' Even the 1961 Jag XKE was really a 140mph car, not a 150mph machine. Apart from *Motor Trend*'s December 1969 'Three Strippers' test, its February 1970 'Theme and Variations' Torino range report, had a warm Drag Pack, non a/c, Ram Air Banana Yellow four-speed Torino Cobra with 3.91:1 rear end. This car scooted through the ¼ mile in 13.99 seconds with trap speed of 101mph!

A 375 horse Drag Pack Torino Cobra with C6 auto and 3.91 rear axle ratio, was played with by *Super Stock and Drag Illustrated*. This car had different carb valving, bigger primary and secondary jets, along with slick tires. This 'little' midsize got a 13.39 second pass at 106.96mph! Drag worthy indeed, and on a stock machine pumping up the Polyglas tires helped 'em bite better off the line. Getting back to earth, the Ram Air and Drag Pack options mayn't have brought the stat performance gains expected. However, they certainly boost the collector value over plainer versions.

The mere act of ordering a car would soon belong to a bygone age. The major

6: Torino the Muscle Car 1970-73

magazine-tested Torino Cobras had plain front fascias. However, one could specify the fancy egg crate grille, hideaway headlights, Laser Stripes, Carousel tach and lots of other items. Building a personal ride was part of the fun!

The multitude of paint, trim and mechanical options, combined with the small 'mom & pop' nature of many dealers, meant that often a car had to be specially ordered. A customer would sit down at a dealer, tick option boxes and then wait for their dream ride to arrive. A buildsheet with all the special, and not so special, choices would follow a car down the assembly line. In accordance with said buildsheet, the appropriate options, like HD suspension and vanity interior lighting pack would be fitted.

Once done, the buildsheet would be stashed somewhere on the car, by Assembly Line Andy. Often under the back bench, sometimes between the roof and headliner, the stowed buildsheet is a key indicator of car originality. It's also invaluable in restoring a car authentically. In modern times special ordering and buildsheets don't exist like they used to. Domestic cars slowly followed the European and Japanese path of limited mechanical and trim options.

Gone were the times of a seven motor lineup choice. With a/c increasingly standard, and presence of a single V6 and V8, perhaps one alternate rear axle ratio, choice was soon limited to exterior color and interior décor. And even here, there was soon little need to special order. Ralph Williams' 1960s Mega Mall Ford dealership, was an indication why. Big dealers had many cars in various hues; with features like cruise control and stereophonic being in many cars on the lot, why go any further?

Reasons to buy Cobra

In 1970 there were still reasons to special order a car, and choose Cobra. Torino Cobra wasn't perfect, axle tramp and weight-affected braking and understeer were problems, but for sporty rides Detroit only built two-door coupes. In March 1968 *Motor Trend*'s Julian Schmidt described Ford Galaxie XL 428. Powerful in straight line acceleration and fitted with six-way power seats, power windows and a/c, but not very sporty. Schmidt mentioned major understeer and a plate-like steering wheel. Even with the second most powerful motor, the 340bhp $244.47 428, 0-60mph was 8 seconds and the ¼ mile 16.4 seconds at 86mph.[13]

Even the $622.97 390 horse 427 wouldn't have made Galaxie sporty, in the enthusiast's manner. Torino Cobra packed a 360 horse 429 standard, included a four-speed at no extra cost, and was cheaper. It was also faster, in spite of the tighter 1970 emissions regs. The same value for money was visible comparing Torino Cobra with

Top left: With all that luxury and refinement, the '70 Torino was the midsize that thought full-size. However, that extra girth took the edge off acceleration a little.

Top right: A family car with 16.2ft³ of trunk, but Laser Stripes and Honeycomb Reflector taillights also. Torino GT was the family racer! (Courtesy Robert J Cuillerier www.facebook.com/pages/Muscle-Car-Classics-MCC/160061237435887)

Ford Midsize Muscle – Fairlane, Torino & Ranchero

Shelby Mustang Cobra! After 1967 the Shelby Mustang became more of a cruiser. The 1968 Cobra 428 cost $4317.39 as a coupe, and came with a 360 horse 10.5:1 comp 428 with one 4bbl carb. 0-60mph was a low six seconds, and the ¼ mile was mid 14s. There were also important options like power steering and power front disk brakes, that would have boosted the price.

Big & small projects – Pinto & Continental MkIII

A four-speed was standard, like on Torino Cobra, but one paid a lot for a Cobra coming from Shelby American. In terms of performance progress, Ford had moved from 390/428s, on to the 429 family. So it paid to visit Henry first for a performance car. It's harder to hit a moving target, and Ford was keeping in touch with industry developments. Mid model year intros, like Fairlane Falcon, avoided the new release rush, and Ford was working on the small car angle too.

Intensifying since the mid '60s, the public were increasingly into small cars. By the dawn of the '70s, almost one million new car sales in North America were small cars. It wasn't just VWs anymore, the general interest encompassed Japanese cars and more. Apart from Falcon, Ford dealt with this development using a captive import. The British Cortina MkII was that car. For Chrysler Corp it was the Plymouth Cricket, aka the British Hillman Avenger. However, as much as these imports were like scaled down versions of US cars, they weren't that well suited to America. Plus, quality was wanting compared to VW, Toyota and Datsun.

Falcon, along with Corvair and Valiant, had seen off most of the imports at the start of the '60s, but now something more was needed. As of January 1 1970, Federal Safety Standard (FSS) requirements would necessitate an ignition switch on a locking steering column. This was going to be too much for Falcon, so Ford had in place a new compact as of April 1969, called Maverick, taking its name from unbranded range animals, and featuring a logo resembling a stylized longhorn cow head.

Maverick certainly had more style than Falcon, a snazzy long hood, short deck look, born of the pony car era. Retailing from $1995, Maverick had budget pop out rear windows, and was aimed at that thrifty VW, Japanese crowd. The trouble was that Ford once again took sales from itself. When Mustang came it reduced Falcon sales, and now Maverick reduced Mustang sales! Mustang and Maverick were Falcon related.

Perhaps the public could see this fact, in any case Ford had trouble getting VW and Japanese conquest sales. Ford Maverick was a sales winner for Henry, 579,000, but at the expense of plummeting Mustang. All the while, Detroit bosses couldn't figure out why folks dug little cars quite so much?! A GM exec at the time even said there must be something wrong with people that like small cars! Detroit management had seen small cars as hardship or poverty specials. That is, cars only bought because the buyer couldn't afford something better. However, there was more to it than that.

By the late '60s, there was a protest against the collective evils of the Big 3. The same sort of sentiment Apple harnessed against 'Big Blue' IBM a decade later. Foreign cars also had exotic charm, and many just didn't want to drive, park and feed a behemoth. With this in mind, Maverick was more Mod Squad funky than Falcon. Opening exterior colors were Anti-Establish Mint, Hulla Blue, Original Cinnamon, Freudian Guilt and Thanks Vermillion.

De-contenting to keep the price down, meant no glovebox until '74 MY! Ford went both ways with Maverick, economy car and muscle car. Both popular concepts coming out of the '60s. Maverick had a performance 'Grabber' package from 1970 to 1975. Cousin Comet offered the Comet GT between 1971 and 1975. The former had a Dual Dome hood, the latter a hoodscoop. Showing the schizoid times, the pleas for performance were as loud as

6: Torino the Muscle Car 1970-73

the ones for economy. Rumor going into 1970 MY, was that Ford was readying a Boss 302 option for Maverick!

In reality, 1970 saw the 250ci 'Thrift Power' I6 as top Maverick Grabber powerplant. It wasn't until 1971 that the 302 arrived underhood, albeit in milder 210bhp trim. With this motor, Maverick Grabber took on Chevy Nova SS 350, AMC Hornet S/C 360, Dodge Demon 340 and all the other sporty fare that tried to deliver muscle, without sky high insurance premiums – economy muscle cars, if you will. Car insurance was deflating the domestic performance car scene, before smog controls and CAFE gatecrashed the party.

All the time, seriously small cars were picking up momentum, and plans were made to bring out subcompacts. GM, Ford and AMC were in the race to answer VW and Japanese imports, with comparably sized economy cars. In the days before the first gas crunch, that meant cheap to buy, insure, maintain and feed. AMC scooped the exclusive with an April 1 1970 Gremlin release; GM's debut for Vega was on September 10 1970, with Ford's Pinto arriving the next day – three small, US made and designed small cars.

Low profit margins and UAW labor costs perhaps, but if you build it they will come, and come they did. By January 1971, over 100,000 Pintos had found new garages to call home. Three small cars, but different approaches, reflecting the corporation at hand. For small car on a budget, AMC cut down Hornet, added distinctive rear styling and called it Gremlin. GM, showing its market dominance and $$$, went clean sheet on Chevy Vega. Scaled down 2nd gen Camaro styling, and a linerless aluminum block I4 headlined this economy act. Reflecting its corporate decline of the time, Chrysler just did captive import.

Ford's eyes were on arch rival Chevrolet and the imports. Although Maverick related, its Pinto subcompact wasn't a small American style sedan. The unconventional shape was by Ford USA's Robert Eidschun, and had a fastback look for style. Pinto incorporated all the elements buyers associated with small imports, apart from VW! Thus, the Ford compact had hatchback, buckets, four on the floor and an I4 motor. Like Chevrolet, Ford didn't take a design from its European subsidiary, but, unlike Chevrolet, did make use of Ford Europe power teams.

Pinto came out with the tried and true Kent OHV I4, found in British Cortinas and Escorts. This was connected to the excellent Ford of Germany four-speed, equaling great thrift and durability. With a nod to Ford's Total Performance era, Pinto, with German 2-liter OHC I4 and four-speed, could do 0-60mph in under 11 seconds. Compared to VW this was warp speed! Compared to Gremlin and Vega, Pinto was the most European of the domestic subcompacts. However, accommodating American preference for more interior space. Pinto was 2-3in wider than a Euro Escort or the Japanese contingent.

Pinto's tagline was "The Little Carefree Car." At $1850 it undercut Vega, and was the cheapest US Ford, since the 1958 I6 family car! Ford also offered some 'do it yourself' service kits, whereby an owner could save a few bucks by doing basic service work, taking advantage of Pinto's simplicity. Henry Ford would have been proud of such economisms! In its September 1970 issue *Car and Driver* billed Pinto as: "An American-Made 'Foreign' Sedan."[14]

C&D joked that Ford had been concentrating so hard on the plain, small sedan concept, where was Pinto GT, Brougham, Country Squire, SportsRoof and Pinto Cobra?! Well, a GT variant, along with plush choices and liftback wagon would eventuate. Pinto based Mustang II would also have Cobra and King Cobra editions, so patience would prove a virtue. Not everything went according to plan. Consumer Reports' first group test of Pinto and rivals showed a quality gap between Ford, GM, AMC and imports. Pinto was delivered with many assembly line defects. The dealer sold

Ford Midsize Muscle – Fairlane, Torino & Ranchero

servicing kit with multi-purpose tool, was of little value.

Trade up to a Conti!

Unfortunately, it seemed like VW was still the Rolls-Royce of small cars when it came to quality. For that kind of bank vault, carved from solid rock nature, one would have to visit Lincoln-Mercury and get comfy in Continental Mark III. This 1968 ride, dubbed 'Baby Lincoln,' was a third attempt to create the ultimate luxury car for discerning buyers. However, it was more affordable than the incredibly pricey 1955-57 Mark II. With this wrinkled leather, dominant grille machine, a semi sensible sticker was chosen for a 15,000 unit per annum sales volume.

In chassis, engine and emissions control, Continental Mark III would have influence on humble Torino, down the road. For the finest ride/handling compromise, with refinement, debate raged on whether unibody construction or separate chassis was optimal. Indeed, at Ford there was much switching between such methods concerning intermediate and full-size lines. For Continental Mark III, separate chassis was the key. The 1970 Lincoln Continental ad spelt it out: "But above all, Lincoln Continental makes this the year of The Ride."

Behind the adcopy was a longer wheelbase, wider track, rubber cushioned driveshaft and four coil suspension. Most of this applied to Continental Mark III, with shorter wheelbase for more nimble handling and improved braking. Brake lock up, especially rear brake lock up and tail slewing, was a problem of the era. Front power disks took care of matters up front, whilst anti lock brakes covered control rearwards. Sure-Track was the first computer controlled anti-skid braking system fitted to a production car. Almost a decade before Mercedes introduced ABS on its S class.

Continental Mark III also came standard with Michelin steel belted radials, for improved ride and handling. For this ultimate, semi-affordable luxo cruiser, an appropriately Kingly motor was needed – the new 385 series 460 big block! As the ad said "At turnpike speed, it is so hushed, so smooth you are scarcely aware it is running." The opening figures were 365bhp at 4600rpm, and 500lb/ft at 2800rpm. A new Autolite 4bbl carb was tailored to the 460 in parallel design development from May 1965.

Ford's new IMCO (Improved Combustion) emissions control was an integral part of the 460 – important, given tightening emissions standards. By 1971 NADA average wholesale prices, indicated that Continental Mark III had the highest resale value of any US-built luxury car. Sure-Track ABS was standard on Continental Mark III, optional on Lincoln Continental; the ad tagline said "The Continentals: the final step up." However, Torino Brougham 429 came awfully close, even with unibody construction, and a long list of options to make the ultimate Torino in luxury. The ultimate sporty Torino nearly made it to NASCAR.

NASCAR 1970 – the sport of kings

On April 18 1970, in North Wilkesboro, Richard Petty won the Gwyn Staley Memorial 400. It was the second NASCAR event televised by ABC Sports. Petty led for 349 of the 400 laps, with every telecast lap showing him leading the pack! At the dawn of the decade, NASCAR was billed as "The Sport of the 1970s." Ultra modern facilities existed, or were being built, across the country by the close of the '60s. Automakers were pouring millions into NASCAR, because 'win on Sunday, sell on Monday!'

At the same time, most licensed NASCAR Grand National drivers were in the Professional Drivers Association (PDA) union. The PDA had concerns about speedway conditions, the astoundingly high speeds attained in modern NASCAR, the amount of time permitted for track car preparation, and venue amenities available to competitors. The different stances and views between NASCAR authority, PDA and race fans created some tension.

In those Aero Wars with the Mopar Marvels, Larry Shinoda and Team Ford slapped an aero nosecone onto Torino Cobra, and, voila ... 1970 King Cobra! (Courtesy RKMotorsCharlotte.com Jeff Spiegel)

So it was that on September 30 1970, the last dirt track NASCAR Grand National race took place at the State Fairgrounds in Raleigh, North Carolina. Richard Petty won the outing in a Don Robertson owned Plymouth. Petty had been lured back from Ford to drive the Plymouth Road Runner – a car designed to tempt Petty back to Camp Chrysler, and to win! Win it did, Petty's part season participation garnered 18 victories in the Road Runner, and it allowed him to come fourth in the championship – beep, beep!

To curb the ever rising speeds, on August 16 1970, at Michigan International Speedway, restrictor plates made their first NASCAR appearance. This race had the curiosity of the #8 Torino Talladega driven by Ed Negre. The funny thing was that this Ford was sponsored by a small Carolina Chrysler Plymouth dealer called Pyramid Motors! Negre's Talladega experienced engine problems and finished 36th.

In spite of the racing restrictions, records were still being set. On February 19 1970, Cale Yarborough and Charlie Glotzbach won the Twin 125 mile qualifiers at Daytona. Yarborough won recording an average speed of 183.295mph. It was an official race speed record that would last 14 years! Then, on March 24 1970, using a Royal Blue Dodge Daytona Chrysler Co #88 car at the Goodyear tire test held at Talladega, Buddy Baker became the first man to break 200mph on a closed oval circuit – the speed achieved was 200.447mph!

In the opening event of the 1970 race season, on January 18 1970, AJ Foyt's Ford narrowly edged out Roger McCluskey's Plymouth Superbird at Riverside. On February 22 at the Daytona 500, Pete Hamilton in the Petty Enterprises Plymouth achieved an upset victory. Hamilton passed Ford's David Pearson with nine laps to go, and won by three car lengths! On March 1, at the Richmond 500, James Hylton beat off a determined challenge from Richard Petty. Hylton achieved his first NASCAR Grand National win. It was his first start in a Ford, after four years in a Dodge.

Pete Hamilton, driving the #40 Plymouth Superbird, was star of the year by claiming both Talladega races and the Daytona 500. However, it was Bobby Isaac in the #71 Dodge that became 1970 NASCAR Grand National Champion. The K&K Insurance Dodge team was owned by

Ford Midsize Muscle – Fairlane, Torino & Ranchero

Sans wind cheating aero covers, King Cobra's famous sugar scoop headlamp cutouts are in evidence. By avoiding mile high tail spoilers, King Cobra was the handsomest aero car, sadly, never to race. (Courtesy RKMotorsCharlotte.com Jeff Spiegel)

Nord Krauskopf. The team started in 1966, with Krauskopf declaring a five year plan to get the NASCAR title, and he did! Isaac won 11 races and amassed nine 2nd places from 47 starts. It was a very competitive NASCAR 48 race season, contested between seven drivers.

Chrysler came to the fore with body addendum clad Dodge Charger Daytona and Plymouth Superbird. Whilst these winged warriors were the latest Mopar shots fired in the Aero Wars, most Ford linked competitors stuck with the 1969 rides. However, Ford hadn't been sitting on its hands; in 1969 it was Holman & Moody that responded to the '69 Dodge Charger 500, with the successful Torino Talladega. Then came the mighty Boss 429 motor, but the return fire came in the form of the mid season Dodge Charger Daytona.

These Mopars outsped Torino Talladega and Mercury Cyclone Spoiler II. However, the Chrysler cars put function ahead of form – they weren't exactly oil paintings on wheels! Ford got to work creating a good looking car, that was aero fast. Larry Shinoda and team added a sleek nose section to Ford's revised 1970 intermediate, the grille opening was beneath the front bumper, and a divided hoodcrease led to pointed prow/bumper fascia. Round headlights resided in sugar scoop headlamp cutouts, with aero covers to cheat the wind, and rivals, during racing.

What the car dubbed King Cobra didn't have, was the skyscraper spoiler of a Mopar machine. From the front King Cobra looked like a big Datsun 240Z! If this was the new wave of aero, it was an attractive one, and integrated well with Torino's existing styling. As with Talladega, the idea was a longer, more sloping nose to reduce frontal area and drag coefficient. Opinion on how well King Cobra worked aerodynamically is divided. Some say the styling may have looked nice, but didn't achieve its aero goal, citing this as a major reason Ford took the car no further.

However, the alternative story is that the prototype, with 700 horse Boss 429 no less, showed early promise. Stock Torino front windshield and rear backlight, were shown to introduce aero instability, so special items were substituted, including a convex backlight in place of the regular concave glass. This is evident on a surviving restored Vermillion King Cobra, on which the front and rear glass were made by Carlite and stamped "Prototype development tooling not to specification."

Initial press and public reaction to the car seemed positive. What was not to like about a cool looking NASCAR aero Cobra, with high output 429? *Motor Trend* subscribed to this viewpoint. The King

6: Torino the Muscle Car 1970-73

Cobra was placed on the cover of *Motor Trend*'s October 1969 issue. The magazine also urged readers to write to Ford, and tell the automaker that they would like to buy a King Cobra. An act that reflected the general enthusiasm for muscle cars at the time, and particular desire to see Ford put King Cobra into production.

History shows Ford didn't put King Cobra into production, and the reasons were more than its aero ability. There was a change in Ford's business direction, Total Performance wasn't accorded the same high priority anymore. Insurance premiums for sporty cars were on the rise, the public's interest in speed was waning, and sales of small cars was a phenomenon Ford couldn't ignore. Lee Iacocca was hip to that small car tune. NASCAR-favoring Bunkie Knudsen was fired from the Ford presidency, with Iacocca taking his place.

Lee Iacocca was focused on a sub 2000 buck, under 2000lb Pinto, to make sure Ford was on song concerning the burgeoning subcompact segment. Upon attaining the Ford presidency, he cut Ford's racing budget by 75%. In addition, NASCAR authorities weren't so enthusiastic about the speed and distance of aero racers from production cars. Ford didn't like the proposed higher 3000 unit homologation number. No way was it going to make and sell, hopefully, that many loss making rides. It fell to Ford Racing Program director Jacques Passino to deliver the bad tidings.

On November 19 1970, Passino said Ford would curtail its factory effort in 1971. In fact Ford was out, factory support wise, by the end of 1970. This left King Cobra, and Mercury Cyclone Spoiler II, in no man's land. Ford built three King Cobra prototypes, a white car, yellow one and Vermillion tester. The firm also did one Mercury Cyclone Spoiler II, red in hue. Today, only the white car is absent, it had a 370bhp Cobra Jet 429. The yellow machine sported Super Cobra Jet 429 375 horsepower, and the Vermillion King Cobra possessed a Boss 429 motor.

Reverence for the protos was in short supply at Dearborn. As a canceled racing program, the nosecone design studio clays were destroyed, and fiberglass mock-ups retained at Holman & Moody's workshop. As for the yellow and vermillion King Cobras, they were simply used as errand cars by Ford staff. Ford associated Trans Am series and NASCAR builder Bud Moore saved the yellow and vermillion cars. The racer saw them while purchasing several Mustangs for the 1971 SCCA Trans Am racing season; he paid $1200 for 'em, and they were brought to the Bud Moore Engineering workshop.

Thanks vermillion!

The yellow car stayed intact throughout the decades, spending much time in the Bud Moore collection. However, the vermillion car had a tougher life. It was purchased by Bud Moore as a blue car, with a damaged nosecone. The car was repaired with a normal 1970 Torino front fascia, and sold to a policeman. This King Cobra was used as a daily driver, until it made its way to a scrapyard. The car was subsequently rescued from a South Carolina field. Two enthusiasts, Steve Danielle and Dennis Roy, heard about this car hull sitting in a field. They went to investigate.

They verified the car's nature from its '69 dataplate, which read XO-429-0058-3. Danielle and Roy added the real King Cobra front fascia, and returned the car to its original vermillion hue. Differences between the King Cobra/Mercury Cyclone

A convex backlight gave aero stability. It was made by Carlite Inc, who stamped it 'Prototype development tooling not to specification.' (Courtesy RKMotorsCharlotte.com Jeff Spiegel)

Ford Midsize Muscle – Fairlane, Torino & Ranchero

The absence of buckets, console and tach underlined the plain nature of Torino Cobra-based King Cobra, versus luxo/sports Torino GT. (Courtesy RKMotorsCharlotte.com Jeff Spiegel)

Spoiler II, and high-performance Fords/Mercurys, were quite small. After all, it was all about that aero nosecone. Thus, expect the same six second 0-60mph time, and mid 14 second ¼ mile pass, from the 375 horse SCJ 429 and Top Loader four-speed power team. There are the respective Ford and Mercury differences, like taillights.

On the King Cobras, the white and yellow examples had the usual Torino Cobra hubcaps and trim rings, on rims of 14 x 7in nature. The vermillion example had the optional Magnum 500 15in styled steel rims. However, this four-speed machine's black vinyl interior lacked front buckets or a tach. This underlined the close relation between King Cobra and Torino Cobra, and the fact such items were Cobra options. Indeed, the vermillion King Cobra even had the usual upscale Torino lower door card woodgrain effect trim, and no center console! There was a Hurst shifter for the Top Loader four-speed though. The red Mercury Cyclone Spoiler II shared its vermillion hue with the restored King Cobra. The Mercury version also had a Boss 429 and Magnum 500 rims. In recent times both the yellow King Cobra and Mercury Cyclone Spoiler II have been owned by Ford enthusiast, and '60s Thunderbolt drag racer, Steve Honnel.

In terms of exterior decals the King Cobra machines sported the usual GT/Cobra asymmetric tuning fork side decal, flat black Cobra hood decorations/hood pins and rear trunklid edge vertical black appliqués. The Mercury Cyclone Spoiler II, on its lower body third, had a black wide

The Vermillion King Cobra proto was rescued from a South Carolina field by Steve Danielle and Dennis Roy. It sports a Boss 429. (Courtesy RKMotorsCharlotte.com Jeff Spiegel)

6: Torino the Muscle Car 1970-73

band stripe, terminating in a "Cyclone Spoiler II" decal callout on the nose. On King Cobra front fender and rear fascia, "Cobra" word decals were replaced with "King Cobra" equivalents. One historical distinction to note, is that an archive Mercury photo shows the sole Mercury proto with a "Cyclone Super Spoiler" decal callout on the surviving car, not "Cyclone Spoiler II."

Apart from the expected Hurst shifter on a Top Loader four-speed, King Cobras had the normal Ford semi-oval tiller inside, and Goodyear Polyglas raised white letter 14in bias belted tires on the outside. The value of King Cobra/Mercury Cyclone Spoiler II lies not in their technical distinction from normal Torinos and Cyclones; it rests in their historical NASCAR importance, and position as the ultimate examples of Ford midsize muscle cars, created in the peak performance year of 1970. In this light, the three surviving protos are invaluable!

1971 – just a Torino!

In the famous Aero Wars between Chrysler and Ford, during 1969 and 1970 racing seasons, special aero racers accounted for 73 victories out of the 102 Grand National races held. These victories were split 37 to Henry and 36 to Walter P. If circumstances hadn't intervened, the King Cobra/Mercury Cyclone Spoiler II might have tipped things Dearborn's way. However, in 1971 Ford was out of NASCAR, and was only concerned with the tally 326,463 units. This was the 1971 model year total for Torino, and just Torino. It seemed the Italian Detroiter had given Fairlane and Falcon nameplates the old Sicilian boot!

Foreign Fairlanes

Although Fairlane was finished in America by the close of 1970 MY, it lived on in Argentina and Australia. In Argentina local manufacture of a low volume, upscale version of 1968-69 Torino, continued through 1981! A luxury sedan alternative to upscale, import duty affected European models. Taking names, and hardware from Ford USA, the Argentine Torino came in base, 500 and LTD forms. Powerplants were a hardy 132 horse 221ci I6, and 185bhp version of the ex US '64 F-series Ford truck Y block 292ci V8.

As usual, in markets with less emissions controls, these older engine designs could make useful power. The most desirable Argentine Torino was the 1978 LTD with Elite option: the height of luxury, and borrowing another nametag from US midsize Fords. Nearly 30,000 Torinos were made in Argentina by the close of production in 1981. The Fairlane lived on longer Downunder. An Australian designed Fairlane came in 1967 as a local luxury car, but with more handling and trimmer size than the luxo US Fords. Dimensions were 196.1in for length and 74.7in concerning width, on a 116in wheelbase.

The size approximated a 1968 Torino, and so did the looks. The Australian Fairlane was like a '68 Torino Brougham with HD suspension. This right-hand drive sedan design was also assembled by Ford in South Africa. The Aussie Fairlane evolved in the '70s, and by 1980 still sported a 200 net bhp, locally made, 351 Cleveland. 1982 saw the final Australian market availability of locally-made Cleveland 302s and 351 V8s, in Australian Fords. This was due to the fuel crisis. Australian engineers then developed an electronic, multipoint fuel-injected version of the US 250ci Ford I6. This featured an aluminum, crossflow cylinder head on top Falcons and Fairlanes.

The aluminum head arrived on the six for 1980, with high comp 250ci I6 (locally called 4.1-litre) making 126bhp net. With fuel crisis fears, Ford Australia contemplated replacing its popular Falcon and Fairlane family cars with a stretched version of Mazda 626, or adoption of the German Ford Granada design. However, popularity of its local cars, saw Falcon and Fairlane continue. Easing conditions post World Fuel Crisis II, saw more Australian buyers flock back to these big cars, with local 4.1 I6 and V8s remaining popular.

Ford Australia still figured fuel prices and pollution laws threatened V8s, so planned

Ford Midsize Muscle – Fairlane, Torino & Ranchero

to drop its 302 and 351 V8s, plus develop the 4.1 I6. The company stockpiled a large number of V8s, thinking it would satiate demand through to the close of 1983 MY. However, so great was the demand, the V8s were gone by the end of '82 MY! In local V8 production days, Ford Australia even built some 351 Cleveland motors with four bolt mains, that resembled US NASCAR practice. With the demise of local V8 production, and end of the 351's Australian racing career in 1984, remaining hardware/tooling was sold and shipped back to America.

Ford Australia developed the popular 4.1 into an electronic fuel-injection edition, that would take over from its former local carb 302 V8. This it effectively did, making 149bhp and 240lb/ft in 1983, versus 200bhp and 306lb/ft for the final 1982 351s. V8s returned to the Aussie market in 1992, in the form of the Windsor 302. This time the motor was in US Mustang spec, fully imported from America. It was simply dropped into the engine bays of Falcons, Fairmonts, Fairlanes and LTDs made in Australia.

For 2003 MY, Ford switched to modular 5.4-liter V8 power. However, the writing was already on the wall, concerning the future of car production in Australia. SUVs and prestige brand import marques eating into lower price segments caused lower sales of normal, rear drive Fords and Holdens (GM subsidiary). Although the Aussie Falcon carried on post the 2007 demise of Fairlane, local production of such rear driver sixes and V8s won't carry on. It seems that just as these models mimicked their US counterparts in the good times, so they matched 'em and market trends on the way down.

1971 choices with Torino!

With all the big changes for 1970 completed, 1971 was a kind of carryover year in Torino land. The range now kicked off with plain butter and egg base Torino, available in two-door hardtop, four-door sedan and four-door wagon. Then one stepped up to Torino 500, with two-door hardtop, SportsRoof, four-door sedan and hardtop, plus four-door wagon. Then, for luxury fiends, sign up for Torino Brougham in two and four-door hardtop guises, or upscale Torino Squire wagon for hauling 2 x 4s down to the country club! As ever Torino Brougham 429, with lovely brocade tricot cloth material, and a long options list, made a powerful argument not to take the Continental 460 route.

The sporty crowd made a beeline for Torino GT, available in SportsRoof and convertible forms. Indeed, 1971 would prove to be the final year for GT ragtop, as fears loomed over the rollover legality of convertibles and pillarless cars. The GT afforded one sports and luxury, with style. However, Torino Cobra remained as the pure performance edition, even if Drag Pack had been deep sixed. It was only available in SportsRoof body, with special mechanical equipment. Blink, and one would miss the cosmetic changes for 1971, so subtle were they.

Cobra was unaffected, but other Torinos got a vertically divided grille, with former GT medallion replaced with oblong plaque. Cobra's matt black hood decal was altered. Formerly a one piece square, pinstriped along the edges, now it was divided up, the middle with body color separating the two segments. There was also a chrome Cobra snake logo, sitting in the middle of the horizontal trim grille divider. There was no emblem in this location on 1970 cars. 1971 Cobras also carried a snake logo and "Cobra" script decal on the rear fenders, above the side marker lights. Once again, such items were absent on 1970 editions.

On 1971 cars, the front lower fender chrome engine displacement callout badge was now absent. Indeed, too much was still absent on Detroit's base family inters. The entry level base poverty specials, lived up to their stripper tags. This included an uncomfortable front bench, that no one could desire by choice. Base engines for these inters were still sixes, and their modest power made the optional first rung V8 practically a mandatory option. Ford's one-barrel 250ci I6 was no better,

6: Torino the Muscle Car 1970-73

or worse, than the others, it promised 145bhp and 232lb/ft at a low 1600rpm on a 9:1 comp ratio, fed with regular gas.

Motor Trend observed these butter and egg machines in June '71. The report, titled "The Invisible Cars," compared a natty Torino Brougham four-door hardtop, with 350 Chevelle SS and puritanical Plymouth Satellite 318 four-door. At the hour, Ford's 351 2bbl V8 Windsor or Cleveland, it was a lottery as to which wound up underhood, was rated at 240bhp at 4600rpm and 350lb/ft at 2600rpm. Once again on a 9:1 comp ratio, and described with gross figures. This powerplant was fitted to the Cruise-O-Matic shifted Torino Brougham *Motor Trend* was evaluating, and elucidated this statement from Jim Brokaw: "Torino actually did some smokey wheel spinning."

The figures were 0-60mph in 9.6 seconds, 16.798 second ¼ mile at 82.87mph and an even 100mph top speed. The two-barrel 351 represented a $45 surcharge over the pedestrian 250 I6. Normally Broughams, Squires and GTs came with 302 V8/three-speed all synchro manual power team. Popular though the 302 was in such rides, including GT, it didn't have much punch in 2bbl form in such weighty cars. *Motor Trend*, *Consumer Report*, et al, mentioned that the base 5-liter V8s in midsize cars didn't cope well with power accessories. As pollution controls got tighter, power steering, brakes, bench, and a/c got burdensome.

Air-conditioning operation affected engine speed on base V8s, so it paid to power up! This was getting harder to do. Mighty GM and California swayed the nation to compression ratio drops as the method of choice to a cleaner, lead free world in 1971. Thus, compared to 1970 all Torino powerplants, bar the Cobra Jet 429s, had slightly lower compression ratios to accept low lead gas. So even the former 300 horse 11 to one CR 351 4bbl Cleveland, now made 285 ponies on a 10.7:1 CR. Torque declined from 380 to 370lb/ft at the same 3400rpm. This motor still needed high test gas, and could still be teamed with a four-speed.

Popular options were $30 F78-14 bias belted WSWs, $95 vinyl roof and a princely $407 for Selectaire a/c. A Trailer Towing Package was an extremely useful option on Torino – such packs on domestic cars had value beyond towing, given they included HD suspension, HD larger radiator and HD alternator. Torino GT brought many standard features, and that usual youth message.

In 1971 Torino GT involved standard non functional hoodscoop, color-keyed dual sports mirrors with left side remote control, tinted rear window, bias belted whitewall Wide Ovals, vent wing avoiding Direct-Aire Ventilation, locking steering column, hubcaps/trim rings, Uni-Lock Harness seatbelts, energy absorbing two-spoke steering wheel and aforementioned 2bbl 302/all synchro three-speed manual power team. Ads commenced with "Provocative.Functional.Durable. – They're a sporting set of better ideas," plus "Torino handles with flair at a price you can handle."

No ball of fire in an inter, but the 302 maximized gas mileage, minimized insurance premiums and saved money for all those other options. The 302 was the V6 of its era! Those tempting options were the familiar Laser Stripe decals, Magnum 500 styled steel 15in rims, Sports Slats louver shade rear window, Hurst shifter topped four-speed or Select Shift Cruise-O-Matic associated with various shorter sport axle ratios, High Back bucket seats and those Hideaway Headlamps. The Hideaway Headlamps were optional equipment on 1971 Torino 500, Brougham, Squire wagon and Cobra too.

On GT one could select the still 11.3:1 comp 370 horse 429 CJ motor, but that would blur the line with Cobra. Although Ford wasn't formally tied to Aston Martin at the time, Ford Torino 1971 Sales Literature carried a top down, front ¾ pose shot of a red GT SportsRoof with Magnum 500 rims. This ride resembled the contemporary Aston DBS. It was the upscale look Detroit was aiming for, with its latest sporty personal cars. The second gen Camaro RS semi bumperless nosecone, was inspired by Jag XJ6. AMC styling boss Dick Teague said 1971 Humpster Javelin had a big money look that marketing wanted. Mustang also had a sleeker, luxury look restyle for '71 MY.

Being fast alone wasn't enough anymore. However, Ford marketing's closing Torino GT line was "Your kind understands it." So Detroit was still pushing the youth message, even though the sporty car scene was quietly deflating under soaring insurance premiums. Important from a collector viewpoint, only 1613 Torino GT convertibles were sold in 1971. The end of the road for the midsize ragtop, luxury continued though, as 1971 Brougham brought more ornamentation outside and in.

Full wheelcovers, extra soundproofing and a front bench backrest angle that could be adjusted. However, that last feature required tools, not an easy seat knob to turn. Still, it was safer to smoke at night if the Courtesy Light Group was specified. This brought an ashtray with a bulb, very practical! Even more useful was Torino Squire wagon, and the 302 V8 it came with. That said, 1971 was probably the last year to be impractical, and impractical started with the word Cobra.

Available only in two-door SportsRoof configuration, Cobra still came with most of the good stuff, although its standard motor had depreciated somewhat. The 1971 base motor was now the 285 horse 351 4bbl Cleveland. Mind you, by now Chevelle SS was on a two-barrel 350 starter, so Henry was keeping things lively on Farm Ford! The other stuff was still handy. Stock equipment encompassed the familiar Hurst shifted four-speed, F70-14 rubber on 14 x 7in hubcapped steel rims, Cobra emblems/decals, Competition Suspension and blacked out grille.

In spite of industry wide, and within Torino range, CR drops, Cobra and some imports held on to the 1970 compression ratio. The 11.3:1 370 horse 429 was around, so too the 375bhp solid lifter 429 according to *Cars*, formerly part of the DP experience. It seemed Ford's 429 made it through intact from 1970. In 1970 a 16 page *Performance Digest* was available through the mail from Ford, or direct from Ford dealers. It showed the supercar hardware Torino offered. In *Cars* magazine's June 1971 issue, staff stated that such Super Cobra Jet parts, like forged racing pistons, could still be had from some dealers in 1971.

Cars tested what it thought would be the final hot Ford, in June 1971. The car chosen was a 1971 Torino Cobra Jet. The power team was the 370 horse 11.3:1 429 and C6 auto tranny. It didn't have the top 375bhp Drag Pack tune, and was loaded with convenience gizmos. These items involved console, stereo, a/c and power windows. Sports Slats backlight louvers, Laser Stripes and Shaker Ram Air induction hoodscoop were all present. This was one of only 3054 1971 Torino Cobras produced, and the only 1971 Cobra tested by a major journal.

It also seemed magazines only tested Cobras sans Hideaway lights. Ford had relaxed restrictions concerning matching hot 429s, with performance rear axles, because *Cars*' test Cobra had 370bhp 429 and Traction-Lok LSD with 3.50 gears. On G70-14 bias belted rubber, with 4100lb weight, this luxo supercar turned a 14.5 second ¼ mile at 102mph, with 0-60mph in 7.4 seconds. Forget about the Road Runner and Super Bee bench seat poverty interiors, with Torino Cobra one rode in style! It seemed Ford had done some special prepping of the yellow test car. It never delivered a trap speed under 100mph, or ¼ mile worse than 14.5 seconds!

The Polyglas GT tires were mentioned as a traction limiting factor. As per many hot cars back in the day, the Cobra had to be walked off the line, then nailed a little ways in! Otherwise it was all tire smoke and no action. Under full throttle the C6 autobox made appropriate changes at 5500-6 grand, just as well, because

6: Torino the Muscle Car 1970-73

the infamous Carousel tach was decried yet again for its lack of functionality. Competition suspension ensured zero roll handling on smooth surfaces. However, the ride was jittery on imperfect ones, with an observation that shocks were incorrectly tuned to springs.

It was fitting that this 'Soul Survivor,' last of the fast cars, was tested out by Joe Oldham. He tried out all the muscle and pony car illuminaries. On this occasion he even lined up the Cobra at the Christmas tree, next to *Cars*' Managing Editor Al Root in a '71 Mustang Mach 1. Both were pretty even in the 1320ft sprint. This magazine, and others on contemporary supercars, didn't much care for Cobra's 'over ornamentation;' however, the 370 horse 429 V8 was described as the best mill, post ye olde 427. It was a lot of car, but at over $5200 it wasn't that cheap. Plus, fewer people wanted this much car.

1972 Torino – Ford puts a better idea on wheels!

The 1971 market threw up an automotive conundrum. Small cars were very popular, and so too were big cars! Increasing numbers sought the benefits of compactness and thrift, but the full-size/luxo segment did none too shabby either. This left inters and ponies stuck in the middle. Torino sales were smaller in the carryover time of '71 MY, and declining pony interest was no new thing. Even though the intermediate segment didn't live up to industry wide expectations, Ford persevered. It thought Interland was still worth investing in, so Dearborn came up with an all-new Torino!

1972 Torino encompassed many style and engineering changes, including major chassis revisions. Taking a leaf out of Ford's big car book, '72 Torino went to a separate chassis. In doing so it took on the lessons learned from Lincoln Continental MkIII; that is, better ride, refinement and even handling could come from body on frame construction. To this end, Torino adopted an insulated perimeter chassis. Fairlane's familiar torque boxes were joined by 14 hollow rubber body mounts. Those mounts did a job damping out vibrations, with their number promoting rigidity.

Concerning rigidity, there were five solid crossmembers. There was an abutment for the front suspension's crossmember, and wagons came standard with an HD frame. Suspension was completely redeveloped; gone was Ford's old mainstay, the front MacPherson struts – instead, front unequal length control arms had computer-selected coil springs on the strut stabilized lower control arms: a setup not unlike the full-size LTD. Out back, apart from retaining the ubiquitous Detroit live axle, it was a whole new game.

From the 1962 inter start, family Fords had rear leafs; now they rode on rear coils, just like full-size Galaxie and LTD since '65 MY. However, Torino used a special four link 'Stabul' system, to locate

Above: An all original '72 GTS, with factory paint and Laser Stripes intact! This one owner GTS with optional Magnum 500 rims was picked up in November 1971. (Courtesy Rusty Rutherford)

Left: The strip speedo of 1970-71 was gone! In came Ford's deep-set, glare-fighting tumbler gauges that it used around the world in this era. The bottom left climate control panel worked an upgraded Torino a/c system for '72. No Performance Instrument Cluster on this luxo chariot. (Courtesy Rusty Rutherford)

aforementioned live axle. Once again, rear coil rates were optimally selected by computer. With lower rear roll center and increased roll understeer, Stabul promised to banish Detroit's traditional axle hop and axle tramp. Reduced acceleration squat, improved directional stability along with improved ride and handling were engineer goals.

One small step for Ford; one great leap for Torino kind!

Torino had made a refinement leap. Before 1972, its general chassis/suspension layout was Mustang like; now, it moved closer to that 'Big Car' feel that Ford started Fairlane/Torino on in 1970. It worked, according to *Motor Trend*'s Jim Brokaw. In March 1972 he gave the road manners edge to Torino, over Chevelle Malibu. Torino's rear suspension roll center being 8in off the ground seemed to contribute to a more stable high speed ride and less ride harshness, with good roadholding at low speed. Indeed, the front coils were rubber cushioned at the top, to stop road and axle noise getting through to the passenger compartment.

A side benefit of dumping MacPherson struts and their associated towers was more underhood space. Many V8 cars were known for tight engine bays maintenance-wise. For steering, the recirculating ball continued, but with many changes. To maintain reasonable feel with power steering Ford chose 'torsion bar link', rather than GM's variable ratio system. As ever, it was wise to specify power steer, now costing $115. It helped resale value, and cut the number of turns lock to lock from an unwieldy 5.7 to 3.7 turns. On resale value '72 Torino was second only to Chevelle in the family inter battle.

Engineering refinement saw a new steering column design introduced. It was the smaller/shorter Ford Pinto 'Mini' system. An energy absorbing design that stopped at the instrument panel's lower surface. The universal joint solid shaft had a special insulator coupling to the steering gear. Torino previously had an external linkage booster type. The new design had fewer moving parts, and was more compact and durable. The wheels that the whole shebang steered were 14in, or 15in on police and sometimes fleet cars.

Safety sells!

If '72 Torino went someway to restoring the Ford family car reputation as a handler, it also reignited Ford's pioneering passive autosafety work. The 1972 Torino, and Mercury Montego cousin, were the only domestic intermediates that came with front disk brakes as standard equipment. They weren't power assisted, that option was standard on 429 powered sedan/coupe and/or wagon, but Ford had a way to make non power disks work on a car this big. Lacking the natural assistance of drums, front non-power disks had been passable only on compacts and subcompacts.

So Ford used a lighter single piston floating caliper, with inner and outer brake pads working on both sides of the 10.72in ventilated disk brake. 10 x 2in drums lived at the ends of the live axle. The larger diameter single piston caliper allowed a 40% reduction in hydraulic line pressures, according to Ford. Thus, one didn't have to press that hard to get brake action. However, magazine reports stated

By going separate chassis during 1972-79, Ford's midsize had that 'Big Car' ride. However, it was very wise to spec the optional HD or even Competition Suspension, to avoid wallow. (Courtesy Rusty Rutherford)

6: Torino the Muscle Car 1970-73

that whilst the non-power disk action was lighter than usual, power disk was still easier, and better on a car this hefty.

Should the worst have happened, '72 Torino's separate chassis had S-shaped front frame members. This part of the frame was designed as a crumple zone, to progressively give way in a front end crash. Shock would be absorbed, with less reaching the passenger compartment. Body on frame construction had been criticized for being too rigid, and not absorbing crash forces like a unibody. Cosmetically, Torino's '72 bumpers had been redone to offer a bit more 'park by ear' protection, compared to 1971 Torinos. 1972 cars also had modification to their door latch override lock buttons.

Flush door handles and side impact door beams also improved safety. Integrated head restraints warded off whiplash. Base Torino seating was a new sculptured front bench. The seatback's outboard positions were raised approximately 8in, thus there was no need for separate head restraints. Ditto Torino's high backed bucket seats! 1972 Torino's electrical system featured a 'locking wedge connector,' and fuse panel with fewer circuits per fuse. The fuse panel was now located in a more accessible place, the left side dash below the instrument panel. Even the revised glovebox had safety type twist open latch!

That's original Ford factory blue! The '429-4V' air cleaner decal callout was more a call to cruise, than a call to arms, with these T-Bird-sourced motors. (Courtesy Rusty Rutherford)

New '72 Torino range variants

Matters kicked off simply with base Torino. Body styles were the usual suspects: two-door hardtop, four-door pillared hardtop, and family four-door wagon. Concerns over possible rollover testing from federal legislation, meant no pillarless four-door. In its place, a sedan with frameless door glass. Torino convertible had been deep sixed too! Move up to mid spec, and one encountered the new Gran Torino. Torino Brougham was now an offshoot option pack, with the expected niceties. These

Part of '72 Torino's new separate chassis was a ladder frame with 14 rubber hollow body mounts. (Courtesy Marc Cranswick)

Ford Midsize Muscle – Fairlane, Torino & Ranchero

By deep sixing the traditional Ford MacPherson struts, Henry created a roomy engine bay. So much so, this GTS' original 429 has been replaced with a Boss 429, backed by a TKO 5 speed manual! (Courtesy Marc Cranswick)

included nylon tricot upholstery, super foam and an extra pad for lumbar support.

Gran Torino and Gran Torino Squire were the upscale wagon versions. The latter came standard with roof luggage rack and translucent exterior wood trim paneling. As before, third row seating and Magic Door tailgate were optional, as were two tow packs. First the lighter duty Class II, rated at 3500lb. This didn't give sedan the HD frame that wagon already had, but came with shorter 3.25 rear axle ratio and required the 2bbl 351 V8 as a mandatory starting point – more tractible than the base 2.75 econoaxle. The Class III option carried a 6000lb rating, and bequeathed HD frame to sedan.

Class III tow pack also brought HD suspension, HD radiator, HD battery, aforementioned 3.25 rear gears and trailer wiring. Class III needed at least the optional 400 2bbl motor. A new addition to the range, the 400 2bbl was a high torque, family motor in the recent 335 Cleveland engine series, like 351C. Publicity material from Ford said 180 horse. However, the headline showroom act was the Gran Torino Sport or GTS; this new sports variant came as a coupe in Formal Hardtop or SportsRoof flavors.

The previous GT and Cobra variants were gone – GTS kinda covered both roles. Indeed, Ford had simplified the Torino range, reducing variants from 14 to nine. 1972 Torino represented a collaboration of Ford engineers, stylists and marketing, to get their intermediate back on the commercial track, whilst other midsize rivals floundered.

1972 Torino had completely new sheet metal, and you couldn't miss that grille. *Mechanix Illustrated*'s Tom McCahill certainly didn't. Uncle Tom noticed a resemblance between Torino's grille and the mouth of famous killer whale Namu, but of course Namu's mouth was smaller! What Henry Ford II thought about this observation is unknown.

'72 MY Torino came with a large egg crate, oval aperture grille. Base models with non full width visage, and Gran Torino sported a hatch hood. Gran Torino had chrome beauty bezels surrounding the front dual horizontal circular headlamps, and body-colored sheetmetal covered the space between its headlamps and grille. Gran Torino regular had dual vertical overrider bumper bars, front and rear. They also had a Gran Torino trunk crest badge, in the middle of said trunk panel's leading edge. GTS cars had one on the driver side front grille, between the hood's Ford 'R' and 'D' chrome letters.

Overall Torino styling was low, wide hipped and long. There was a kick up over the rear wheel housings. Flared fenders on a family ride? It suggested mechanical muscle! For practicality Ford leaned out the roof, there were slimmer A pillars, and SportsRoof had its C pillars canted. Thus, in spite of a 60 degree windshield angle rake, this was one inter that the driver could see out of! Plus, there were no vent wings to obstruct side vision. This last fact implied Ford's DirectAire ventilation system was standard across the range.

1972 Torino dimensions

However, it was often noted how sporty SportsRoofs' rear styling was a detriment to rear headroom. This explained why some GTS buyers chose the Formal

Hardtop route. As for space, outside and in, Ford followed Big 3 rivals by having separate wheelbases for two- and four-door variants. GM was first on this street, and Chrysler did the same for '71 MY. Now, two-door Torinos rode on a 114in wheelbase, with four-doors on 118in. Many thought different wheelbases were good for looks, and made the four-door sedan and wagon more commodious.

A two-door hardtop was 203.7in long, 79.3in wide and 51.8in high. Fancier GTS was 207.3in long, and Gran Torino wagon 215.1in long. Two-door 79.3in width was 2.5in up, and the 80in of wagon was 4.6in greater. To help handling, front and rear track were also increased. On sedan front and rear track of 62.8in/62.9in were 2.3in and 2.9in up respectively, versus the '71s. Concerning wagon, front and rear tracks now rested at 63.9in front and 64in rear. These were 3.4in and 4in increases over the '71 stats. Two and four-door sedans were slightly lower in height. At 54.7in, wagon was 1.4in down too.

1972 Torino lived up to the American ideal of long, low and wide. It was refined, with the new car acknowledged as having low wind noise, and NVH transmitted to occupants. It was a body of good aero, but the refinement quality carried a weight penalty. The model weight range was 3629lb to 4183lb. Trunk volume was 14.8ft³, with gas tank capacity at 22.5 gallons. With the changing '70s inflation/energy picture, it was up to buyers to decide if a V8-powered midsize was still practical.

'72 Torino powerplants
There was an amended range of motors for '72 MY. This was due to tightening emissions law, and the associated drop in compression ratios. The future looked like zero lead, so, to start with, Ford's fleet had to run on 91 octane regular low lead gas. Those muscle car high test days were fast disappearing in the rear view mirror. With GM being behind this route to a greener planet, it's no surprise its '71s could sup no

The all-new Gran Torino Sport had a starring role in the Barry Newman movie *Fear Is The Key*. This GTS wears the 2B Bright Red color, made famous by the *Starsky & Hutch* GTS. It also came 351W 2bbl-equipped. (Courtesy Kevin Dohner)

This 351W has Comp Cams XE274 hydraulic cam, Trick Flow TW heads, 10:1 Hypereutectic pistons, and Ford Duraspark electronic ignition. (Courtesy Kevin Dohner)

lead gas! Ford literature made no mention on its 1972 engines being safe for no lead. Thus, like AMC owners, the Ford crowd filled with leaded every fourth tankful, just to be on the safe side.

The precaution was to ward off VSR (Valve Seat Recession). Using leaded gas deposited lead on the base of the valve, protecting it from wear. In the absence of lead, hardened valve seats are required. It seems Ford engines of this era weren't ready for no lead, because owners running motors like a '72 2bbl 351 Windsor on unleaded, have experienced valve damage. Ford's '72 engine changes were right out of the emissions control playbook. The idea was to get a better running engine, leaner fuel mix, and more thorough burn.

To that end, transmission spark control, mechanical fuel bowl vents on two-barrel carbs, staged carb choke action, and new carb heat system to speed carb warm up, jumped on Henry's wagon. The last item tried to get the motor off choke sooner, to improve emissions. To battle the increased thermal load, a new 28in crossflow radiator was introduced. A new 14in diameter air cleaner topped off the engine bay. As per others, Ford's '72 powerplants carried net flywheel horsepower ratings. This made the 1971 to 1972 transition seem worse than it actually was.

Try 113 horse for the increasingly humble 250ci I6 or 130bhp for the 2bbl 302. The latter was the base motor in Gran Torino Squire and Gran Torino Sport. Next up were 351W (Windsor) and 351C (Cleveland), with those two-barrel engines sporting a 165bhp power label. The handy, all purpose 400 two-barrel V8 was a Cleveland family member, with 180 horse attributed. Then came Ford's two performance motors, which early literature named as possessing 220 horses. These were the four-barrel 429 and 351CJ. Gone were the premium fuel swilling high CR 429s. This 429 was luxo Thunderbird derived, not a NASCAR mover and shaker.

More hopeful was the Cobra Jet Cleveland 351, which many considered the only real performer supercarwise. Ford carefully developed this motor to deliver high output on 91 octane juice. The specification sheet, suggested Ford had the right stuff. Although a hydraulic lifter V8, one would still find four bolt mains, large oval intake and exhaust ports, plus an intake manifold, designed to center the intake ports of the 750 CFM Motorcraft 4300 D carb, that Henry included. But wait, there was more! Sports cam worked with special valve springs/dampers, with exhaust gases exiting courtesy of a 2.5in dual exhaust system. Sounded good, even on regular!

Motor Trend sampled a couple of the engines in March 1972. A 2bbl 351 in Torino GTS and 429 in a Broughamed four-door. Quoted figures were 161bhp at four grand and 276lb/ft at two grand on an 8.6:1 CR for the 351. The big incher belted out 205 horse at 4400rpm, with 322lb/ft at 2600rpm on 8.5 CR. In 1971 the base 429 still had 10.5:1 comp and made 360 gross ponies. The *Motor Trend* GTS weighed 4040lb, did 0-60mph in 10.7 seconds with the ¼ mile accomplished in 17.9 seconds at 80mph. 1970 equivalent figures were 3551lb, 8.7 seconds and 16.5 seconds at 86.6mph. The 1972 429 Brougham four-door held up better. A grand 4250lb, but 0-60mph in 10.1 seconds and the ¼ mile in 17.3 seconds at 82mph. Once again 1970 equivalent stats for a like bodied car were 3913lb, 8.8 seconds and 16.7 seconds at 86.1mph. Big inch torque seemed to slow the performance decline. However,

Bored over 0.030, and drinking through a QFT SS735 aluminum carb. The V8 exhales through dual mandrel bent 3in exhaust, with ceramic pads and shoes bringing the GTS to a halt. (Courtesy Kevin Dohner)

6: Torino the Muscle Car 1970-73

Motor Trend's 1972 Pontiac GTO 455 HO weighed a mere 3885lb.

This indicated the price Gran Torino paid for being so grand, with that big car feel. No major publication sampled a GTS with the 429 big block. They all focused on 351CJ-motivated editions that were grabbing the headlines. Quoted power and torque figures for the regular gas 351CJ motor were all over the place: *Car and Driver*'s September 1971 Gran Torino Preview article reported 280bhp at 5800rpm and 345lb/ft at 3800rpm on a 9:1 comp ratio; testing a four-speed, 351CJ SportsRoof GTS with performance 3.50 rear end, 0-60mph in a scant 6.8 seconds was gleaned!

This was lineball with the also previewed Fairlane GT/A 390 that *Motor Trend* covered in October 1965. However, 6.8 seconds in 1972 was a greater achievement given pollution controls and Gran Torino's luxo girth – and you could have Ram Air induction. The GTS came with a hoodscoop, like on 1970-71 Torino GTs. It was a broad, forward facing, non-functional item as stock. However, some GTS cars were specified with functional Ram Air. It was available with 351CJ and 429 V8 options, but didn't alter the GTS' exterior appearance, and was pretty rare. No shakers in 1972, and 1972 would prove to be the final year for fresh air induction. California drive-by noise regulations were a factor in Ford (and others) planning to drop the feature!

From the driver's seat!
Inside, one couldn't miss the new dashboard, with functional, circular instrumentation. No more strip speedo or Carousel Tach! The new dashboard had a top trim panel made of steel, foam padding for the top and vertical panel face. All covered by a one-piece injection-molded ABS plastic overlay. Standard '72 Torinos had an extreme left circular dash aperture, for the standard DirectAire vent system. Next were speedo/odometer and clock, plus the usual 'too late to help' idiot lights. However, spring for optional Performance Instrumentation, and one received an additional bank of five small circular gauges, displaying vital readouts.

By the time an idiot light starts blinking, it's already game over! However, Ford's two in the top row, three in the second lower row, provided some peace of mind. From top left, they told of fuel level, then water temp, and on the second row were ammeter, oil pressure and clock – never underestimate the importance of an accurate timepiece in the '60s and '70s! It had the traditional sporty car white markings, on black gauge faces, and deep set, canted instrument tubes, aimed at a single driver eyeline focal point. Ford were using this deep set circular instrument style

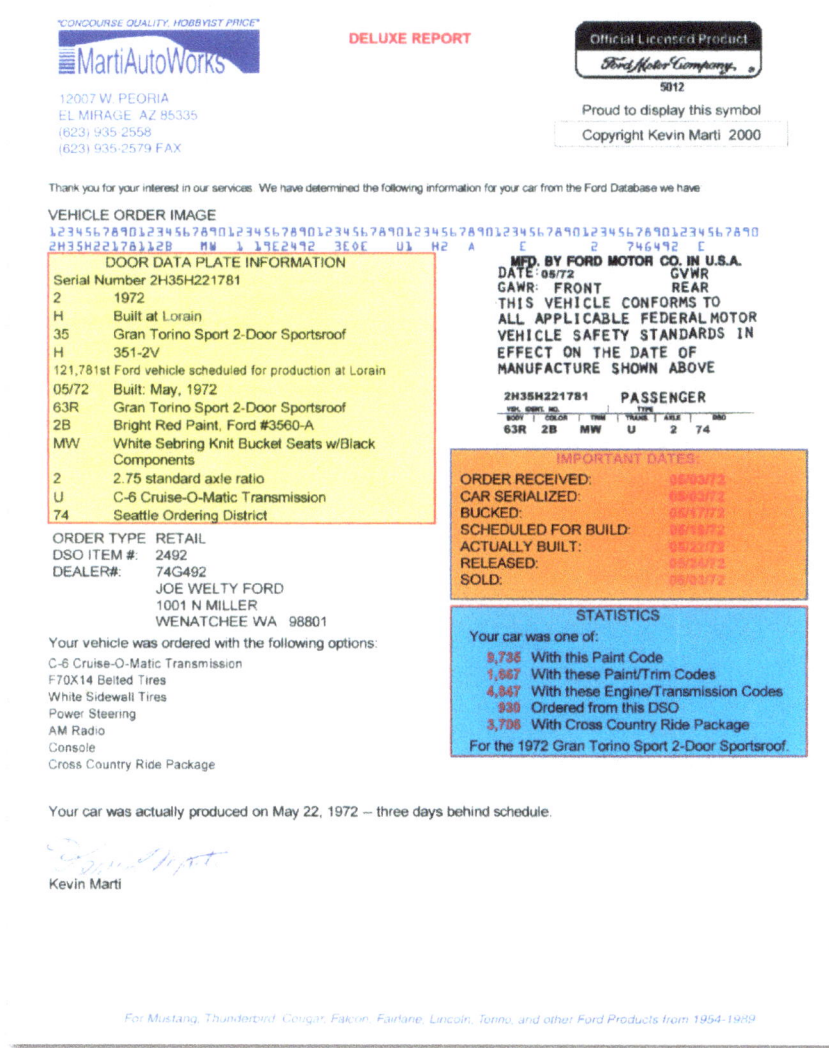

This Marti Report confirms the 2B Bright Red exterior, and 351W motor. Not so the American Racing rims! (Courtesy Kevin Dohner)

in German, English and Australian Fords. Along with deep set tubes, the hooded, cliff face style dashboard molding, avoided sunlight reflections, in theory.

The deep set gauges could be a little hard to read, if you were shorter than the typical male driver such cars were designed for. However, regardless of legibility, designers probably reasoned that owners would spend more time checking out a hot chick at the traffic lights. Another reason to specify automatic transmission?! You see, Ford engineered a special C6 for the hi po 351CJ. Specifically a 10¼in diameter torque converter, with 2500rpm high stall speed, tailored to 351CJ's peak power operation. Combined with the Traction-Lok LSD still available, and 3.50 rear gears, Ford were making sure one's GTS hooked up just right!

Driving the new Torinos!

A high-performance scenario calls for a cool head, and beyond standard DirectAire Henry had Selectaire. At $412 it cost five bucks more than in 1971, but had been completely rejigged for more performance. A larger condenser, new evaporator, icing control system, new operator control head and high placed vent outlets. Ford claimed the new setup provided nearly 21% more airflow. It was part of Ford's plan from 1970, to make midsize as appealing as full-size. There was zero doubt stock Torino suspension was comfy, but the land yacht wallow was alien to the once good handling family Fords.

Critics felt that roadability made the HD suspension option practically mandatory. This added the usual HD springs and shocks. When *Car and Driver* sampled preview GTS cars for its September 1971 article, it tried versions with and without Competition Suspension. The second GTS tried had the Competition Suspension, and was judged to make GTS handle and ride better. It didn't make GTS a slot car racer, just more acceptable as an overall roadcar. Perhaps the American Supercar was growing up? Magazine consensus was that pre 1972 optional suspensions created real teeth rattlers.

Competition Suspension used HD suspension's firmer shocks and stiffer springs, added a larger diameter front swaybar and a 0.072in rear swaybar. Smaller, firmer bushings for front suspension link connections, were also part of the equation. This was the first time Torino had received a rear swaybar. Before, handling was done by just stiffening the suspension. However, '72 Torino chassis meant good handling could come from control, rather than harshness. Apart from the insulation effect of 14 hollow rubber body mounts, insulation packs kept Torino refined.

1972 Torinos had a new optional deluxe sound insulation package that weighed 40lb more than Torino's stock pack, and 15lb over the deluxe pack of 1971. Ford predicted 85% of '72 Torino variants would feature the optional pack. It was created using state of the art electronic acoustic equipment. So it was that the new Torino, especially Gran Torino, embodied modified rapture: some sport and lots of luxury. Insurance companies and smog law put paid to the youthful dream that was 10mpg, 400 horse, 4000lb, laser striped hedonistic benders of old!

Actually, those Laser Stripes were still on the option sheet, and now ran the entire length of the car. Then there was Ram Air induction. However, *Motor Trend*'s March 1972 report showed that not all GTS cars were flyers. The GTS had the 2bbl 351, Windsor or Cleveland, it depended what was in stock on the assembly line. Auto trans along with manual Torino disk/drum brakes were standard equipment too. Those in the know specified their GTS with the Rallye Equipment Group. Normally a GTS SportsRoof came with F70-14 tires, the hardtop with E70-14s. However, Rally Equipment Group (REG) brought G70-14in rubber for the 14 x 6in steel rims. No 7in-wide rims by this hour.

REG also implied a 351CJ motor or 429 V8, both four-barrel engines, teamed

6: Torino the Muscle Car 1970-73

with a genuine four-speed, Competition Suspension and Performance Instrument Cluster. *Road Test* titled its September 1971 preview article on the '72 Torinos appropriately, "Ford de-emphasizes performance!" Before, advertising spelt out which was the hot setup. Now, it was understood informally that the 351CJ, was the motor to have. *Car and Driver* observed in September 1971, that it wasn't happy up to 3500rpm, but came on song thereafter.

In December 1972, *Cars* magazine, pointed out the also informal understanding that one had to bypass REG's stock four-speed. Instead, go for the specially calibrated C6 reserved for the 351CJ. One paid a small surcharge for the slushbox. REG's four-speed offered one of the few places in 1972 Detroit, to nab a car with four on da floor … and duals! You had to concede its effectiveness. *Cars'* December 1972 report on an automatic REG 351CJ GTS SportsRoof, showed a 15.4 second pass at 86mph. *Motor Trend's* June 1972 quartet comparo article had a four-speed Pontiac GTO 455 HO, with 300 net horses on 15.4 seconds at 92mph.

GTS on the silver screen & racetrack!

In 1972 it seemed fast class went with fast glass, a/c and an acoustic chamber pack. It also made GTS a star on the big screen. In 1971 actor Barry Newman famously drove a white 1970 Dodge Challenger R/T 440 in *Vanishing Point*. It seemed to cement that ride's already established high-performance image. Not so well known, is the fact that the following year Barry Newman also starred in an action thriller, which also featured an iconic muscle car doing outlandish stunts. The movie was 1972's *Fear Is The Key*.

In *Fear Is The Key*, Newman played a man trying to bring to justice, the people behind the death of his family. The movie contained a rough and tumble car chase sequence, over seven minutes long. Here, Newman's character purloined a street parked '72 red GTS 351CJ SportsRoof

automatic, to evade cops. One car was used for the stuntwork. It was just as well Henry brought back a sturdy, shock absorbing separate chassis, because this machine took one heck of a pounding! This included a jump onto a departing river ferry, that saw the trunklid pop open on landing!

More worrying was the bent frame the Gran Torino Sport suffered. Somehow the vehicle was fixed up to carry on with part

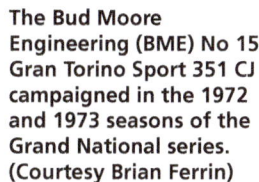

The Bud Moore Engineering (BME) No 15 Gran Torino Sport 351 CJ campaigned in the 1972 and 1973 seasons of the Grand National series. (Courtesy Brian Ferrin)

The iconic Top Loader four-speed, worked by racing legends David Pearson and Bobby Isaac. Pearson secured a 4th at Atlanta in 1972. (Courtesy Brian Ferrin)

Grand National World Champion Bobby Isaac managed a 2nd at the Daytona 500. It was his second outing in the BME GTS. He was runner-up to Richard Petty, no less! (Courtesy Brian Ferrin)

two of the chase post ferry. Obviously the same car, with windshield cracks consistent with the ones picked up earlier from traversing 'thank-you-m'am' big bumps, there were no Bullit style Mustang beauty shots possible, once the dust had settled. Just one beat up GTS slithering away from vanquished cops! Equaly risky maneuvers were visible on the nation's racetracks, courtesy of Bud Moore Engineering, Bobby Isaac and '72 GTS!

Even though the years of big Ford involvement had passed, that '72 GTS SportsRoof was in NASCAR. Raced by heroes like Dick Brooks and Bobby Allison at speeds over 150mph, and using a hot 429 like you couldn't get in a production car anymore. There was even a Jo Han created red model version of this era of racer. However, even more noteworthy was the version campaigned by Bud Moore Engineering. Bud Moore's operation had achieved success in SCCA Trans Am racing. The famous 1970 championship victory with Parnelli Jones, in a Boss 302 Windsor Mustang.

Concerning handling, Bud Moore understood the benefits of less weight in the nose. A small block V8 typically weighs 200lb less than a big block. It's like having a large man strapped to the hood of your ride – definitely going to promote understeer! On a race car it spelt a harder life for tires. Even on ovals, handling matters, so Bud Moore applied small block virtue to what was the Grand National series at the time. Not a Windsor, but the slightly larger Cleveland 351CJ. The kind that occupied top dog status, in the 1972 Torino road car performance options list.

Quite something, seeing that high output '351CJ' signage on the hood. It foretold the American V8's modern, small displacement future. Bud Moore was just testing the waters in 1972. However, in nine race outings David Pearson did bring the GTS 351CJ home in 4th place at Atlanta. A full scale campaign took place in 1973. Bud Moore Engineering got major sponsor Sta-Power, and star power in the form of Bobby Isaac.

1970 Grand National World Champion Isaac was signed up as a full time driver. He stepped into the No 15 GTS 351CJ that BME ran in the 1972 and 1973 racing seasons. Isaac's first race, at Riverside, resulted in a DNF after 61 laps, due to engine trouble. However, his second race, at the Daytona 500, saw Isaac finish 2nd to Richard Petty. Bobby Isaac chalked up five top five results, six in the top ten. Then came the infamous 1973 Talladega 500. There was a halfway distance, 21 car

6: Torino the Muscle Car 1970-73

racing accident, that claimed the life of racer Larry Smith.

A few laps later, Isaac pulled into the pits and told Bud Moore he was retiring from racing. Bobby Isaac then left the track, although he did return to racing again for the 1974 season. Concerning the remainder of the 1973 racing season, Darrell Waltrip took over the GTS 351CJ. Waltrip managed a best showing of 8th at Darlington. After the 1973 racing season, BME sold the white and blue liveried No 15 GTS 351CJ to D&M Engineering in Florida. The car then went to Ron Spohn of Monroe, North Carolina, who did ARCA races then stored it in his shop.

In 1986 Bill Bradford of Huntsville NC purchased the GTS, and commissioned Kim Haynes of RACEtorations, to restore the No 15 classic. It was then unveiled at SAAC-23, held at Lowes Motor Speedway, and subsequently featured in a Sunoco TV commercial. The car was displayed at the North Carolina Motorsports Museum from 1990 until 2008, and was then purchased by a collector who entered it in Historic Grand National Group racing.

As a sign of what the Cleveland V8 was producing back in the BME days, the No 15 car's 351CJ was tuned to make 475 net horses and 440lb/ft in such historic racing. It was also backed by the classic Top Loader four-speed. A veteran of two Wine Country Classic events, the No 15 GTS 351CJ is the only surviving BME Torino. In 2009 it was displayed at the Monterey Motorsports Reunion event called 'The Quail. A Motorsports Gathering.' Track success heartened Henry, but showroom prowess made money for Ford, and here '72 Torino delivered.

As the only new inter for 1972, Torino notched up 496,645 sales, outselling mighty nemesis Chevelle for the first time since that Chevy's 1964 debut interwise. Ford's efforts in sticking with the midsize concept seemed to have paid off. 1972 Torino even garnered a Consumer Guide '72 'Best Buy' award. Apart from such practicalities, it seemed the public just plain dug the Torino's wide hipped, broad shouldered look, in a segment where style mattered. This was a big part of why Torino was tops, and clean looking Olds Cutlass edged out Chevy in the 1972 sales stakes. It seemed that 1972 intership had sailed, sans GM!

1973 Torino – keeping Allstate happy!

If anything was going to upset Ford's Torino mantra, it was the insurance companies. Not happy about paying out for low speed parking lot snafus, the insurance companies applied political lobby group pressure to get Detroit, and

With its SCCA Trans Am know-how, BME believed in the handling benefits of a lightweight motor. This 351CJ makes 475 horse net! (Courtesy Brian Ferrin)

129

Ford Midsize Muscle – Fairlane, Torino & Ranchero

Top: A 1973 Goldglow Gran Torino 351C wagon. To haul over 4000lb, the optional Cleveland V8 was a necessity, not a luxury.

Bottom: In wagon we trust! Before SUVs came along, the family wagon was the dependable truckster: just ask Clark W Griswald! (Courtesy Flip van Swaay)

others, to beef up bumper bars. Plus, redesign front and rear fascias, so lighting, a/c condensers, and grille work were less likely to get damaged. This way they could keep insurance premiums, and not have to pay anything out. It was like a modern day loaves and fishes miracle, except Joe Q Public wasn't getting any fish or bread!

So it was that the '73s had to withstand front 5mph impacts and 2.5mph rear shunts, sans safety related equipment damage. The insurance companies promised this would lead to lower long-term premiums, but no one was holding their breath! The front 5mph/rear 2.5mph bumper law made '73 MY domestics look unbalanced. Imports got around the rulebook until 1974. The new laws required Ford and others to do much re-engineering. Unfortunately, that meant straightening, and stiffening, Torino's formerly 'S' shaped, controlled collapse front separate chassis frame members.

Ford's 1972 chassis got around the usual criticism, that 'body on a frame construction' was too rigid, and transferred too much shock to the passenger compartment. The 1973 changes undid that good work, and reinforced the belief that the new bumper laws were about protecting the car, not the occupants. Those new bumpers upset weight distribution, and introduced vibration on rough roads, during initial '73 Torino trials. So Ford, using computer assistance, had to work out optimal

6: Torino the Muscle Car 1970-73

adjustments to spring rates, spring travel, shock absorber length, wheels, tires, plus body and engine mounts.

All the changes, so consumers wouldn't notice any difference. In ultimate form, a GTS SportsRoof with Competition Suspension, *Car and Driver* in July 1973 judged Ford's ride/handling compromise as superior to Chevy with GM's sports suspension. However, the bumpers added over 100lb, mostly to the front, and made Torino more of an understeerer than previously. Horsepower was down across the industry, but all dimensions and weight were up! Length ranged from 208-215.6in for wagon. Sedan and coupe were 79.3in wide, with the wagon narrower at 79in. Height went from 52.1in to 54.9in, weight from 3731lb to 4213lb. Trunk capacity had minimum of 14.8ft^3 to max of 16ft^3.

Optioning up Torino!
Like Chevelle, the '73 Torino's styling wasn't judged as favorably as the '72s. The front bumper was a substantial impact beam, with vertical bumper guards optional. The rear bumper looked like the 1972 item, with the addition of a horizontal impact pad lying between taillights and vertical bumper guards. The firewall forward sheetmetal was new, with distinction between Torino and Gran Torino being that between regular and upscale highline. On Torino a wider full width grille surrounding headlamps, with parking lights placed on the outer fascia edge, in plastic fender caps.

Gran Torino continued with classy separate beauty grille, with parking lights moved from '72 bumper position to horizontal placement within aforementioned rectangular grille. As before Gran Torino had dual round headlights, surrounded by chrome bezels. Gran Torino medallion was moved to mid grille, with said item returning as trunklid lock concealer. Hood and front fenders were shared between Torino and Gran Torino, to keep the bean counters happy! The upscale Gran Torino Brougham made 'em even happier!

Brougham was a distinct model once again, after its 1972 option pack status. The luxo two-door hardtop and frameless four-door brought the finest in upholsteries, including fine nylon cloth fabrics and leather like vinyl. Standard front bench, had a fold down armrest. Instruments lived in a woodgrain panel, plus there were deluxe steering wheel, electric clock, bright pedal pad trim and dual note horn, to complete that Continental feeling! Complimenting Brougham, was a like trimmed Gran Torino Squire wagon. This highline suburban chariot came with the expected simulated side wood trim and chrome roof rack.

Nice, but enthusiasts would look to the Gran Torino Sport. For '73 MY, GTS was offered again in Formal two-door Hardtop and two-door SportsRoof. GTS

This '73 GTS Formal Roof Hardtop has all the good stuff. That is, 351 CJ V8, Competition Suspension, G70-14 tires, on $116.99 Magnum 500 rims. Plus, Laser Stripes, Rally Equipment Group with Sports Instrumentation Group. Even the $21.35 surcharge for motor matched Select-Shift COM automatic! (Courtesy Michael Liebenberg)

The 351 CJ motor was the last specialist high performance motor in Ford's midsize lineup; it was shared with Pantera. Like Chrysler's Magnum 340 and Pontiac's W72 400, Ford went into smaller V8s for speed, in the smogger/gas crisis years. (Courtesy Michael Liebenberg)

Ford Midsize Muscle – Fairlane, Torino & Ranchero

This '73 MY GTS shows Torino's carryover dash design from 1972. The infamous 'Carousel Tach' departed at the close of '71 MY. (Courtesy Michael Liebenberg)

The rear fascia of 1973 was just like the previous year, save for the addition of 'between the taillights' impact pad and vertical bumper guards. (Courtesy Michael Liebenberg)

and Gran Torino Squire, came with the 2bbl 140 horse 302 V8 standard. All other range cohorts were fitted with the humble 98bhp 250ci I6! The only big standard item was price – on Gran Torino figure $3094. Fortunately, one could still jazz up GTS, with body length running $37.99 Laser Stripe decal, now designed to ride higher on said body. Ivy Glow paint was another $37.99 option, as were $402.24 a/c and $32 leather wrapped steering wheel.

There was one essential option on many Torinos, a gearbox. 250/302ci powered cars came with a three-speed manual standard, Cobra Jet cars the four-speed stick. However, manual transmission wasn't available on 2bbl 351, 400 or 429ci motors. Given automatic transmission was an option, technically such motorvated Torinos and Gran Torinos came minus a gearbox! This canny sleight of hand produced a lower, more attractive base sticker price. The $385.37 Rally Equipment Group was an enthusiast must-have. Applied to Gran Torino two-door it brought high output 351CJ 4bbl Cleveland V8, Competition Suspension, Performance Instrument Cluster, G70-14 tires on 6in wide rims and that four-speed.

One of the last chances to get a muscle car factory equipped with four on the floor and duals. However, there was a $21.35 cover charge for the performance 351CJ calibrated Select Shift Cruise-O-Matic sports autobox with 2500rpm lock up torque converter. This automatic maximized the acceleration of a motor shared with De Tomaso Pantera! Less glamorous, but important, were the detail improvements Ford put into '73 Torino. For security, the hoodlatch mechanism, now resided inside the car. The windshield washer bottle had its capacity boosted to 80 fluid ounces.

Coolant recovery system and the usual HD radiator were Torino options, standard with Class III Trailer Towing Package. A spare tire lock was optional. New federal standards mandated less flammable seating surfaces. So, said surfaces were treated, with flame retardant chemicals. This made cloth seating more prone to soiling and color fading. Going into '73, a new 460 four-barrel 'Interceptor' Package was available to cops. Given the 429 4bbl was down to 208 net horses, performance fiends were wise to frequent police auctions, and fleet disposal outlets, looking for an ex 460ci cop car!

Hello 400M!

'73 Torino continued with manual front disks as standard equipment, and added

6: Torino the Muscle Car 1970-73

Being named after Italy's Detroit, Torino was right at home next to Enzo's finest! More than that, '73 GTS' 351CJ V8 was shared with that Italian Stallion known as Pantera! (Courtesy Michael Liebenberg)

larger 11 x 2.2in rear drums. Important, given the '73 MY weight additions. Safety also, from low back bench seats, with separate head restraints which improved rearwards vision. The high back buckets continued as before. Sensible too, was the 400 2bbl V8 powerplant. For those not into racer Cobra Jet, but liking the 385 series torque combined with Windsor gas mileage, 400M was the ticket.

From '72 MY, Torino featured a safety twist open glovebox latch. In its July '73 issue, *Car and Driver* noted its GTS 351 CJ SportsRoof auto was one decibel quieter at 70mph than an 11 grand Jag XJ12! (Courtesy Michael Liebenberg)

Present in the Torino lineup from 1972, 400M made 1971 debut, as the last new OHV passenger car V8 designed by FoMoCo. The M-block V8 (Modified) achieved its 400ci by having the tallest deck height (10.297in) and longest stroke of any small block Ford V8. Indeed, the motor was actually 402ci. This versatile member of the 335 family, had the Cleveland's integrated timing cover casting at the block's front, to which the radiator hose connects. However, it also had an automatic gearbox bell housing pattern like a 385 series big block, so a high torque C6 could be harnessed.

Finding the real 351CJ!
Some M-blocks came with a dual style bell housing, allowing them to connect to lighter duty FMX auto, in lower horsepower, weight saving applications. The 400M utilized Windsor size 3in main bearing journals, plus featured 4in bore and stroke. Good value for the family car man, but, in the smog era, speed freaks had to search out that hot setup. On the surface, this was the 351CJ/auto power team, but what could it really do? *Car and*

Ford Midsize Muscle – Fairlane, Torino & Ranchero

If it looks like a muscle car, and quacks like a muscle car, then, in the case of this 100% stock '73 GTS 351CJ SportsRoof, it IS a muscle car! (Courtesy Alan & Robin Aaskov www.alyssasmotel.com)

Left: The final year for Ford's Laser Stripe decal (1970-73). Combined with 4 on da floor, 351CJ and Magnum 500 rims, how else would one order their muscle car? According to Ford's order blanks, let me count the ways …!

Right: In '73 MY, the hi po 351CJ motor was limited to two-door Formal Hardtop and SportsRoof. Four-speed was standard, and the only four-speed power team Ford offered in '73 midsize. (Courtesy Alan & Robin Aaskov www.alyssasmotel.com)

Driver's September 1971 preview of a pre production four-speed GTS SportsRoof suggested 0-60mph in 6.8 seconds – the same time as the pre production '66 Fairlane GT/A 390 *Motor Trend* tried in October 1965.

Quite an achievement given the emissions hurdles for 1972. Ford's publicity pictures for GTS SportsRoof 351CJ, including one with smoky burnout, all involved one automatic transmission car with Competition Suspension. This was the second car *Car and Driver* tried, after sampling the four-speed non Competition Suspension GTS. That car had more pitch and roll than a 1930s ocean liner crossing a stormy Atlantic! The 351CJ motor's introduction in 1972 Torino was delayed, by said motor's inability to meet Californian smog dictates. How many of the promised 280 ponies actually made it through?

The 351CJ four-barrel V8 had been seen in the latter stages of 1971 MY Mustang. The Q code 351CJ four-barrel V8 was a low compression ratio hydraulic lifter, four bolt main motor available from May 1971 to 1974. Like the solid lifter R code 351s, all 335 series Cleveland V8s either had four bolt mains, or provision for them. There were high CR and low CR R code 351Cs, and like Q code 351CJ, they were open

6: Torino the Muscle Car 1970-73

Left: Optioning a 351CJ guaranteed one a gearbox! With Ford chicanery, an engine of 351ci, or larger, technically didn't come with a gearbox, unless one optioned Cruise-O-Matic. The Fair Trade Commission never troubled Henry over the suspect base sticker!

Right: Hurst-shifted four-speed and 'Love Bench' may have seemed incongruous. However, kissing over a console was just plain awkward. Bucket seats spelt lonely! (Courtesy Alan & Robin Aaskov www.alyssasmotel.com)

chambered. Q code's 750 CFM 4300-D Motorcraft carb and dual point distributor spelt 280 horse, in those '71 Stangs.

Once the smog haze had cleared, 1972 Mustangs and Torinos, with aforementioned Q code, were rated at 266bhp and 248bhp, respectively. That smoky burnout '72 GTS SportsRoof that Ford liked to show off, had 280bhp. According to *Cars*' December 1972 report on GTS SportsRoof with 351CJ, the numbers were 266 horses and 0-60mph in 8.9 seconds, for an automatic. This article gave compression ratio as 9.2:1; however, early 280bhp Ford material said 9:1. Clouding matters further were the stats recorded in *Car and Driver*'s July 1973 report on a '73 GTS SportsRoof automatic.

By 1973 Torino's 351CJ V8 was down to 246bhp on an 8:1 CR, Mustang remained on 266 ponies. However, C&D's GTS was pretty fleet of foot. 0-60mph in 7.7 seconds. 0-70mph in under 10 seconds, OK, only just at 9.9 seconds, and 16 second ¼ mile at 88.1mph, with fuel economy range of 10-13mpg. Satisfactory gas mileage pre-fuel crisis, and those figures were recorded on 'vin ordinaire' regular gas. C&D noted that Torino shared this motor with Pantera, but still felt this Cobra Jet mill paled next to those hot 429s of old.

However, realise that this was a 4308lb inter with mere 351 lugging a/c, fast glass and 32 buck leather wrapped tiller. The 1973 $5169.56 GTS 351CJ recorded a mere 80dBA, with pedal to the metal. An 11 grand Jag XJ12 registered 79dBA. C&D's test example had $116.99 Magnum 500 chrome rims, with its $385.37 Rally Equipment Group guaranteeing G70-14 rubber on the 6in wide, 14in five bolt chrome plated rims. Wearing Goodyear Polyglas bias belted tires C&D's GTS beat out Chevy Monte Carlo S, Olds Cutlass S, and even little AMC Hornet X Hatch, in a braking comparo from 70mph. At 188 feet, GTS stopped 20ft shorter than its nearest rival. Front/rear brake bias was judged perfect. 1973 saw radials become available for the first time in the Torino line. However, GTS' braking, ride and handling were pretty good on bias belted tires. GTS was more than a one trick pony!

Car and Driver kicked off its GTS article, mentioning Ford dealers were saying Torino more times than an Alitalia booking agent! Such was Torino's popularity, and in the bumper sales year of 1973 Torino was still a good way to fly. At the time Mustang was fading, with Pinto based Mustang II waiting in the wings. Ready to inject better commercial, if not underhood, performance. 1973 Torino stepped up with 496,581 unit sales, nearly 170,000 stronger than Chevelle, and you can bet GM was counting! The success wasn't limited to Torino. It had cousins in dealerships close, and not so close, to home.

Montego, Cyclone & Road Warrior Falcon!

The 1968 Mercury Cyclone GT ad spelt it out loud and clear, "Mercury Cyclone GT. Fast-backed, 4-stacked. Radial-tracked." Truth to tell, radial tires weren't around, and one has to suspend belief a little,

Ford Midsize Muscle – Fairlane, Torino & Ranchero

By '73 MY, it was Torino, not Mustang, that was bringing home the bacon for Ford. The fact that Chevrolet messed up '73 Chevelle's launch helped Henry. Headroom-wise, Formal Hardtop was more amenable. (Courtesy Alan & Robin Aaskov www.alyssasmotel.com)

with badge-engineered rides. The Lincoln-Mercury Division link was alluded to as "The Fine Car Touch inspired by the Continental." More like inspired by Ford Torino GT! The top 4bbl 'Marauder' 390 GT V8 looked familiar, as did base 302 and mid-level 2bbl 390. Still, at a time when each division more than contributed to the bottom line, the bean counters were okay with those variations on a theme. The GT suspension package of stiffer springs, HD shocks, large front swaybar and 6in-wide rims on Firestone Wide Ovals looked familiar, as did the turbine-type wheel covers. Today, collectors can marvel at the subtle differences from what was a Torino GT cousin. Apart from GT body profile striping and black grille paint, try a unique rear fender 'Cyclone' puffed script decal! In 1968 the Mercury Montego arrived as an upscale cousin of the Comet, and, just like Ford, the Montego replaced Comet after 1969. It was a similar deal to the Fairlane-Torino transition.

1968 Montego came in the usual two-door hardtop, convertible, four-door sedan and wagon bodystyles. MX was the '500' equivalent option up trimline, with 1969 MX Brougham offering Conti level, super lux. The exterior faux wood-paneled MX Villager wagon was along the same lines as Squire in Torino land. In the go-faster late '60s, Cyclone was the ultra performance variant. It remained the super sporty Montego, until the end of 1971 MY. After 1971, Montego adopted the mechanical and cosmetic alterations seen with 1972 Torino.

Thus, Montego went on to two wheelbases, 114in for two-door, 118in for four-door and wagon. Coming along for the ride were Torino's new body on frame construction, and thin B pillar/frameless glass of the latest pillared four-door hardtops. Montego GT served as both a Cyclone replacement, and Gran Torino Sport kissing cousin. Once again featuring SportsRoof fastback. Like Torino, Montego sales were strong in 1972 and 1973. 1972 Montego sales were 136% up on the 1971 MY range, with the biggest rise attained by MX Brougham. Indicative of the rising following for smaller size luxury, and decreased interest in sporty variants.

6: Torino the Muscle Car 1970-73

When it came to that sporting touch, 1970 and 1971 Cyclones were known for their aggressive front fascias. Unlike '72s, concealed headlamps were still available in this earlier time. They could be specified on Broughams and Villagers. Styling differences from Torino were even functional. Mercury Cyclone's front fascia allowed it to cleave through the air more effectively than the already proficient Fairlane fastback. It explained both cars' excellence in the 1968 NASCAR Grand National racing season. In particular Cale Yarborough's Daytona 500 win that year, in the Wood Brothers Cyclone!

Henry rides shotgun with Mad Max!

Montego/Cyclone collector interest, comes from owning a rarer Torino relation, with those subtle badging, decorative differences. That said, there was one Ford muscle car North American FoMoCo fans couldn't get hold of. The Road Warrior Mad Max V8 Interceptor! That was because the car was made by Ford Australia! The iconic, post apocalyptic V8, was based on an Australian Ford Falcon XB GT 351 V8 Coupe. A car that was also central to the *Love The Beast* documentary done by actor Eric Bana.

By the late '60s Australia's Falcon had greatly deviated, from what was a RHD CKD version of Henry's 1960 compact. It was not that much smaller than a US intermediate, featured 302 and 351 power, and ended its XY version, with an ultimate incarnation called Falcon Phase III GT-HO. The GT-HO (Handling Option) had a 385bhp Cleveland 351 V8, and was, at 142mph, the fastest four-door sedan on the planet. Uniquely Downunder, four-door muscle cars were favored, and raced in roadcourse touring car races. The pinnacle of which was the annual Mount Panorama held Bathurst spectacular. The Phase III GT-HO won it in 1971, naturally!

1972 saw the Aussie debut of the all new XA Falcon range. Public pressure, fanned by a media campaign, put the Phase IV GT-HO 351 four-door, and other next generation Australian Supercars on ice. However, the new XA range did have a two-door hardtop GT Coupe, available with locally made 302 and 351 V8s. Mad Max and the feral kid could rest easy! Some of the Phase IV hardware had to be used up, and made its way onto the 1972 XA GT. Under the RPO 83 order code, this involved larger gas tanks for endurance races, winged sumps and 15 x 7in Globe aluminum rims.

The revised 1973 XB Falcon carried the slogan "The Great Australian Road Car." It was fit for Road Warrior Mad Max, since the GT Coupe had four wheel disk brakes, hood locks, dual circular headlamp pairs and scoops integrated into the power bulge hood. In keeping with the psychedelic era, two tone paint schemes saw body in contrasting color to power bulge, wheel arches and rocker panels. Most popular combo was a Yellow Blaze body, with other parts in black. Front fender 'GT 351' stencilled callouts, in contrast color, also featured on GTs. Purple was another popular external color.

Engine wise, all 351s were initially US imported, then worked up for special pavement pounders. However, from mid '72 The Ford Australia Geelong foundry knocked out 351s for automatic cars. There was also a 302 Cleveland. This, being cheaper to make locally at Geelong, than import a Windsor 302 from North America. This motor provided a more cost effective competitor, for the 308 V8 made by General Motors Holden (GMH) in Australia. Locally produced 302Cs, continued to be available in Aussie Fords, going into 1982.

Performance-wise, the fuel crisis, and pollution controls took their toll. In a comparison magazine article, evaluating an imported 1974 Pontiac Trans Am L75 automatic, and local Falcon GT 351 automatic coupe, getting the latter to its 5200rpm redline was an unhappy task. The 351 got out of puff and sounded busy. The cars recorded high 14s, and an exact 16 second ¼ mile respectively.[15]

That Aussie Cleveland 351 had closed

combustion chambered quench heads, and smaller 2bbl ports to boost CR on said 351. The first 211 XB Falcon GTs were assembled with the big port US-built 351C, then switched to the small port Aussie version. All the while the GT was available in two-door hardtop or four-door sedan variants, affirming this market's liking of four-door muscle cars. Many of these machines sported steel 12 slot rims. In July 1976 the lightly restyled XC Falcon was introduced. The GT variant was gone, but milder GS (Grand Sport) version continued in two-door hardtop and four-door sedan editions.

In December 1977 13 special order XC Falcon two-door hardtops were created. The cars carried homologation race parts. These were fitted at the Parts & Accessories Workshop of Ford Australia's Broadmeadows operation. Front and rear spoilers, reverse hoodscoop, transmission oil cooler, spring tower brace, and 25mm extended rear fenders were some of the included goodies! This led to the final incarnation of the Falcon Coupe: the 1978 XC Falcon Cobra. 1978 was also the last year for Falcon's rival, the Aussie Chrysler Charger Coupe. GM-Holden's Monaro Coupe had also stopped earlier. With Falcon approximating the size of a pre-1974 Mustang Mach 1 351 V8, this heralded the demise of the traditional muscle car in the southern hemisphere, as the world got ready for the cold cyber '80s.

1978 Ford XC Falcon Cobra was inspired by the 1-2 formation finish to Ford's winning of the seminal, annual Bathurst touring car race. This limited edition two-door model used up the final 400 hardtop coupe bodies, and could be specified with Cleveland 302 or 351 V8. Based on the humble Falcon GS Coupe, the Cobra's exterior featured noticeable white exterior paint, with body length, over the hood/roof/trunk panel dual blue stripes. Not unlike a Mustang II Cobra, but you couldn't get a 351 in one of those!

Falcon Cobra came with 15in 'Globe' Ferrari copy aluminum rims, four wheel disk brakes, ER70 HR rated radials, full instrumentation, hood scoops and dual exhaust. Falcon was radial ready, in response to Holden's late '70s adoption of Pontiac's RTS (Radial Tuned Suspension). Ford's 'Touring Suspension' for its rear drive, live axled chassis was first standard on Fairmont GXL, an upscale Falcon.

Radial suspension was standardized on all Falcon sedans and hardtops during the 1978 ½ XC face-lift. Ford Australia showed the worth of 'Touring Suspension' by getting local legend Fred Gibson to drive a XC sedan slalom … around fellow Ford racing drivers! The human cones could trust Touring Suspension, and so could local Ford buyers! Mad Max and the feral kid weren't too concerned about radial tires. No XC radial suspensioned XCs were used in the first Road Warrior film.

There was Max's XB Falcon two-door hardtop, and yellow XA and XB sedan cop cars. By the time the 1979 movie came out, Ford Australia was onto the reskinned, revised XD Falcon. Looking like a big MkII West German Ford Granada, this Falcon could still have 302/351 V8 action, 200bhp DIN net with the latter, but no two-door hardtop. It was the end of an era. No wonder Max was mad!

7

1968-1979 Ranchero. From Cobra Jet to Disco Delight!

Ford kept its Ranchero up to date with Fairlane/Torino. In 1968 that meant matching the new Torino's front grille. (Courtesy Paul Vankerhove)

Ranchero always symbolized Henry's thrift. The front fenders, hood and grille were the kind one would find on the same year Falcon/Fairlane sedan, whereas the rear third of Ranchero sheet metal was wagon-sourced. Modified wagon quarter panels kept tooling costs low. So it was that 1968 Ranchero took on that year's much revised Fairlane/Torino makeover. These sleeker, 114in wheelbase riding pickups involved base, Ranchero 500 and GT: equivalents to Fairlane/Torino trim level counterparts. New outside and in, since Ranchero afforded the same revised quad circular instrument pod.

Third pod moving left to right could have the optional tach, seen on sporty Torinos. A new seatbelt warning light lit briefly in the extreme left pod when turning over the motor. It was part of the federally mandated 1968 MY safety gear. These included wraparound front side marker lights, and rear fender equivalents. The steering wheel crashpad was shared from Ford's '68 compacts and inters. Active safety came courtesy of the starter V8, Ford's revered 2bbl 289: Henry also wanted Ranchero folks to be comfy!

'68 Ranchero, like Torino, had no quarter mini vent windows. However, it also missed out on the inter's flowthrough vent system. Ranchero's narrow B pillars, meant it wasn't feasible to fit exhaust relief valves – so, drive with windows part open, or specify Selectaire climate control a/c. Regular Ranchero had underdash fresh air vents, but Selectaire pickups had a special built in 'Fresh' air vent system. This system could also blend in heat from driveshaft tunnel outlets, and make use of waist-high cooler vanes. Such sophistication didn't come cheap. Ford Selectaire Conditioner cost over 100 bucks more than escalating from base I6 to T-Bird FE 390 four-barrel V8!

However, it was effective at keeping one cool. When it came to keeping one's cool, revised suspension geometry was cool aid! And mid '68 MY revision to Fairlane front suspension brought better stability and steering feel to related Ranchero. Ranchero was increasingly all about fun. There was the same 'GT' crest grille badge, and a symmetric tuning fork profile decal that could also be found on Torino GT. Same optional four-barrel FE 390 V8 with 10.5:1 CR, 325 horse at 4800rpm and 427lb/ft at 3200rpm!

The Ranchero GT's 1968 interior had sportscar vibes. Apart from two-seater

Ford Midsize Muscle – Fairlane, Torino & Ranchero

Chrome vent decorative grilles at the base indicate an a/c specified rig. (Courtesy Paul Vankerhove)

nature, the faux stitching circling the instrument pod gauges, steering wheel crashpad and four on the floor provided Porsche 911 ambience! In the June '68 issue of *Hot Rod*, a Ranchero GT 390 four-barrel with three-speed auto and 'Equa-lock' lsd, available across Ranchero's range, and weighing 3375lb, did a 15.6 at 91.8mph. To achieve this, the old drag racer tricks of removing the air cleaner lid, disconnecting a/c compressor and power steering belts were invoked! Dimension-wise, 1968 Ranchero had 203.9in length, 74in width and 55.2in height. Front and rear tracks were 58.8in and 58.1in respectively, and price as *Hot Rod* tested $4012.76.

Ranchero speeds up to more big block V8

Base price for Ranchero 390 GT was $2964.26, but as with Chevy El Camino, the fun was in the optioning! El Camino's sportscar like flying buttress B pillars,

In its September 1968 'Death Valley Days' truck/van comparo, *Motor Trend* found Ranchero V8 to be a nimble, tidy handler on Mojave Desert sandy trails. An off road T-Bird? An all-purpose sports car? You call it! (Courtesy Paul Vankerhove)

7: 1968-1979 Ranchero. From Cobra Jet to Disco Delight!

predated Jag XJ-S by 7 years! The semi hemi 'Porcupine' head 396 V8 was an option. No one really needed vehicles like these. '68 Ranchero was a long way from Plain Jane '61 Falcon Ranchero. To match the Bowtie Brigade, and keep in touch with Torino, the Cobra Jet 428 was a mid '68 MY Ranchero option. 1969 brought a slight restyle, involving flatter three-piece grille. The GT grille badge was relocated to the lower driver side grille corner, just like Torino GT. The exterior Ranchero script badge was moved from the rear quarter panels to the front fenders.

Inside, as per Fairlane/Torino, the instrument panel saw a redecoration from black numerals on a white dial face, to black markings on brushed aluminum. There was a slimmer two-spoke steering wheel and crashpad, like other '69 Fords. Sitting on a standard bench or optional bucket, one saw a purloined Torino GT broad hoodscoop, on Ranchero GT's hood. Substancewise, 69 'MY brought 351W (Windsor) and 351C (Cleveland) availability. Each motor, and only these two in the Torino/Ranchero line, could be teamed with the new medium duty FMX autobox.

1968 and 1969 Rancheros were constructed at Ford's Lorain, Ohio and Atlanta, Georgia factories. A very special GT from '69 MY was the Rio Grande. This variant could be painted in Maverick Grabber colors of Wimbledon White, Poppy Red or Calypso Coral. The pickup had partially blacked out hood with scoop, profile stripes, decorative bed rails, Ranchero's optional vinyl top and 'Ford Ranchero Rio Grande' wheel centers. Around 900 copies were made. Rio Grande had Ford's Special Performance Vehicle ID on the data plate, regardless of power team combo.

The Rio Grande had a blank where the trim code would normally be. However, there was no doubt the 1969 Ranchero that Mario Andretti took to the Bonneville Salt Flats was a true performance vehicle. This 428ci 335 horse specified rig, achieved 191.7mph, for a two-way Bonneville average. This feat made it officially the "Fastest Truck In The World." In all this time Ranchero was legally road registered as a truck, but Ford analysis showed consumers judged it as a car. With the new 1970 Ranchero Squire, who could blame them?

The Ranchero Squire was a new, luxo, fourth model in the revised 1970 pickup range. With the exterior woodgrain appliqué, it was equivalent to the upscale Torino Country Squire wagon. The semi transparent wood effect paneling, permitted a slight amount of body color to show through. Another visual attraction in '70 MY, were the optional Hideaway Headlamps. Just like Torino's toys! Yet

In 1968 Ranchero started with 200ci I6, and was transitioning from 289 to 302 as the base V8. The four-barrel FE 390 was the top dog. (Courtesy Paul Vankerhove)

This 1971 Ranchero 500 was originally built in Atlanta, Georgia. Specified with 210bhp 302 V8, it was taken to Germany from the Netherlands in 1994. (Courtesy Marc Cranswick)

Ford Midsize Muscle – Fairlane, Torino & Ranchero

In the style of the '71 GT, this rig has custom hoodscoop with open air filter. Headers and sidepipes expel unwanted pollutants! (Courtesy Marc Cranswick)

Even a Road Warrior enjoys the comforts of a love bench! Narrow B pillars meant Ranchero and Torino wagon couldn't have flow-through ventilation. So lower a window, or order a/c! (Courtesy Marc Cranswick)

another car touch in a restyled range, echoing the curved, muscle car look of new '70 Torino. Ranchero GT could have fresh air induction, courtesy of a Mustang borrowed hoodscoop.

Like Torino, Ranchero could have the same high output, premium gas 429s. Inside, 1970 was the first year Ranchero got model specific badging. It now said Ranchero or Ranchero GT, where formerly Fairlane or Torino script had adorned glovebox locations. Either way, from 1970 MY onwards Ranchero would only be made at Lorain, Ohio. Suspension-wise, Ford had put its money on rear leafs, rather than El Camino's rear coils. Rear leafs were judged to give better ride, handling compromise, especially with a load.

Hot Rod's Steve Kelly said Ranchero was more controllable than El Camino in June 1968. In September 1968, *Motor Trend*'s Julian G Schmidt, said its test Ranchero GT 390 handled like a sportscar on loose dirt surfaces, and outhandled some supercars in general. However, in the May 1971 issue of *Motor Trend*, Jim Brokaw remarked that he felt 1957 Ranchero's loaded state handling was still superior to the latest model. Unlike El Camino, Ranchero didn't offer factory air shocks. In 1968 these came courtesy of the aftermarket, in the form of GM Delco Pleasur-Lifts (part No P3044) – a little poke in the eye for Henry!

1969 and 1970 Ranchero had 0.72in front swaybar and rear Hotchkiss four leaf setup. Standard front/rear spring rates were 225lb/in and 126lb/in respectively. However, 429 V8 variants had stiffer front coils. Plus, whereas stock brakes were 10 x 2.5in drums, 10 x 2in drums front/rear, 351 and 429 rigs sported larger 10 x 2.5in rear drum stoppers. As with most domestic cars, HD suspension was much recommended to improve ride and handling. The option cost $14 in 1971, and improved load rating from 1035lb

The final year for strip speedo in a Ranchero, or Torino. Steering wheel and trick shifter are custom touches. The owner plans to restore the original 'three on da tree' shift! (Courtesy Marc Cranswick)

to 1245lb. The Ranchero provided an insurance premium loophole too.

Ranchero goes Gran Torino!
One could option 429 SCJ RA motor, four-speed, power front disks, Traction-Lok, lsd, full instrumentation, HD suspension, buckets/console, Laser Stripe and get a lower premium than a like spec Torino! With the '72 MY the 11.3:1 CR 429 was gone, as Ranchero followed Torino on to the new separate chassis. Staying faithful to family wagon links, '72 Ranchero rode on the longer 118in wagon wheelbase. It also adopted the fancy 'Namu Mouth' Gran Torino grille, for a simplified range that went Ranchero 500, Squire and sporty GT.

The revised range adopted the 351CJ four-speed power team as a fast pickup option. Low CR 429 and the new 400ci V8, were also borrowed from the Torino range. The story continued with the adoption of Gran Torino's 5mph impact bumper front fascia, on '73 MY

Rancheros. '73 Rancheros also brought owner comments critical about poor gas mileage, and carb maladies, on the latest models. Michael Lamm mentioned this, in the July 1973 issue of *Popular Mechanics*. The grievances in this PM Owners Report, were related to industry wide tighter smog tuning.

Owners also raised an old bugbear, it

In February 1959 *Hot Rod*'s Ranchero with top 352/COM combo did 0-60mph and ¼ mile in 9.9 and 17.2 seconds, respectively. In February 1971, *Road Test*'s Ranchero GT 351 improved to 9.3 seconds for 0-60mph, and 15.9 seconds in the ¼ mile. (Courtesy Marc Cranswick)

Ford invested a lot in the 351 Cleveland. However, '71 Ranchero kicked off with 1bbl 250ci I6. This pickup's 2bbl 302 was a 9:1 regular fuel V8, making 296lb/ft at 2600rpm. (Courtesy Marc Cranswick)

Ford Midsize Muscle – Fairlane, Torino & Ranchero

The decals suggest a Boss Mustang connection! However, with 114in wheelbase and 209in length, '71 Ranchero was midsize, not compact. (Courtesy Marc Cranswick)

A 450lb cargo gives a small block V8 Ranchero even weight distribution, and neutral handling. Stock rear '71 Ranchero suspension had a 1035lb load rating. Optional HD springs increased that to 1245lb. (Courtesy Marc Cranswick)

would have been nice to get the spare tire out of the old traditional cab location. In June 1968 *Hot Rod*'s Steve Kelly, said Ranchero embodied the old Ford ad line "quieter than a Rolls" and in 1973, as ever, that dual car/truck nature was a combo drawcard. Ranchero and El Camino always attracted positive glances. However, it seemed the market for a coverall, leisure oriented ride, was limited in the pre SUV era. In the PM Owner's Report only 0.4% chose base Ranchero 250ci I6, and only 0.7% went for three-speed manual. A mere 0.7% optioned four on the floor, 35.2% took the base V8 302 route, with a mega 57.8% selecting that great all rounder, the 400 V8!

98.5% of buyers homed in on automatic transmission. This was up from the 75% figure, mentioned in *Road Test*'s February 1971 report on Ranchero GT 351C four-barrel. Another trend was the rise of the Japanese mini-truck. Smaller, more affordable and cheaper to feed, Datsun L'il Hustler, Toyota Hilux, et al, had their uses in tight areas. They did achieve some conquest sales from midsize domestics, prompting the Big 3 to adopt captive imports. Even AMC considered six cylinder Hornet and Pacer derivatives.

This 1972 Ranchero 500 was completed at Ford's Atlanta plant on October 25 1971. Options fitted run to: hoodscoop, Magnum 500 rims, C4 auto, power front disks and Appearance Protection Group. (Courtesy Andrew Koromhas)

7: 1968-1979 Ranchero. From Cobra Jet to Disco Delight!

One needed the optioned two-barrel 351 to handle the fitted Ford Selectaire a/c, load drainwise. New Torino/Ranchero HVAC had 21% greater airflow, versus '71 MY. (Courtesy Andrew Koromhas)

From a collectability standpoint, in 1971 Ford High Performance magazine, did an article titled "Light's Hauler" on Jim Light's restified '57 Ranchero – a chromed ¼ mile screamer, with worked '67 427!

Starsky's Ranchero 1974-76

The Light's Hauler article mentioned how few fullsize Rancheros still existed, by the start of the '70s. The Ranchero name and pickup spirit, even made its way to South Africa, courtesy of Ford Australia. Ford Australia made right hand drive versions of the early '60s US compact Falcon Ranchero. This vehicle was simply called, Falcon Ute (utility).

The Aussie Falcon and pickup, evolved away from its US counterparts, as the '60s wore on. In 1968 Ford South Africa started CKD assembly of the Aussie Falcon Ute, but named it Ford Ranchero! Available with Ford I6 and 302 V8 motors, this pickup mirrored Ford Australia production changes. This included transition from the XY to the Road Warrior XA Falcon based pickup by 1973, as well as production of the Australian Cleveland 302 V8 in South Africa. Free of the draconian US smog controls, this 2bbl Autolite carbed 302 was making 230 gross ponies, going into 1974. It took advantage of 98 octane leaded gas, and a 9.8:1 CR! By January 1973 14,880 Ford Rancheros had been sold in South Africa.

For 1974 American Rancheros adopted the front fascia style of the *Starsky & Hutch* TV Gran Torino. *PV4* magazine praised Ranchero for doing so, feeling it gave Ford a styling edge over El Camino, in a Ranchero versus El Camino April

Like Torino, Ranchero deep sixed '72's Namu mouth grille for '73 MY. With era correct 14 x 8.5in ET Slot Mags, this mildly modified '73 Ranchero GT has a stainless steel dual system, coming off Headman Headers. (Courtesy Martin Fowler)

Ford Midsize Muscle – Fairlane, Torino & Ranchero

The iconic 351 Cleveland connected to FMX automatic. The most fuel efficient Ford midsize power team for real world driving. Handy, with the upcoming fuel crisis. (Courtesy Martin Fowler)

This '73 Ranchero GT 400 has upgraded handling, courtesy of Addco front swaybar with polygraphite control arm bushings front, plus rear upper and lower equivalents. Moog upper and lower balljoints join 255/60R/15s front and 275/60R/15s rear on respective 8 and 9in rims. Front coils have had a ⅝in shim job. Plus, rear progressive rate Torino four-door sedan coils have been retrofitted. (Courtesy Carl Anderson)

the 429 as the top Ford motor for '74 MY. As ever, the kind one would find in a T-Bird. Concerning midsize rides, Ford was initially Aston Martin quiet on the motor's power and torque figures. However, in '74 Ranchero they were disclosed as 195bhp at 3800rpm and 355lb/ft at 2600rpm, using an 8:1 CR.

Many considered that 460, Ford's last big block for a production car, was the finest motor Henry was offering in this era. However, the hi po 351 V8 was still around in midsize Fords. By 1974 it was down to 255 net ponies, and could no longer be four-speed teamed in a Ranchero, but still made more horses than the 460. By 1974 1974 comparo article. In red and with optional Laser Stripe it looked like, and perhaps inspired, Dave Starsky's Flying Red Tomato?! Starting price for base Ranchero 500 was $3029, GT being $3264 and let the optioning commence! Sizewise Ranchero measured 215.7in long, 79in wide and 53.1in high. Suspension stuck with front independent A arms, coils, tube shocks and at the rear semi-elliptic leaf springs and tube shocks, kept that live axle in check.

In 1968 Ranchero relied on 200ci I6 base motor, with 289 V8 the first option. In '69 MY these motors were replaced with 250 cube I6 and 302 V8 respectively. In 1974 V8 power became standard, for the first time. The 302 V8 had 8:1 CR, making 140bhp at 3800rpm and 230lb/ft at 2600rpm on 91 octane gas. Pay 44 bucks to upgrade to 162 horse 351 power, $135 for the 8.4:1 400 and $274 for Big Daddy 460 V8! The 460 had replaced

Ford's versatile 400M, with an added 600 CFM Holley 4bbl, dual plane intake manifold and Petronix electronic ignition. Exhaling through duals/glass packs and backed by a C6 auto. Street moxie aplenty! (Courtesy Carl Anderson)

7: 1968-1979 Ranchero. From Cobra Jet to Disco Delight!

El Camino still had a manual four-speed on offer, but Ranchero only had three-speed manual for base 302, auto for all other motors.

Surveys suggested light construction hauling and fishing topped the list of respective task and leisure uses for car-based pickups. To that end, Ranchero's load area measured 77.7in x 48.5in x 16in. Power brakes and power steering cost $48 and $112 respectively. Standard a/c was $424, climate control a/c $487, with tint lightening the wallet to the tune of 42 bucks. Best tire and rim combo involved HR78 x 14B radials on optional 14 x 6in wheels. *PV4* magazine's test Ranchero GT kept the Ford dealer happy with 460, radials, a/c, Traction-Lok lsd and $94 full instrumentation pack. It cost $5756, and *PV4* was impressed how much refinement, value and all purpose ability Ranchero, and El Camino, brought to the party on and off road.

In testing at Orange County International Raceway, Ranchero gave best to El Camino. Ford's 9.9 second 0-60mph and 17 seconds at 78mph ¼ mile, couldn't touch the Chebbie's respective 9.2 second and 16.5 second at 84mph clockings. It seemed Chevy V8s still had an edge, with Bowtie 454 outpunching that Blue Oval 460. However, with Olivia Newton-John singing on the 8-track audio deck, who cared?!

In Xanadu they all drive Rancheros!

According to *PV4* magazine, its tester maintained the crispness of his leisure suit, with Ranchero GT 400's climate control a/c. He inserted Olivia Newton-John's latest tape into Ranchero's fantabulous AM/FM stereophonic radio/8 track machine. Perfect for a trip to Xanadu in the disco era! By now Ranchero maintained its midsize synch, by adopting the styling/mechanical properties of the Torino replacing LTD II. That meant popular stacked square quad headlights, and rear coil suspension.

Still on the wagon 118in wheelbase,

For '74 MY, Ranchero took on the S&H Flying Tomato styling, in a Ranchero 500, GT and Squire range trio! (Courtesy Davy Klijnsma)

Like Torino, Ranchero could have Ford's 1974-76 star motor, the $274 195 net horse 4bbl 460. This engine made 355lb/ft at 2600rpm. (Courtesy Davy Klijnsma)

Ford Midsize Muscle – Fairlane, Torino & Ranchero

In '74 MY the base Ranchero 500 retailed for $3029. Starter engine was the 302, with 351 two-barrel a $44 option. A 1975 Ranchero 500 351W is at hand.

Above: In its April 1974 comparo, *PV4* magazine considered Ranchero's 1974-76 look superior to El Camino style! (Courtesy Eric Dejan)

Right: Ranchero owners enjoyed the same sporty ambience as Super Cop Dave Starsky! (Courtesy Eric Dejan)

Ranchero had length/width/height stats of 220.1in/79.6in/53.5in, and 58/42% weight distribution with 400M motor installed. Performance figures for the time, were an excellent 0-60mph in 10.7 seconds, and ¼ mile in 18 seconds at 78mph. About the same as a BMW 733i automatic, costing over 20 grand, which made *PV4*'s Ranchero GT 400 loaded with options, a steal at just $7049! Even so, the recession, fuel crisis/gas lines, gas hog debate etc, brought some introspection. It all motivated *PV4* to title its May 1977 report "Guilt Complex: Ranchero GT Ford's blend of temperature control, tape deck and brute horsepower …"

Brute horsepower it was, with the 460 deep sixed, and the $156 optional 400M 8.0:1 CR V8 making 173bhp at 3800rpm and 326lb/ft at 1600rpm. For reference Corvette's base 350 in 1975 made 165bhp! This made Ranchero GT the better of the US two-seaters performancewise! Completing the GT's performance portfolio were $130 sports instrumentation, $54 lsd and $33 Handling Suspension Package. Top tire/rim combo were HR78-14 Bs on 14 x 7in rims. Even base Ranchero provided much.

$4618 brought 302 V8 and Cruise-O-Matic, power steering, power brakes, chromed 5mph bumpers and interior carpeting. Squire added vinyl cladded moldings, simulated body profile/tailgate woodgrain paneling, deluxe wheel covers, wood decorated instrument panel, electric clock and black vinyl concealer flaps for the behind the seats stowage area. The starting price was $4971, GT cost more at $4984, but included more useful standard stuff.

Ranchero GT was considered top model and had remote control dual racing mirrors, wheel trim rings/hubcaps, 'Flight' bench seat with folding armrest, informative 'Instrumentation Group', engine turned instrument cluster appliqué and deluxe JC Witney steering wheel to complement the Disco Dash! In the era of paint and tape, GT had its own adorning bodysides and tailgate. Contrasting decals

7: 1968-1979 Ranchero. From Cobra Jet to Disco Delight!

As per sibling LTD II, 1977-79 Ranchero boasted the refinement of rear coils. (Courtesy Michael Calhoon www.mjcclassiccars.com)

Below left: Was it a truck, or a car? Even in 1978 the debate continued!
Below right: As before, if one didn't look rearwards, this could have been a full luxury LTD II sedan. The carlike refinement of this Ranchero even ran to a/c. (Courtesy Michael Calhoon www.mjcclassiccars.com)

for sail panel and lower third body profile were distinctive, as was the 'GT' script decal on the rear fender upper third, inline with the rear side marker light.

351M – FoMoCo Frankenstein small block!

On the serious side, Ford tried to keep Ranchero within light truck duty emissions class. FoMoCo worked out the Ranchero's Gross Vehicle Weight Rating (GVWR) differently to a normal truck. This probably explained why payload jumped from 750lb to 1250lb when HD suspension, which included rear swaybar, was optioned. Option a 351 V8 and a surprise lay underhood. Either Ranchero would turn up with a 351 Windsor van spec motor with 8.3:1 CR making 149bhp at 3200rpm and 291lb/ft at 1600rpm, or 351 modified pickup spec V8 using 8.0:1 CR and offering 161bhp at 3600rpm and 285lb/ft at 1800rpm. The lsd was only available with the optional 3.00:1 final drive. California was limited to the 2.50 rear axle ratio.

Ford Midsize Muscle – Fairlane, Torino & Ranchero

Top: During the LTD II era, Ranchero base motor was the 302 displayed. By the late '70s/early '80s, trucks and vans were increasingly the only place to get a V8 rear driver.

Bottom: With the downsizing, CAFE dominated cyber '80s, Ranchero's luxo interior got replaced by swathes of gray plastic! (Courtesy Michael Calhoon www.mjcclassiccars.com)

The Cleveland V8 bid the Torino/Ranchero line farewell, at the end of '74 MY. From 1975 onwards, Ford had the 351W and 351M. This was the first year for the industry wide adoption of the catalytic converter. Thus, it was also the first time a Ford V8 was unleaded ready. To save weight and boost gas mileage post gas crunch, all post '74 MY small blocks had lighter castings, which weren't as strong. With an eye to replace the 390FE, and satiate the excess demand for 351Ws, Ford created the 351M (Modified). 351M borrowed the 400M's taller deck height of 10.297in, but was destroked with a 351W crank, plus used Windsor conrods and intake manifold. This combination of Cleveland 400 and Windsor related hardware, led to the 'Modified' designation.

The special 351s and 400s had the bell housing flexibility to accept HD C6 and lighter duty FMX. From 1975 on the M blocks (351M and 400) were made at the Michigan Casting Center at Flat Rock, or at the expected Cleveland Foundry. At first, confusingly, Ford marketed 351M under the Cleveland banner, to take advantage of that name's positive notoriety. In 1977 Ford replaced FE 360/390 in light duty truck applications, with 351M and 400. This light truck use saw a stronger block, to be shared with all 'M' V8s in 1978 MY. 1982 saw the final usage of 351M and 400 in FoMoCo cars.

Hasta la vista Ranchero!

CAFE and falling demand for V8s, saw the demise of the final Cleveland vestige. 351 Windsor took up the slack thereafter. The M block's emissions control forward thinking, also proved its downfall. Ford designed the M block with smog controls in mind. Thus, EGR and Thermactor were built in and neat looking. However, when stricter 2nd gen pollution controls were needed, they couldn't be incorporated easily. It was more cost effective for Henry to call it a day on the M block, and by 1982 Ranchero had already been bid adios.

The writing was on the wall with the success of Ford's F series pickup. By the end of '78 MY it was America's best selling ride. It was the start of the trend to pickup and SUV dominance by the mid 1990s. Being subject to less stringent truck economy and emissions federal dictates, it was good to be an F series! Unlike Ford's new downsized LTD, the truck could have 2bbl 400 and 4bbl 460 motors … teamed with a four-speed! 1979 MY F series options wouldn't have looked out of place on a car either. The complement stock new rectangular headlamps, sports/convenience options ran to decal tape and stripes, special paint with blackout treatments and

7: 1968-1979 Ranchero. From Cobra Jet to Disco Delight!

How long was a pre-downsized LTD II based midsize Ranchero? Try 220.1in! Size classes were in a late '70s state of flux, as lines got redrawn for the econo '80s. (Courtesy Michael Calhoon www.mjcclassiccars.com)

Despite the mods and pleas of owners and magazines alike, Ford kept that spare behind the passenger side, all the way from 1957 to 1979. (Courtesy Michael Calhoon www.mjcclassiccars.com)

In January 1979 *Road Test* magazine put the US car-based pickup market at just 75,000 units. It correctly predicted Ford wouldn't do a new downsized LTD based Ranchero – and noted '79 Ranchero might prove a sound collector car investment. (Courtesy Michael Calhoon www.mjcclassiccars.com)

a tilt steering column. Life wasn't so easy for Ranchero.

Ranchero had always been outsold by mighty Chevrolet. El Camino sold more in fullsize days, and even since returning as a midsize. In 1970 it was 38,286 versus 20,537. Entering 1979 MY, the Ranchero was looking much the same as its 1977 LTD II style makeover, and selling at one half El Camino's rate. That Chevy would sell on into the '80s, but Ranchero was doubtful. In January 1979 *Road Test* predicted Ford wouldn't do a Ranchero version of its new LTD, once Torino based LTD II shuffled off this mortal coil: "… it's unlikely Ford will continue this model after it retools its LTD II for 1980. Might be a good investment."

So it was that 1979 was the last year for Ranchero, 6.6-liter Trans Ams and V8 AMC cars. There seemed little place for fun, as the industry geared up for the practical, front drive and fuel efficient '80s. This left a legacy of 508,355 Rancheros.

8
Torino Moves from Turin to Lincoln Type Design 1974-1979

The 1977-79 LTD II stacked headlamp visage proved most popular amongst Ford niche fans. After a commemorative 1979 ½ Ranchero finale edition, some dealers catered to continued interest in the pickup car concept, by selling aftermarket converted Fairmont Futuras and Mercury Zephyr Z7 Sport coupes. And there the Blue Oval car pickup remains, waiting to be revived by Henry!

Torino had proved midsize dynamite, and as popular as Jimmie Walker for Dearborn. So Ford saw fit to keep investing in the Turin inspired intermediate, going into '74 MY. The federal forced adoption of 5mph bumpers front and rear that year precipitated a restyle. The tail saw wraparound lamps that were shorter and squarer than before. These were protected by a low set, square bumper bar capable of seeing off any Consumer Reports bash test! Torino's gas filler door had been seen below the bumper, and behind the license plate. Now, it was above said bumper, behind a mid-fascia access door under the trunk lock.

Big changes at the front for Gran Torino, a fancy new visage. The 1974 grille was bigger, and divided into eight equal sized vertical sections. A new design Gran Torino badge lay on the driver side grille. The grille was decorated with finer mesh, with parking lights being the outermost vertical sections, nearest the pairs of circular headlamps. Gran Torino's bumper was more pointed now, with more centrally located bumper guards. The license plate holder lived on the driver's side of the front bumper.

The normal Torino featured the same 1973 style grille, but with amended '74 type 5mph 'Gran Torino like' bumpers. However, the license plate was in the center. Upscale Gran Torino Brougham had a full-width rear taillight lens cover, although the center part was non-functional. Both Brougham and Gran Torino Squire wagon had stand up hood

Coming into '74 MY Torino was sitting pretty having outsold Chevelle by almost 170,000 units! 496,581 Torino sales in '73 MY, and 426,086 in 1974 was midsize magic for Ford. (Courtesy Davy Klijnsma)

8: Torino Moves from Turin to Lincoln Type Design 1974-1979

ornaments, not GTS' grille emblem. Length dimensions of two-door models were 213.1in long, four-door sedans were 215.4in, with wagons at 222in. Width for the hardtop coupe and four-door sedan was 79.3in, and the wagon a trimmer 79in. Height was 52.8in on a normal two-door.

Torino trinkets

Two and four-door editions kept riding on their respective 114in and 118in wheelbases, with weight range being in the 3509lb to 4250lb vicinity. Unlike in 1972-73, Torino two-door had fixed rear windows. Luxo options included leather wrapped steering wheel, split bench seat, power sunroof and handy steering wheel mounted cruise control buttons. Gran Torino could be optioned with newly available opera windows. Opera windows were standard on Brougham. New optional rear fender skirt could be applied to Gran Torino two-door hardtops and sedans.

Side moldings now lay on the rocker panels, not the lower doors. Broughams and Sports featured an extra chrome molding on the lower fender edge, between front wheelwell and bumper. Squires had no lower body moldings. Gran Torino Sport could have rear fender skirt plus opera windows, on vinyl roof optioned cars. However, that SportsRoof option had vanished. The GTS emblem continued in the usual locations: grille, C pillar, fuel filler door, with "Sport" script placed next to the C pillar's GTS medallion. However, no such emblem lay on opera window optioned GTS, and the sport script was moved under the Gran Torino fender nameplate badge on such rides.

The institution Laser Stripe option, gave way to a lower body, multi-colored non-reflective stripe. To satisfy FoMoCo's accountants, the GTS now had the same vinyl door trim card as other Gran Torinos. That said, such door cards and seats were highlighted with colored stripes. Low back buckets with separate head restraints were a '74 MY GTS option. Base sticker price for a '74 Torino was $2811, with this including the federal mandatory 'wear your seatbelt … or else' Interlock safety system – a one-year-only industry requirement – 'or else' meant the car wouldn't start if the driver didn't satisfy that logic sequence computer.

Standard stuff!

For convenience, Ford upped gas tank capacity. From 22.5 to 26.5 gallons on hardtops/four-door sedans, and 21.5 to 22 gallons on wagons. All tanks had been reshaped, with less expansion space at

Top: A 1974 Gran Torino Sport, Ford's performance leader of the day. SportsRoof body was gone, but 351CJ/four-speed and 460 motor options were abound.

Bottom: A complete restyle for '74 MY, with low, square-shaped rear 5mph impact bumper. Shorter, squarer, wraparound taillights maintained visibility, and the gas filler door was now above the bumper. (Courtesy Davy Klijnsma)

153

Ford Midsize Muscle – Fairlane, Torino & Ranchero

This all original 1974 GTS 460 coupe has done just 3500 miles, with intact factory 3D paint and Marti Report to prove it! (Courtesy Alan & Robin Aaskov www.alyssasmotel.com)

A console, my kingdom for a console! A desirable option at the time, and one coveted now during muscle car rebuilds as a retrofit. (Courtesy Alan & Robin Aaskov www.alyssasmotel.com)

1974 was the first year for front and rear 5mph bumpers, but the new 460 option was great enthusiast compensation! (Courtesy Alan & Robin Aaskov www.alyssasmotel.com)

the top. With industry vehicle weight on the rise, Ford fitted larger 11 x 2.25in rear drums to all wagons specified with optional engines. To combat said weight, Torino's standard power team was the 302 and three-speed manual column shift combo. However, industry repair manuals (Chilton and Motor) and observed '74 cars, suggest that some came with the 250ci inline six.

As for optional motors the 351 2bbl/4bbl, 400 2bbl and 460 4bbl came with Ford's new solid state ignition system. This was the final year for hi po Cleveland V8. The special 351 was the only motor combinable with a four-speed. It was no longer called Cobra Jet, but at 255 bhp net, was still stronger than that 460 mill! Ford were quiet on what the big block could do. The 385 series 460 had 3.85in stroke, 4.362 bore, 8:1 CR and Ford's '73 figures said 338lb/ft at 2800rpm.

In the January 1974 issue of *Motor Trend*, Gran Torino Brougham 460 faced off against Chevelle Malibu Classic, Cutlass Salon, Buick Regal and Matador X 401. At 8.3 seconds for 0-60mph, it offered the quickest sprint for that group stat. Not bad considering the Conti style luxury, and the highest weight (4615lb) on test. The Brougham wore Firestone HR78-14 steel radials and stock suspension.

This gave land-yacht like handling, but *Motor Trend* commented the Torino's reputation for good feel power steering was maintained. For better suspension, Ford combined former HD and Competition Suspension into one HD pack. This had larger than stock front swaybar, HD springs and shocks, along with a rear swaybar. Initial Ford model preview info said the pack was available on all 11 Torinos, with HD shocks a possible separate hardtop option. However, in practice it seems it was only available on non wagon models.

An elite Torino

Standard Torino rubber was a G78-14 bias belted blackwall. Gran Torino Brougham,

8: Torino Moves from Turin to Lincoln Type Design 1974-1979

Squire and Sport, came with HR78-14in steel belted radials standard. The F78-14 was deep sixed, but performance G70-14 and H70-14in Wide Oval bias belted rubber, could still be had. That said, performance was increasingly off buyer's minds. Folks wanted luxury in a smaller package. Thus, with an eye to budget T-Bird fanciers, FoMoCo introduced Gran Torino Elite. A rival for Chevy Monte Carlo, Elite had unique front sheetmetal, twin headlamps with chrome bezel surrounds, parking lights on front fender outer edges. Plus, big grille rectangularly arched across the front.

Quarter panels and doors were shared with kissing cousins Merc Montego/Cougar, but Torino's sweeping bodyline look, was absent. Larger tailwidth wide taillights had a non-functional center. Standard features involved Westminster cloth trim, woodgrain dash, full instrumentation, split bench, opera windows, 351 2bbl V8, Cruise-O-Matic and radials. However, HD suspension was unavailable. Elite was a hit, contributing 96,604 units to Torino's mega 426,086 total. Ford honored this result by making Elite a stand alone iteration for '75 MY, which had new steering wheel design and newly optional 'Fuel Sentry' vacuum gauge in the wake of the gas crunch.

Like the '75 Ford ad said, "Announcing a mid-size car in the Thunderbird Tradition. The 1975 Ford Elite." Power moonroof and other 'T-Bird' options were stated as being at hand. Continuing the big luxury in small car theme, there was Ford's Falcon/Maverick related Granada, and compact Merc Monarch twin. "What looks like the latest Cadillac and is priced like the newest VW? Ford Granada. 1975's best-selling newcomer." The optional 351 V8 was described by Ford as "action-packed." Unlike midsize, Granada could still have that thrifty 200ci I6!

More functional were the continuing Magnum 500 rims optionable on GTS. For Ford '74 MY, said rim possessed a revised chrome wheel trim, with polished trim ring and Argent painted spokes. However,

1974 400M and 460 V8s had Ford's solid state ignition. Mustang couldn't even have a V8 that year, except for Mexico, so all performance paths led to Torino! (Courtesy Alan & Robin Aaskov www.alyssasmotel.com)

the hi po 351 Cleveland 4bbl was off the table in 1975, and with it the chance of '4 on da plush pile!' There seemed fewer reasons to grab a GTS by now. The basic Torino adopted the Gran Torino's front grille/fascia, reducing range differences. A mere 5126 GTS cars rolled out of the door in 1975!

1975 represented the industry wide adoption of the catalytic converter to meet the strict planned federal smog laws. Also, as with rivals, weights were going up. The 1975 Torino range went from 3987 to 4456lb according to Ford. To combat all the above, the 351 two-barrel became Torino's base motor, with a lottery as to whether one would get a Windsor or Modified edition. The trend towards luxury and small rides was borne out by the 1975 sales figures. 195,110 Torinos and 123,372 Elites, as folks started liking compacts and subcompacts a whole lot more. 1976 Torino didn't offer much more than new options, and range rationalization.

Arrivederci, Turin!
All 1976 two-doors could savor opera windows, and landau roof style. Onlookers had time to enjoy the decorations, because a revised 2.75 econoaxle was standard on all! Some engine spark ignition advance, and EGR fettling, liberated more pep on 351 and 400 2bbl V8s, but the 460 was slightly down. Power trunk release and automatic parking brake release were new

Ford Midsize Muscle – Fairlane, Torino & Ranchero

This *Starsky & Hutch* Gran Torino replica, eschews that iconic 2B Bright Red exterior, in favor of a factory burgundy. (Courtesy John Mohrlein Jr, http://forum.grantorinosport.org/75granmans-gran-torino-w-3k_topic6099.html)

options. One could also nab a Gran Torino two-door with center console, if buckets were specified. Formerly, center console was for GTS only, but now there was no GTS!

May the (police) force be with you!

GTS' role had effectively been taken by Granada Sports Coupe and Monarch S in 1976-77. Then came 1978-80 ESS (European Sport Sedan) as small became the new big. It was the end of the line for Torino, with 1976's 193,096 units being the nameplate's final production year. Not quite the final curtain for this midsize platform, or high-performance. However, with the latter it helped to be with the fuzz! For law enforcement, all the good stuff that had been legislated away with smog law, and discontinued due to insurance premiums and fuel crisis, were still around.

Most common cop cars were full-size Galaxies, but Ford had a complete portfolio. This included wagon, van, ambulance and even Police Bronco! Naturally midsize was in the mix too. Depending on purpose, Torino models involved Sentry, Ranger, Pacer, Trooper and Interceptor. Sentry invoked thrifty one-barrel 250 I6; Interceptor, a police-use-only 460, concerning '73 MY Torinos. Highway patrol cars have always had strict acceleration, top speed and handling requirements. The California Highway Patrol (CHP) even has its own test facility. To this end Ford's cop 460 had high CR, big cam, special high rpm balanced crank, special conrods, forged aluminum pistons, special engine oil cooler, HD oil pump, electric fuel pump and four-barrel carb on a special intake manifold.

Going with the cop 460 was a mandatory police HD C6 automatic, with first gear lockout, and the ability to hold second. The 460 exhaled through duals, and could be teamed with 3.25 final drive and 90 amp alternator, along with suitable upgrades. Ford's stout 9in differential (with 4 pinion and 3.00 ring

8: Torino Moves from Turin to Lincoln Type Design 1974-1979

Originally an Ohio car, with a spec resembling that of Ford's own '76 S&H replica. That is, 2bbl 351W, C4 auto and 2.75 gears. However, this Striped Tomato has been 'heated up' since! (Courtesy John Mohrlein Jr, http://forum.grantorinosport.org/75granmans-gran-torino-w-3k_topic6099.html)

and pinion), 11in flared rear drums with HD linings, park brake warning light, heavier duty California Brake Package and engine coolant recovery system. Maximum handling suspension and rear swaybar, plus H78 15in tires on 6.5in wide steel rims kept things in control, with help from Ford's Traction-Lok lsd.

Cop car seriousness was borne out by front mount oil cooler for the power steering pump, and 140mph speedo accurately calibrated in 2mph increments. There were air scoops, feeding cooling air to the uprated brakes. Plus, the cop brake booster involved a higher placed brake pedal, with longer pedal travel, so drivers didn't ride the brakes in traffic. Along with HD alternator and battery, there was even HD front seat and vinyl upholstery! Ford normally fitted Torino with soft foam and coverings for comfort. However, to cope with harder police usage, more durable substitutes were on hand.

Ford's Special Order Department could meet a custom car order, like two-door hardtop with buckets and four-speed, if there were enough orders placed. Special cop cars would carry a DSO (Domestic Special Order) tag. In 1977 there was even a Maverick Police Package. However, it wasn't sufficiently upgraded, and sold

Factory spec brought 'Love Bench' and column shift. It now has the correct buckets, and floor shifted Top Loader four-speed. (Courtesy John Mohrlein Jr, http://forum.grantorinosport.org/75granmans-gran-torino-w-3k_topic6099.html)

under 400 units. Ex-police cars make their way to police auctions – recall Jake and Elwood's Dodge experience in *The Blues Brothers* movie – or fleet disposal specialists. These in turn sell job lots to dealers, making for speedy Easter eggs … just waiting to be discovered!

Striped tomato – the *Starsky & Hutch* Gran Torino

For four seasons on ABC, the TV cop show *Starsky & Hutch* starred Paul Michael Glaser as Dave Starsky, David Soul as Ken 'Hutch' Hutchinson, Antonio Fargas as Huggy Bear, and Bernie Hamilton as Captain Dobey. A key ingredient to the show's appeal was a certain white-striped, mid '70s cherry red (according to Starsky)

157

Ford Midsize Muscle – Fairlane, Torino & Ranchero

For season two, Paul Michael Glaser requested a Gran Torino with buckets, to stop David Soul sliding into him during spirited cornering! (Courtesy John Mohrlein Jr, http://forum.grantorinosport.org/75granmans-gran-torino-w-3k_topic6099.html)

Gran Torino two-door hardtop, driven by the crime-fighting duo. A Spelling-Goldberg production, the studio's switchboard was inundated with calls concerning what kinda car was that, and where could it be bought? This was in spite of Chevrolet and Dodge being the show's sponsors!

Aaron Spelling asked Spelling-Goldberg Productions transportation chief George Grenier for a special car, for the show. Grenier looked at Ford's entire line, since the company used FoMoCo's Studio-TV Car Loan Program, and chose the Gran Torino. He also went for the red paint job, and designed that vector stripe! Really arresting for a cop show! American Racing Indy 15in slotted mag rims, oversize tires,

Even though the performance choice of the day was a 351CJ, the movie car had a worked 351W. That said, for seasons two to four of the S&H TV show, a pair of 460 Gran Torinos did most of the work. (Courtesy John Mohrlein Jr, http://forum.grantorinosport.org/75granmans-gran-torino-w-3k_topic6099.html)

air shocks and rear hi-jackers, gave the car a purposeful raked look. In fact, to prevent the tire maker getting free advertising, the raised white letter part was turned axle inward! A shorter final drive ratio bestowed extra pep for stunt work, and probably explained why at least one second season car, had a "Do Not Exceed 50mph" dash label.

Given California smog law, no engine mods were done. The opening title sequence, had hi po V8 engine roar, dubbed in! Paul Michael Glaser did normal driving, with stunt coordinator Chuck Picerni stepping in for chases and mild stunts. In the show, detective Starsky was portrayed as a car enthusiast, and doting Gran Torino owner. Hutch drove a beat up '73 Galaxie, and couldn't have cared less for Starsky's ride. Hutch even derogatorily called the Gran Torino a striped tomato! In real life it was Glaser that didn't think much of the Gran Torino.

In an interview given around the time of the 2004 *Starsky & Hutch* movie, Glaser mentioned how Aaron Spelling took him to one side, and said they got a neat ride for the show, presenting Glaser with the Gran Torino. Glaser wasn't impressed with this contemporary smog controlled, 5mph bumpered midsize. He considered Torino to be one of the poorer examples of this vehicle type, and openly vowed to destroy the car during film sequence driving! Hence the overt kerb bashing! By the second season Glaser and Soul asked for a bucket equipped car, because the early bench seat Gran Torino saw Soul slide into Glaser during cornering!

The show's pilot movie *The Word On The Street* was filmed in spring 1975, and utilized two VIN code H '75 351W powered Gran Torinos. For the first season two '75 Gran Torinos with 400Ms, VIN code S, were ordered. One car had a roof mounted camera, for the S&H perspective. For the second 1976 season, two '76 Gran Torinos were ordered, with stout 460 V8s (VIN code A) for stunt work. These cars were ordered via Ford's Fleet Program, so the 2B Bright Red exterior paint could be

8: Torino Moves from Turin to Lincoln Type Design 1974-1979

chosen to maintain continuity. This color had been discontinued from the regular 1976 Torino line. The early 351W machine, was kept as backup.

From mid second season, Ford's own P122 S&H replica was leased as a second backup. The VIN code H 351M powered car (Unit PS 122), had its original 351M replaced by a 429 V8 overnight, post stunt damage. The '75 cars had the vector stripe running along the body crease, the '76 cars had the stripe going underneath. It was thought Spelling might have the Gran Torino written out of the show, being wrecked in season two. The Torino replacing LTD II, was coming out for '77 MY. However, the 'striped tomato' had a longer shelf life! Stuntwork is hazardous, and the cars got damaged at least once per episode. So the S&H Gran Torinos were looking pretty tired by 1979! With the show sadly over, the two 1976 Gran Torino 460s were returned to Ford and auctioned off!

These season two to four Gran Torinos, were both built on February 16 1976 at Ford's Lorain, Ohio factory. They had consecutive serial numbers, and the same options. However, car number two had the buckets to prevent the aforementioned sliding problem that Glaser and Soul complained of. All TV show cars had slushboxes. Earlier than that, the general public wanted a S&H car. FoMoCo answered the call of duty, with their Limited Production (LP) Starsky & Hutch Torino! It was the first time a TV show spawned a production car. 1000 units, plus one Chicago Auto Show unit and three pre-production cars were made. The latter

A Ford mechanic for over 25 years, owner/restorer John Mohrlein Jr found this Ohio car in October 2010. In wishing to create a S&H replica, this example was 'The Holy Grail,' a rust-free, two-door hardtop! (Courtesy John Mohrlein Jr, http://forum.grantorinosport.org/75granmans-gran-torino-w-3k_topic6099.html)

Torino was Ford's hot seller during the early to mid '70s. However, the S&H TV show jammed the TV studio's switchboard with enquiries: "What car is that, and where can I get one?" (Courtesy John Mohrlein Jr, http://forum.grantorinosport.org/75granmans-gran-torino-w-3k_topic6099.html)

159

Ford Midsize Muscle – Fairlane, Torino & Ranchero

A view afforded many, given the performance upgrades. A bored and stroked 351CJ is 393ci. This Cleveland V8 is connected to the iconic Top Loader four-speed, and Ford 9in differential, with Traction-Lok and 3.50 rear gears. (Courtesy John Mohrlein Jr, http://forum.grantorinosport.org/75granmans-gran-torino-w-3k_topic6099.html)

Left: Gran Torino Sport had an additional Gran Torino crest badge on the front grille. Regular Gran Torinos had them as trunk lid badges alone. Right: Between the Great Depression and 1981, North American Ford vehicles didn't feature an exterior Blue Oval badge! The Fox platformed '82 Granada marked its return! (Courtesy John Mohrlein Jr, http://forum.grantorinosport.org/75granmans-gran-torino-w-3k_topic6099.html)

four vehicles in late January, early February 1976. Some enterprising dealers even pre-dated FoMoCo, and made a few clones of their own!

Production took place at the Chicago Assembly Plant. It used to make full-size Galaxie and LTD, but the rise of the inters saw a switch to Gran Torino Elite after the December 1973 holiday shut down. So popular was Elite, that it was the only model made here in 1974 and 1975 MYs. By mid '76 MY (December 1975) it was apparent Torino and Elite would have to be made here to avoid lay offs. That included the LP mobile from March 1976, which necessitated deluxe bumper group ($67) and dual color keyed sport mirrors ($46) as mandatory options. The S&H paint scheme was down as $164.20.

Unlike the TV car, no decal vector stripe was layed on, with LP that stripe was paint! According to plant employee Bill Maynard the LP got two coats of Ford production white in the Main Paint Spray Booth. Here, areas destined to be white (door middle, ¼ roof and part of roof top) were shot white. Then in the masking area, maskers would apply a special decal developed by 3M for Ford, to keep white areas white! The body was then sanded for adhesion and sent to the two-tone paint booth, for three coats of '76 fleet only color 2B Bright Red. Painting red second stopped bleed through.[16]

The cars then went to the two-tone paint booth oven for curing. The cars were then checked, had the masking tape removed and received final trim. Front fenders and hood were painted on the plant's east side, in the Small Parts Paint area. Production stopped early June, since FoMoCo wanted to be ready for the late July LTD II model changeover. The LPs had a special engine compartment tag on the right side, along the passenger cowling, that said PS-122. Two digits were followed by a 0022 DSO number suffix on the door tag. 100 cars were earmarked for Canada, with these rides having an 8000 suffix. Some also had the PS122 ID code on the metal data plate in the engine bay, near the passenger side windshield. These PS122 ID code and 0022 DSO items, were repeated on the buildsheet. The buildsheet of an LP car would state "STARSKY AND HUTCH UNIT PS122" at the bottom. With only 1000 cars made, and the pre-production units scrapped by

8: Torino Moves from Turin to Lincoln Type Design 1974-1979

Ford, they were hard cars to find used, even as early as 1977/78. The vector stripe looked slightly different to the TV cars, and LPs were delivered with humble Torino wheelcovers! However, many owners optioned Magnum 500 rims, or fitted aftermarket slot rims and air shocks to match that TV show stopper!

In 2004, a big screen Hollywood movie called *Starsky & Hutch* revived the legend. It starred Ben Stiller and Owen Wilson, although Paul Michael Glaser and David Soul did make cameos. For the movie a 1874 mile 1974 Gran Torino I6 was converted to S&H style. Originally a red car with black vinyl roof, cloth bench front seat and column shift, it was given a Viper Red paint job and that vector stripe! It also received a built up 435 horse 351W, using a lot of parts from the Edelbrock catalogue. Black vinyl buckets, center console, floor shift and 15 x 8.5in mags were also done mods.

This, and a second 'Hero Gran Torino,' were built by 'Movie' Mike Walsh's San Fernando California Premiere Studio Rentals business. Both were described in the March 2004 issue of *Hot Rod* magazine, and both experienced front end damage during filming. Those 5mph bumpers got a real workout! Mike Walsh kept Hero Gran Torino #1, upon which Ben Stiller and Owen Wilson signed "The Best CAR EVER!" and "All the Best Yr Pal," respectively, on the underside of the trunklid. The #2 car was based on a 1976 LP Unit PS122 edition, and was sold to Barry S in Nevada. Several additional cars were built for the movie by Ray Claridge of Cinema Vehicle Services, serving as stunt cars, tow cars etc. All were sold to private buyers after filming was completed.

LTD II – Lincoln Type Design midsize!

By the late '70s, Ford's midsize needed some fine fettling. The move to upscale luxury in a smaller, more fuel efficient package, with less emphasis on performance and more on refinement,

called for a different kind of inter. Plus, 1969-73 Torinos had displayed surprise rust, paint orange peel, and general reliability issues, once the newness had worn off. In stepped LTD II! This upscale midsize was a reworked, restyled Torino replacement, that worked from the engineering basis of the 1972-76 Ford inter. On the surface, squared up, stately LTD styling, with distinctive stacked headlamp visage.

Underneath, the refinement of rear coils. Underhood the 302 Windsor rejoined as base midsize motor, for the first time since 1974, a nod to demand for better MPGs. Or, option up to 351W or 351M, even 400M for that deep breathing T-Bird performance of old. Along the same

The 1974-76 Gran Torino Brougham, its final era, included HR78 14in steel belted radials. Standard on Gran Torino Squire and Sport, too. Most figured one rode better on radials. (Courtesy Stanley Spadowski)

This '76 Gran Torino Brougham has 351M V8, power windows, seats and a/c. Accoutrements one would expect of a Brougham, a fine town carriage, no less. (Courtesy Stanley Spadowski)

Ford Midsize Muscle – Fairlane, Torino & Ranchero

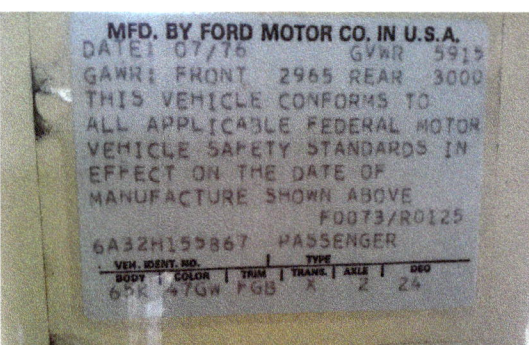

The 7/76 maker's plate signifies this as one of the last Gran Torinos made. Ford had the even more luxury-oriented LTD II waiting in the wings! (Courtesy Stanley Spadowski)

Above: Brougham luxury implied woodgrain dash appliqué for the driver's pleasure, and opera windows, plus rear wheel spats for passers-by. However, the viewpoint on luxury was changing to Europeanesque ideals. That is, Mercedes 450SEL.

Left: Gran Torino Brougham opened the door to midsize luxury, and optional 460 V8. In a gas crunch, why go Conti?!

Bottom left: Mid '70s Brougham was a 4500lb vehicle – 300lb over domestic midsize rivals. Downsized 1979 LTD did pretty much the same job, at 700lb less! Oh, those sacred CAFE mpgs! (Courtesy Stanley Spadowski)

engineering lines of C6 auto, light duty C4 helped get more shiftless MPGs. This box used an aluminum three-piece case, and simplified Simpson planetary gearset. Bodywise it was two-door hardtop, four-door sedan, and for '77 MY only, four-door wagon. The first on the familiar 114in Torino wheelbase, and latter two on same's 118in wheelbase, 302W was a California no show.

LTD II was made for three model years, at Georgia's Atlanta Assembly Plant, now demolished, and Ohio's Lorain Assembly Plant. By 1979 MY, the 400M was off the option sheet, but for all three years, two sporty packages were available on two-door LTD II. The final hurrah for Ford's traditional muscle car. More commonly found was the Sports Appearance Package with single solid exterior color. Rarer was Sports Touring Package, in two-tone exterior paint. Decorative striping was applied to roof and B pillars.

8: Torino Moves from Turin to Lincoln Type Design 1974-1979

The great downsizing debate & nameplate shuffle!

Unfortunately, the refined personal car style LTD II brought, got lost in general market confusion and a welter of ads trying to convince buyers more was more. The Ford LTD and LTD II ad said it all "For 1977 some car makers will offer you only shorter, narrower, lighter full-size cars. Ford has a better idea. Choice: LTD The full-size car that kept its size. The trimmer, sportier LTD II at a trimmer price." Basically, Ford said its full-size and inters of yesteryear, were better than GM's Caddy DeVille and downsized '77 full-size of today, respectively.

Trouble was, folks wanted new designs that were smaller on the outside, bigger on the inside, and lighter to save on gas after the fuel crisis. Plus, CAFE was coming! Ford said LTD and LTD II came standard with V8, automatic, power steering and power front disks. Radials and Dura-Spark Ignition also. The old skool domestics were priced nice, but if a car is lighter it can get by with a base I6. Plus, people would pay a premium for efficiency. Ford's new downsized '79 LTD was 15in shorter and 660lb lighter. Starter price was $6058, $5677 for LTD II.

Trouble on Henry's farm

Losing market share to high end European imports, low priced Japanese imports and having to spend hundreds of millions of dollars on a downsized, CAFE friendly '80s range, weren't Henry's only woes. In light of the Pinto's vulnerable gas tank litigation, Ford did a 1978 recall, fitting protective plastic shields and redesigning the gas tank filler neck. However, as No 2 automaker, Ford was a lucrative target. Ron Wakefield of *Road & Track* wrote about the 1984 $1.8 million out of court settlement paid to a female driver, who received permanent brain damage after a frontal crash in her '75 Pinto. The car had three young women, not wearing seatbelts and occupying the two front buckets of said Pinto. Ford was accused of not providing airbags (passive restraint) to prevent injury. Feeling a jury would be sympathetic to the young woman, Ford paid out.(17)

Not many '70s cars of any price had airbags, but many had auto transmissions, and Ford had trouble with those. Many FMX equipped cars had stories of the shifter jumping out of park, whilst the motor was running. Compared to 27 fire related Pinto deaths, there were 180 concerning the transmission problem. This was why many late '70s Ford midsize and full-size carried prominent dash decals, warning the driver to turn off the motor, if leaving the car unattended in park. Plus, to apply the park brake as well.

Lee Iacocca presided over rushing Pinto into production, even though engineers warned him about the vulnerable gas tank. By 1974 he was proudly standing next to Pinto based Mustang II, luxo Granada/Monarch compacts too, saying a guy wouldn't buy a car anymore, just because it had a long hood. Worryingly for Henry, by 1978 Iacocca was saying this kind of thing at Chrysler. Iacocca claimed he was fired from Ford for being too successful. Whatever the truth, as boss of reborn Chrysler, Iacocca and the federal assisted K car put the heat on Ford for the '80s.

Those midsize spin-offs!

Troubles aside, Ford kept on badge engineering, to get the most out of the

A mint 1977 Mercury Cougar XR7 302 automatic. By 1974 Cougar had moved on from upscale compact Mustang cousin to midsize Torino platform sports/luxo personal car. (Courtesy Lee Rehorn www.YouTube.com/watch?v=iw0Y4clUtNw)

By the mid '70s Cougar had morphed into a mini budget Thunderbird, before the T-Bird itself moved to the Torino platform for '77. During 1974-75, the Torino platform Cougar was UK market available in XR7 coupe form only. (Courtesy Lee Rehorn www.YouTube.com/watch?v=iw0Y4clUtNw)

Torino platform. Mercury Montego for one, with Torino engine options, including 460 during 1974-76. Montego sold well going into 1974, but got bitten by Cougar that year. Monarch's '75 MY entry, also put the pressure on Montego to abdicate! Cougar moved up from compact to midsize in 1974, displacing Montego. And they were all Cougars by '77 MY. Performance-wise, 460ci Cougar XR7 Coupe was top cat, and only XR7 Coupe was UK market imported during 1974-75. The real sales winner for Ford was 1977-79 Thunderbird.

7th gen T-Bird went from full-size to midsize, taking on hot selling Monte Carlo and Olds Cutlass in the personal car battle. Starter V8 was 302W, no 400M for '79, but no one cared. This T-Bird was top bird, a full bird General that outsold Colonel Saunders! 955,032 when America still cared for T-Bird. It built on the success of discontinued Elite, had wide fixed B pillar but retained frameless glass. 1978 saw Diamond Jubilee Edition to celebrate Ford's 75th birthday. It was a super pricey option pack, nearly doubling the price to almost 12 grand! Standard with all, bar moonroof and engine block heater. A '79 MY Heritage Edition signed off on the 7th gen.

On ABC TV show *Charlie's Angels*, John Bosley famously drove a green 7th gen T-Bird. However, *Car and Driver*'s Patrick Bedard felt the XR7 Cougar version, to offer a sporty alternative to the staid prestige of T-Bird. *C&D*'s short

XR7 was upscale, but this example came with no power toys and 302 V8. Many buyers combated '70s inflation by passing on auto options. (Courtesy Lee Rehorn www.YouTube.com/watch?v=iw0Y4clUtNw)

8: Torino Moves from Turin to Lincoln Type Design 1974-1979

test involved a loaded version, on whose base $5274 escalated to $8770, thanks to $934 MoonRoof and GT Pack. The latter involving engine turned dash panel, sports three-spoke tiller and seven gauge Sports Instrumentation Group. HD 'Cross Country' suspension wasn't fitted. Bedard noted traditional Detroit suspension of limited travel, and good ride only on smooth surfaces. Acceleration of the 161 horse 351/auto power team, was rather unenthusiastic above the federal 55mph limit.[18]

In all that was transpiring at Ford, Henry wasn't too bothered about continuing the Torino/LTD II platform into the '80s. Apart from the new full-size Panther platform, the new front drive Mazda related Escort, was getting ready for '81 MY. In the May '76 issue of C&D, it was stated that three of Ford's top execs, including Henry Ford II, were running around in Euro sport sedans like Grand Monarch Ghia! New Fairmont took over LTD II wagon duties for '78 MY. For '81 MY, Granada went onto the Fairmont platform. Ford's next true midsize family car, after this tumultuous time, was the front drive I4 and V6 Taurus.

Torino/LTD II V8 lovers kinda moved to Fox platform T-Bird 5.0s in the '80s, the 10th gen Superbirds thereafter. That good sized, V8 available, rear driver two-door had independent rear suspension! However, not even this could stop the rise of the SUV/pickup segment, that saw to Superbird's '90s demise. In the 2000s, Mercury Marauder challenged the reincarnated Impala SS. However, being

In light of auto accidents related to auto transmission use, Ford put a procedure decal on '70s midsize and full-size cars. The driver of this '77 Cougar wagon, was Ford-warned not to leave the car unattended in park with the motor running. (Courtesy Lee Rehorn)

By the late '70s sport was out and luxury was in, so Henry re-engineered Torino into LTD II. Still on the familiar midsize separate chassis, but now with added pizzaz! (Courtesy Scott Goodrich)

Ford Midsize Muscle – Fairlane, Torino & Ranchero

This $6300 1978 LTD II 351 two-door hardtop was one of the last '78s made. Produced at Georgia's Atlanta Assembly Plant, just days before that year's 4th of July holiday. LTD IIs were also built at Ohio's Lorain Assembly Plant during 1977-79. (Courtesy Scott Goodrich)

Top right: LTD II engine options ran from 302 to 351W/351M, and the desirable 400M, the last choice ending in 1978. Combined with the decorative sports pack, these rides were the final traditional Ford muscle cars. (Courtesy Scott Goodrich)

an auto only, two valve 4.6 Mod motor four-door, with limited rear axle ratios, it was more Crown Vic with attitude, than a true muscle car. Therefore, of limited commercial import.

V8s continued to be developed for CAFE lenient truck and pickup markets. Some aftermarket sources like to chime in with names and engine sizes, invoking hallowed past icons. However, these have limited engineering links to the FEs and Clevelands of old. With the tightening of CAFE initiated by President Obama, and the central place of Mustang at Dearborn, it seems traditional Ford midsize muscle, will only exist in historical literary tomes of knowledge. Plus, cruise nights, and the very fevered imaginations of car fiends, the universe over!

This 1978 LTD II has the rarer of the two sports packages. Sports Appearance Package had a single, solid exterior color. The rare Sports Touring Package, present here, had two tone paint. Decorative striping appeared on the roof and B pillars! (Courtesy Scott Goodrich)

Appendix

Ford's four on the floor!

1957 Ford Custom Ranchero (two-door Ranch Wagon-based pickup)

List Price:	$2224.44
Motor:	Y-block 'Thunderbird; 292 2bbl all cast iron OHV V8, 9.1:1 CR, 212 bhp (gross) @ 4500rpm 297lb/ft @ 2700rpm, cast iron manifolds, dual exhausts.
Transmission:	Ford-O-Matic three-speed torque converter automatic (3.56 final drive).
Front Suspension:	Independent ball-joint (Lincoln-Mercury type), single unit upper and lower arms, swaybar, coils, airplane style shocks.
Rear Suspension:	Five leaf semi-elliptic springs, diagonally mounted shocks, live axle.
Size & Weight:	203.5in length/77in width/58.7in height (with max load)/116in wheelbase/3640lb (test weight).
Brakes:	11in hydraulic drums.
Wheels & Tires:	14 x 5.5in steel 5 bolt rims/14in tires with 8in footprint.
Performance & Economy:	0-60mph 11.3 seconds & 14.6mpg (*Motor Life* July 1957).

1957 was really the first year that Fairlane was a nameplate, rather than a trim level. Ford's latest family car had related Ranch Wagon, and Ranchero pickup spinoffs. The latter two-seater could be specified with T-Bird motorvation. Chevrolet had only one two-door sports car, Henry had two!

1964 Ford Fairlane 500 Sports Coupe

Base Price:	$2725.75 (standard features: buckets, console, HD suspension, 260 V8 & heater)
Motor:	Windsor small block 'K code' 289 4bbl (manual choke 595 CFM) all cast iron OHV V8 (solid lifter), 11:1 CR, 271 bhp (gross) @ 6000rpm, 312lb/ft @ 3400rpm, free flow headers, dual exhausts – Premium (99 octane) gas required.
Transmission:	Four-speed manual 1st (2.74:1), 2nd (2.04:1), 3rd (1.51:1), 4th (1.00:1), (4.11 final drive ratio available, 3.25 ratio tested).
Front Suspension:	Independent, upper A-arm and single lower control arm with strut, swaybar, coils, direct acting tube shocks.
Rear Suspension:	Five leaf semi-elliptic springs, direct acting tube shocks, live axle.
Brakes:	10 x 2.5in four-wheel hydraulic, duo-servo powered drums.
Size & Weight:	197.6in length/75in width/55.5in height/115.5in wheelbase/3155lb.
Wheels & Tires:	14 x 5in five-bolt steel rims/14in 2-ply tires with 7in footprint.
Performance & Economy:	0-60mph 7.5 seconds (*Popular Mechanics Car Facts* 1964 annual) & 19.1mpg (*Motor Trend* January 1964 – testing Fairlane 500 Sports Coupe four-speed with base 9.0:1 CR 195 bhp 289).

In 1962 Fairlane became an intermediate. By '64 MY, '4 on da floor,' and the new 271 horse K code 289, made the Sports Coupe variant, a GTO muscle car contemporary. Fairlane got K code before Mustang! Folks were saying again that Henry's midsize family car was 'The Right Size Ford.'

Ford Midsize Muscle – Fairlane, Torino & Ranchero

1970 Torino Cobra 429 Ram Air Drag Pack Coupe

Base Torino Cobra:	$3249.75, 370 horse Ram Air 429 ($229), Drag Pack (375 horse hardware + performance rear axle – $155)
Motor:	385 series big block (with four bolt mains) 429 4bbl (780 CFM Holley) Ram Air (RA) + Drag Pack (DP) configuration – all cast iron OHV V8 (solid lifter), 11.3:1 CR, 375 bhp (gross) @ 5600rpm, 450lb/ft @ 3400rpm, free flow headers, dual exhausts – Premium (99 octane) gas required.
Transmission:	Four-speed manual with Hurst shift linkage 1st (2.32:1), 2nd (1.69:1), 3rd (1.29:1), 4th (1.00:1), (3.91 final drive ratio on test, 4.30:1 a no cost DP choice).
Front Suspension:	Independent, unequal length control arms, coils, tube shocks and swaybar.
Rear Suspension:	Semi-elliptic leaf springs, staggered shocks (DP), live axle.
Brakes:	11.3in vented disk (front), 10 x 2in rear drum + duo servo power assisted.
Size & Weight:	206.2in length/76.8in width/51in height/117in wheelbase/4185lb.
Wheels & Tires:	14 x 7in five-bolt steel rims/Goodyear Polyglas F70-14in tires.
Performance & Economy:	0-60mph 6 seconds, ¼ mile 14.5 seconds @ 98.5mph, 120mph estimated top speed, 7-10mpg range on premium (99 octane) (*Car and Driver* December 1969).

1970 was the performance zenith for Ford, and Detroit in general. Smog controls and gas mileage dictates would slow things thereafter. The '70 Torino Cobra 429 RA DP, was a four-wheeled distillation of Ford's finest hardware. All that larger '70 midsize refinement made for a luxo racer!

1977 Ranchero GT 400M

Base Ranchero GT:	$4984, 400M ($156), additional test car options: Brougham split bench ($187), Sports Instrumentation Cluster ($130), LSD ($54), Handling Suspension Package ($33).
Motor:	Ford 400M (Modified) 4bbl, all cast iron hydraulic lifter OHV V8, 8.0:1 CR, 173 bhp (net) @ 3800rpm, 326lb/ft @ 1600rpm, 87 octane unleaded gas (catalytic converter fitted).
Transmission:	C6 three-speed torque converter automatic, 1st (2.46:1) 2nd (1.46:1) 3rd (1.00:1), (LSD with 3.00:1 mandatory rear axle ratio).
Front Suspension:	Independent A-arms, drag struts, coils, tube shocks and swaybar.
Rear Suspension:	HD coil sprung live axle, 4 longitudinal control arms, rear swaybar.
Brakes:	10.7in vented disk (front), 11 x 2.25in rear drum + power assisted.
Size & Weight:	220.1in length/79.6in width/53.5in height/118in wheelbase/4215lb (curb weight).
Wheels & Tires:	Mag 500 14 x 7in five-bolt rims/H70-14B tires (Goodyear Polyglas Bias Belted).
Performance & Economy:	0-60mph 10.7 seconds, 94mph top speed, ¼ mile 18 seconds @ 78mph, City/Highway 14.7mpg (*PV4* May 1977).

Ranchero was now surfing the newly popular pickup, customized van and leisure vehicle late '70s era. Increasingly, the only place to get a potent four-barrel V8. Sadly, El Camino's stronger sales, plus the imminent demise of LTD II, meant Ranchero was about to say "Adieu monde cruel!"

Appendix

Ford muscle car websites

Ranchero USA
www.ranchero.us
A website dedicated to all years of Ford's car-based pickup (1957-1979). Member forums include technical help, VIN decoder and production history.

The Ford Torino Page Forum
forum.grantorinosport.org
Covering all Torino variants, from the introduction of the upscale midsize in 1968. All Mercury cousin models, and Ford spinoffs up to 1979 are also catered for.

Muscle Car Classics Facebook
https://www.facebook.com/pages/Muscle-Car-Classics-MCC/160061237435887
An auto enthusiast site devoted to the classic American muscle car. Involving domestic rides from the late '50s, to the mid '70s. Factory originals, and upgraded cars featuring factory options/aftermarket hardware of the era, are welcome.

Ford Muscle Forums
www.fordmuscleforums.com
Billed as the "Ultimate Ford Performance Community," the site offers discussion and help concerning classic enthusiast postwar Fords. It has Fairlane/Torino and Ranchero subforums.

'57 Fords International
57fordsforever.com
A forum for lovers of Henry's 1957 model range. A tidal wave design change that influenced Dearborn's direction until the mid '60s!

Ford bibliography

Bedard, Patrick. "Short Take: Mercury Cougar XR-7." *Car and Driver*, May 1977.
Bentley, John. *All The World's Cars 1954*. New York: Cornell Publishing Corp, 1954.
"Detroit Spotlight." *Motor Trend*, April 1967.
"Ford and Chevy level their sights on Volkswagen." *Car and Driver*, September 1970.
Given, Kyle. "And Now A Word From Our Sponsor." *Car and Driver*, September 1969.
Harvey, Chris. "Bandwagon GTO." *CAR*, August 1984.
Holder, Bill, & Kunz, Phillip. *GTO*. MN: MBI Publishing Co, 2003.
"Inside Detroit." *Motor Trend*, March 1968.
Ludvigsen, Karl. "Fuel-injection: One Answer To Smog?" *Motor Trend*, March 1968.
Maynard, Bill. "1976 Starsky & Hutch Gran Torino Update." *Fairlaner,* Vol 16, No 6, November-December 1996.
"Ours Versus Theirs." *Muscle Cars,* No 2, 1974 Special.
Quammen, David. "People of the Horse." *National Geographic*, March 2014.
Schmidt, Julian. "The Most Grueling Test of All." *Motor Trend*, March 1968.
Skinner, Phil. "Swedish-Style Ford 1953 Customline." *Cars & Parts Annual,* 1999.
Wakefield, Ron. "USA." *Motor*, May 16 1984.
Whipple, Jim. *Popular Mechanics CAR FACTS*. New York: Popular Mechanics Company, 1963.
Willson, Quentin. *Great Car*. New York: Dorling Kindersley, 2001.
Woron, Walt. "Ford's new all-purpose Ranchero." *Motor Trend*, April 1957.

Ford Midsize Muscle – Fairlane, Torino & Ranchero

Footnotes

(Indicated by superscript numbers in the main text)

(1) Chris Harvey, "Bandwagon GTO" *CAR* (August 1984): p160.
(2) Karl Ludvigsen, "Fuel-injection: One Answer To Smog?" *Motor Trend* (March 1968): p70.
(3) Phil Skinner, "Swedish-Style Ford 1953 Customline" *Cars & Parts Annual* (1999): p40.
(4) John Bentley, *All The World's Cars 1954* (New York: Cornell Publishing Corp, 1954): p112.
(5) Quentin Willson, *Great Car* (New York: Dorling Kindersley, 2001): p224.
(6) Walt Woron, "Ford's new all-purpose Ranchero." *Motor Trend* (April 1957): p51.
(7) Jim Whipple, *Popular Mechanics CAR FACTS* (New York: Popular Mechanics Company, 1963): p44.
(8) Bill Holder, & Phillip Kunz, *GTO* (MN: MBI Publishing Co, 2003): p95.
(9) "Detroit Spotlight." *Motor Trend* (April 1967): p21.
(10) "Inside Detroit." *Motor Trend* (March 1968): p12.
(11) Kyle Given, "And Now A Word From Our Sponsor" *Car and Driver* (September 1969): p70.
(12) David Quammen, "People of the Horse" *National Geographic* (March 2014): p117.
(13) Julian Schmidt, "The Most Grueling Test of All" *Motor Trend* (March 1968): p48.
(14) "Ford and Chevy level their sights on Volkswagen" *Car and Driver* (September 1970): p28.
(15) "Ours Versus Theirs" *Muscle Cars* No 2 (1974 Special): p26.
(16) Bill Maynard, "1976 Starsky & Hutch Gran Torino Update" *Fairlaner* Vol.16 No.6 (November-December 1996): p14.
(17) Ron Wakefield, "USA" *Motor* (May 16 1984): p25.
(18) Patrick Bedard, "Short Take: Mercury Cougar XR-7" *Car and Driver* (May 1977): p114.

Mercury Cyclone. (Courtesy Roger Pirtle)

Appendix

(Courtesy Ford Motor Co)

Ford Midsize Muscle – Fairlane, Torino & Ranchero

Paul Michael Glaser at the 2016 Claremont Show. (Courtesy John Mohrlein Jr)

Also from Veloce –

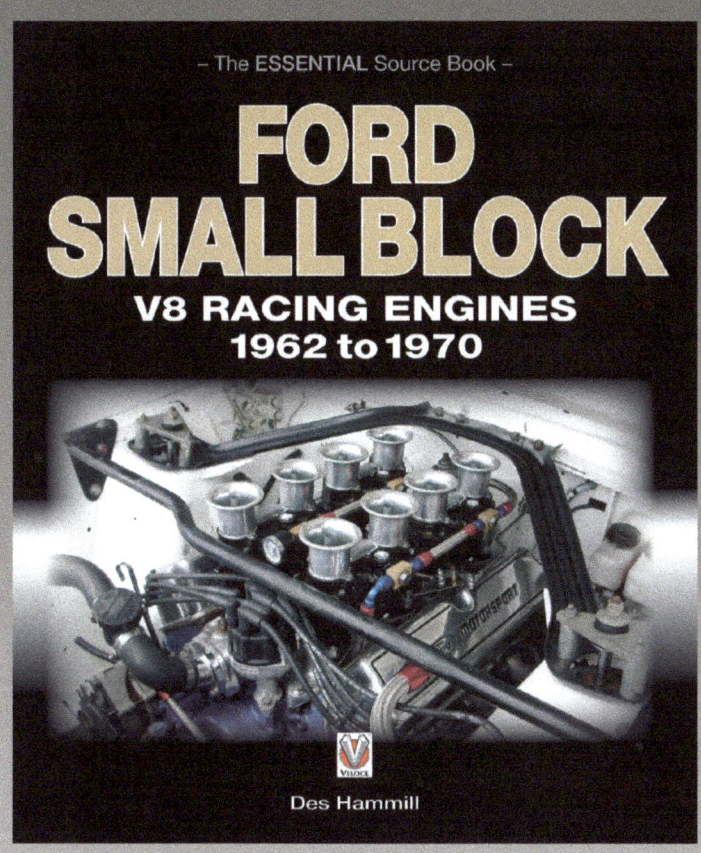

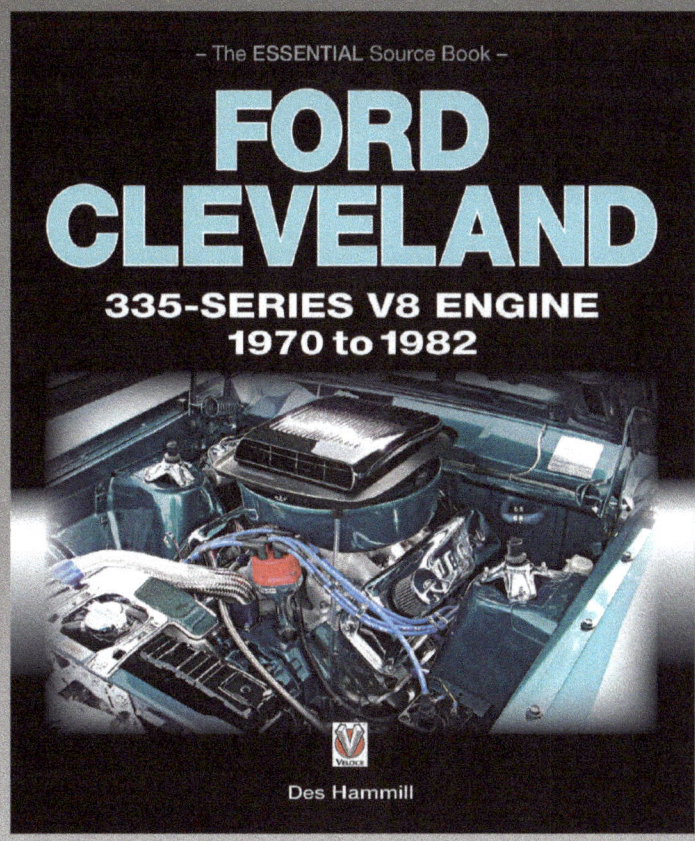

A rare insight into the confident, logical approach of Ford's Engine & Foundry Division engineers during the 1960s racing programmes – a time when outstanding technical decisions led to many events being won.

ISBN: 978-1-845844-25-7
Paperback • 25x20.7cm
• 112 pages • 125 b&w pictures

Years of meticulous research have resulted in this unique history, technical appraisal (including tuning and motorsports) and data book of the Ford V8 Cleveland 335 engines produced in the USA, Canada and Australia, including input from the engineers involved in the design, development and subsequent manufacture of this highly prized engine from its inception in 1968 until production ceased in 1982.

ISBN: 978-1-787110-89-2
Paperback • 25x20.7cm
• 96 pages • 46 colour and b&w pictures

For more info on Veloce titles, visit our website at www.velocebooks.com
• email: info@veloce.co.uk • Tel: +44(0)1305 260068

A LIMITED EDITION OF 1500 COPIES

GRAND PRIX
FORD
FORD, COSWORTH AND THE DFV

GRAHAM ROBSON

A limited edition of 1500 copies. In 1965, Colin Chapman persuaded Ford to underwrite development of a V8 engine for the new 3000cc Grand Prix formula. Built by Cosworth, the new DFV engine won Lotus four World Championship Grands Prix in 1967. A year later, and now available to other constructors, the engine began its domination of Grand Prix racing.

ISBN: 978-1-845846-24-4
Hardback • 25x25cm
• 272 pages • 313 colour and b&w pictures

For more info on Veloce titles, visit our website at www.velocebooks.com
• email: info@veloce.co.uk • Tel: +44(0)1305 260068

Index

ABC (American Broadcasting Company) 110
AC Cobra 16
A/FX (drag racing) 50, 52
Air Suspension (Fairlane Fullsize) 18, 22, 25
Allison, Bobby 128
AMC Ambassador 60
AMC Gremlin 109
AMC Hornet 109, 135, 145
AMC Javelin 98, 118
AMC Matador 154
AMC Pacer 145
AMC Rebel 60, 64, 105
Andretti, Mario 75, 141
April Love (1957 movie) 30, 32
Ash, L David 30
Aston Martin DB5 118
Automatic:
  Cruise-O-Matic 14, 17, 20, 26, 27, 35-38, 57-59, 63, 66, 67, 74, 78, 80, 81, 83, 84, 92, 98,100, 117, 131, 132, 135, 143,148, 155
  Ford-O-Matic 8, 9, 14, 17, 20, 30, 35, 42, 44, 54, 55, 57, 67, 167
  FX 14
  MX 14, 67
Automobile Manufacturer's Association 15

Baker, Buddy 111
Bana, Eric 137
Bandt, Lew 29
Beadle, Tony 106
Bedard, Patrick 164, 165
Bentley, John 19
Blain, Doug 22
BMW 733i 148
Bob Ford (dealership) 51
Bolster, John 22, 25
Boone, Pat 30, 32, 35
Borg Warner 14, 45, 67
Bowsher, Jack 85
Boyer, Bill 8, 30
Bradford, Bill 129
Brickhouse, Richard 94
Brokaw, Jim 117, 142
Brooks, Dick 128
Bud Moore Engineering 113, 127, 128, 129
Buehrig, Gordon 29, 30
Buick Regal 154

California Brake Package 157
California Highway Patrol (CHP) 156
California Premiere Studio Rentals 161
Caminito, Jerry 52
Carlite 112, 113
Carousel Tach 96, 101, 106, 107, 119, 125, 132
Challenger (Hi Po Windsor V8) 43
Chapman, Colin 75
Charlie's Angels (TV Show) 164
Chevrolet Camaro 82, 93, 95, 104, 106, 118
Chevrolet Cameo 31
Chevrolet Chevelle 72, 74, 96, 105, 117, 118, 129, 131, 135, 136, 152, 154
Chevrolet Corvair 26, 40, 47, 108
Chevrolet Corvette 6, 18, 30, 34, 35, 38, 39, 74, 85, 98, 148
Chevrolet El Camino 36-39, 53, 58, 140, 142, 144-148, 151, 168
Chevrolet Impala 36, 37, 39, 166
Chevrolet Malibu 120
Chevrolet Monte Carlo 135, 155, 164
Chevrolet Nomad 30
Chevrolet Nova 109
Chevrolet Vega 109
Chrysler 300B 6
Chrysler K car 163
Cinema Vehicle Services 161
Clamshell Buckets 96
Claridge, Ray 161
Cobra Supercharger (Shelby American) 47
Comfort Weave (upholstery) 77, 99
Competition Suspension 87, 90, 103, 118, 119, 120, 126, 127, 131, 132, 134, 154
Conelrad (radio stations) 11
Consumer Reports 47, 48, 55, 69, 80, 109, 117, 152
Corning Glass 64
Courtesy Light Group 118
Cross Country Suspension 165

D&M Engineering 129
Danielle, Steve 113, 114
Datsun L'il Hustler 144
Dearborn Steel Tubing Co (DST) 51
De Tomaso Mangusta 87
De Tomaso Pantera 132, 133, 135
DeLorean DMC 12 52
DeLorean, John Z 6, 52, 92
Detroit Lions 84
Detroit Locker (LSD) 52, 72, 81, 85, 88, 104, 106
Dillinger, John 8, 41
DirectAire (ventilation) 96, 99, 100, 117, 122, 125, 126
Dodge Challenger 127
Dodge Charger 93, 102, 112
Dodge Daytona 93, 111, 112
Dodge Demon 109
Dodge Super Bee 90, 118
Donilson, John 52
Drag Pack 88, 101, 104-106, 116, 118, 168
Dual Range (Cruise-O-Matic) 17

Edsel 6, 20, 21, 23, 26, 35, 40, 50, 53, 61
Eidschun, Robert 109
Elder, Jake 75
Electra 'Rat Fink' bicycle 55
Engines:
  Ford 335 series Cleveland Small Block V8 24, 86, 87, 95-103, 115-118, 122, 124-129, 132-135, 137, 138, 141, 143, 144, 146, 153-155, 158, 160, 166
  Ford 385 series Big Block V8 97, 99, 100, 102-104, 108, 110, 112-114, 116-122, 124, 125, 127, 128, 132, 133, 135, 142, 143, 146-148, 150, 153-156, 158, 159, 162, 164, 168
  Ford FE V8 6, 15-18, 20-22, 24, 27, 33, 37, 38, 42, 44, 45, 47-50, 52, 58, 60-62, 64-73, 79-90, 93, 107, 108, 119, 136, 139, 140-143, 150, 166
  Ford MEL Big Block V8 50
  Ford Modified Small Block V8 (351M & 400) 122, 124, 132, 133, 143, 144, 146-150, 154, 155, 158, 159, 161, 162, 164-166, 168
  Ford Modular V8 16, 166
  Ford Flathead V8 6, 7, 9, 41, 42, 70
  Ford Windsor V8 13, 41-49, 51, 55-66, 70, 72, 76, 77, 79-84, 86, 87, 90, 91, 97, 99-101, 116, 117, 124-126, 128, 132, 133, 136, 139, 141, 143, 144, 146-150, 154, 155, 157-159, 161, 162, 164, 166, 167
  Ford Y block V8 6-10, 13-15, 19, 20, 24-27, 30, 31, 33, 34, 36, 39, 45, 115, 161
  Ford Y block 272 V8 'Power Package' 6-8
Equa-Lock (LSD) 46, 60, 140
Estes, Pete 6
Ethridge, John 66, 68

Fargas, Antonio 157
Fear Is The Key (1972 movie) 123, 127, 128
Ford Bronco 99, 156
Ford Capri 77
Ford Cortina 108, 109
Ford Econoline (truck) 49
Ford Escort 109, 165
Ford Falcon 65
Ford F100 30
Ford Fairlane 500 5, 7-11, 13, 17-20, 22-28, 30, 31, 40, 42-44, 48-52, 61, 66, 67, 73, 76, 88, 90-93, 99, 136, 139
Ford Fairlane (Argentina) 76, 115
Ford Fairlane (Australia) 22, 23, 24, 115, 116
Ford Fairlane (South Africa) 22, 28, 115
Ford Fairlane Cobra 83, 87-91, 102
Ford Fairlane Crestline 6
Ford Fairlane Crown Victoria 6, 7, 8, 10, 23, 32
Ford Fairlane Custom 11, 13, 16, 17, 18
Ford Fairlane Custom 300 11, 12, 14, 15, 22
Ford Fairlane Customline 7, 8, 13
Ford Fairlane GT 59, 64-67, 70-72, 74, 80, 90, 139
Ford Fairlane GT/A 59, 60, 65-70, 72-74, 80, 82, 84, 125, 134
Ford Fairlane Falcon 98-100, 108, 115
Ford Fairlane Mainline 7, 8, 13, 30
Ford Fairlane Sports Coupe 43, 44, 46, 55, 63, 65, 167
Ford Fairlane Thunderbolt 27, 47-53, 70, 73, 114
Ford Fairlane XL 61, 65, 71, 74, 90, 115
Ford Fairmont 116, 138, 152, 165
Ford Falcon 15, 22, 24, 26, 40-42, 45, 53-56, 58-60, 75, 92, 99, 108, 116, 137, 138, 145, 155
Ford Falcon Club Wagon 55
Ford Falcon Sprint 44, 55, 56
Ford Falcon Station Bus 55
Ford Fiesta 77
Ford Galaxie 22-28, 40, 42, 44-48, 55, 64, 70, 72, 76, 107, 120, 156, 158, 160
Ford Gran Torino 122, 123, 125, 130-132, 143, 145, 147, 152, 153, 156-160
Ford Gran Torino Brougham 121, 122, 131, 152-154, 161, 162
Ford Gran Torino Sport 119-123, 125-129, 131-136, 152-156, 161
Ford Granada 64, 77, 115, 138, 155, 160, 163, 165
Ford Granada ESS 156
Ford Granada Sports Coupe 156
Ford GT40 16, 33
Ford LTD 119, 120, 151, 160-163
Ford LTD II 5, 147, 149-152, 159-163, 165, 166, 168
Ford LTD (Australia) 116
Ford Maverick 92, 99, 108, 109, 155, 157
Ford Model A 29, 41, 70
Ford Model T 22, 48, 50
Ford Mustang 10, 15, 16, 34, 37, 40, 45-47, 53, 54, 56, 58, 60, 63, 67, 69, 74, 75, 79, 82, 84, 87, 90, 95, 96, 98, 99, 104, 108, 118-120, 128, 134, 136, 138, 142, 144, 166, 167
Ford Mustang II 109, 135, 138, 163
Ford Pinto 109, 110, 113, 120, 135, 163
Ford Popular 22
Ford Ranch Wagon 8, 29-31, 33, 35, 37, 39, 44, 76, 79, 167
Ford Ranchero (compact) 53-62, 141, 145, 169
Ford Ranchero (full-size) 29-38, 53-55, 99, 145, 167, 169
Ford Ranchero (midsize) 59-62, 73, 75, 139-152, 168, 169
Ford Ranchero GT (midsize) 139-149
Ford Ranchero Rio Grande (midsize) 141
Ford Ranchero Squire (midsize) 141, 143, 147, 148
Ford Ranchero (South Africa) 145
Ford Special Order Department 157
Ford Special Vehicle Dept (SVD) 48
Ford SVT Cobra 103
Ford Taurus 92, 165
Ford Thunderbird 7-10, 13, 18, 20, 26, 30, 33-37, 40, 41, 43, 44, 55, 58, 60, 67, 70, 74, 99, 121, 124, 139, 140, 146, 155, 161, 164, 165, 167
Ford Torino 5, 76, 77, 95, 96, 115, 116, 120, 122, 123, 131, 132, 136, 145-147, 152, 154, 156, 159, 160, 164, 165, 169

175

Index

Ford Torino Brougham 99, 100, 103, 110, 116, 117, 118
Ford Torino Cobra 97, 98, 100-108, 114, 116, 118, 122
Ford Torino Elite 115, 155, 160, 164, 171
Ford Torino GT 77-79, 83, 84, 90-92, 100-105, 107, 114, 116-118, 122, 125, 136, 139, 141
Ford Torino Interceptor 156
Ford Torino King Cobra 111-115
Ford Torino Pacer 156
Ford Torino Ranger 156
Ford Torino Sentry 156
Ford Torino Squire Wagon 77, 100, 116-118, 136, 141
Ford Torino Talladega 93, 94, 98, 111, 112
Ford Torino Trooper 156
Ford, William Clay, Sr 84
Foster, Sidney 52
Foyt, AJ 85, 93, 111
Freers, Howard 66

Garlits, Don 'Big Daddy' 50
Gibson, Fred 138
Glaser, Paul Michael 157-159, 161, 172
Global Financial Crisis (GFC) 92
Glotzbach, Charlie 85, 93, 111
Gomer Pyle (TV show) 52
Goodyear Polyglas Tire 90, 97, 101, 104, 106, 115, 118, 135
Gray, Pat 52
Grenier, George 158
Gurney, Dan 93

Hamilton, Bernie 157
Hamilton, Pete 111
Harvey, Chris 6
Harvey, Paul 51
Haynes, Kim 129
Heathfield, Dick 8
Hershey, Frank 30
Hertz 56
Hillman Avenger 108
Holden 116, 137, 138
Holland, Bill 8, 10
Holman-Moody 70, 71, 74, 75, 82, 85, 112, 113
Honnel, Steve 114
Hylton, James 93, 111

Iacocca, Lee 46, 47, 56, 64, 87, 95, 103, 114, 163
IMCO (Ford Pollution Control) 88, 110
Indianapolis 500 84
Isaac, Bobby 85, 111, 127, 128, 169

Jaguar XJ6/12 118, 133, 135
Jo Han 128
Jones, Parnelli 128
Jones, Shirley 30, 32

Kelly, Steve 142, 144

Knudsen, Bunkie 113
Krauskopf, Nord 112

Lamborghini Marzal 101
Lamm, Michael 143
Laser Stripe 100, 101, 104, 107, 117-119, 126, 131, 132, 134, 143, 146, 153
Laugh-In (TV show) 92
Le Mans 24 Hour Race 16
Lifeguard Design 10, 23
Light, Jim 145
Limited Production (LP) Starsky & Hutch Gran Torino 159-161
Lincoln Continental MkVIII 110, 119
Lorenzen, Fred 75
Love The Beast (documentary) 137

Mad Max V8 Interceptor 137, 138, 145
Magic Doorgate (Torino wagon) 76, 100, 122
Magnum 500 (Sport Rims) 103, 114, 117-119, 131, 134, 135, 144, 155, 161, 168
Mashigan, Chuck 8, 30
Maynard, Bill 160
Mazda 626 115
McCahill, Tom 8, 34, 122
McCluskey, Roger 111
McGuire, Bob 30
McNamara, Robert 10, 24, 26, 38, 40, 53, 55, 58
McVay, Bob 56
Mercedes 190SL 20
Mercedes S class 60, 64, 70, 110, 162
Mercury Comet 41, 42, 54, 58, 63, 64, 70, 108, 136
Mercury Cougar 47, 84, 155, 163-165
Mercury Cyclone 1, 52, 63, 85, 86, 89, 93, 94, 135, 136
Mercury Cyclone GT 79-81, 135-137, 170
Mercury Cyclone Spoiler 94, 137
Mercury Cyclone Spoiler II 112-115
Mercury Grand Monarch Ghia 165
Mercury Marauder 165, 166
Mercury Meteor 42, 63
Mercury Monarch 155, 163, 164
Mercury Monarch S 156
Mercury Montego 86, 89, 120, 136, 137, 155, 164
Mercury Montego GT 89, 136
Mercury Montego MX Brougham 136, 137
Mercury Montego MX Villager 136, 137
Mercury Zephyr 152
Middlestead, AJ 30
Moonshine Fest 2012 (car show) 39
Moore, Bud 113, 129
Motorama (GM car show) 34

Nabors, Jim 52
Nader, Ralph 26, 49, 50, 61
NASCAR Racing Kit (312 V8) 14
Naughton, John 95

Negre, Ed 111
Newman, Barry 123, 127
Nissan 300ZX 103
Nourse, Ted 74

Obama, President Barack 166
Oldham, Joe 119
Oldsmobile 442 72, 101
Oldsmobile Cutlass 129, 135, 154, 164
Oldsmobile Rallye 350 101

Panther platform 165
Passino, Jacques 113
Patriot Performance 72
Paxton (supercharger) 13, 14
PDA (Professional Drivers Association) 94, 110
Pearson, David 83, 85, 94, 111, 127, 128
Penske, Roger 93
Performance Instrument Cluster 119, 125, 127, 131, 132, 168
Petty, Richard 85, 93, 94, 110, 111, 128
Picerni, Chuck 158
Plaza Fiberglass 52
Plymouth Cricket 108
Plymouth Road Runner 87, 90, 93, 105, 111, 118
Plymouth Satellite 117
Plymouth Suburban 30
Plymouth Superbird 84, 111, 112
Plymouth Valiant 20
Police Interceptor V8 15, 16, 24, 25, 80, 82, 83
Pontiac GTO 6, 13, 15, 39, 45, 60, 64-67, 69, 70, 72, 73, 83, 101, 105, 125, 127, 167
Pontiac Firebird 84, 95, 98, 103, 105, 106, 131, 137, 151
Pretz, PH 8

RACE-torations 129
Rallye Equipment Group (Gran Torino Sport) 126, 127, 131, 132, 135
Rambler American 20, 26, 41
Rambler Electrojector V8 6
Rim-Blow (steering wheel) 96, 106
Road Warrior Movies (*Mad Max*) 137, 138
Robertson, Don 111
Root, Al 119
Roth, 'Big Daddy' Ed 55
Rotunda Division 65
Roy, Dennis 113, 114
Royal Pontiac Bobcat 83

Schmidt, Julian 107
Selectaire (a/c) 74, 92, 117, 126, 132, 139, 140, 145
Shelby American 47, 56, 82
Shelby, Carroll 47, 56, 82, 87, 92
Shelby Mustang 47, 56, 104, 108
Shenk, Bill 95
Shinoda, Larry 111, 112
Shore, Dina 30

Skelton, Ed 59, 60
Skyliner Fairlane Convertible Option 6, 12, 13, 21-25, 30
Smith, Larry 129
Soul, David 157-159, 161
Southern Wheels N' Motion 2012 (car show) 100
Spelling, Aaron 158, 159
Spelling-Goldberg Productions 158
Spohn, Ron 129
Sports Appearance Package (LTD II) 162, 166
Sports Touring Package (LTD II) 162, 166
Squire (Ford wagon & Ranchero trim level) 44, 64, 122, 131, 132, 152, 155, 161
Stabul (Gran Torino suspension) 120
Starsky & Hutch (TV show) 123, 145-147, 156-161
Starsky & Hutch (2004 movie) 158, 161
Stiller, Ben 161
Studebaker Golden Hawk 6
Studebaker Lark 20
Sunbeam Tiger 64
Sunliner Fairlane Convertible Option 22, 23
Super Stock (drag racing) 50-52
Sure-Track (ABS) 110

Tasca Ford 48
Teague, Dick 118
Teletouch (automatic) 20
The Blues Brothers (1980 movie) 157
The Hot Rod Factory 73
Thermactor (smog air pump) 62, 66, 80, 150
Toyota Hilux 144
Traction-Lok (LSD) 88-91, 101, 104, 118, 126, 143, 147, 157, 160
Trailer Tow Pack (TTP) 100, 117, 122, 132

Wait, Rich 73
Wakefield, Ron 163
Walsh, Mike 161
Waltrip, Darrell 129
Wangers, Jim 6, 69, 83
Wheeler Racing 72
Whipple, Jim 20
Williams, Ralph 92, 107
Wilson, Owen 161
Wilson, Waddell 75
Woods, Damon 30
Woron, Walt 31, 32, 34
Wright, Jim 42, 44

Yarborough, Cale 85, 93, 94, 111, 137
Yarbrough, Lee Roy 93, 94
Youngren, Harold 14

Vanishing Point (1971 movie) 127
VW Beetle 17, 20, 26, 41, 98, 108, 109, 110

www.ingramcontent.com/pod-product-compliance
Lightning Source LLC
Chambersburg PA
CBHW041411300426
44114CB00028B/2978